The
COBOL 85
Example
Book

The
COBOL 85
Example
Book

Jerome Garfunkel

A Wiley-Interscience Publication
JOHN WILEY & SONS
New York / Chichester / Brisbane / Toronto / Singapore

Library of Congress Cataloging-in-Publication Data

Garfunkel, Jerome.
    COBOL 85 example book.

    "Wiley-Interscience publication."
    1. COBOL (Computer program language)   I. Title.
II. Title: COBOL eighty-five example book.

QA76.73.C25G37   1986   005.13'3   86-1716
ISBN 0-471-80461-4 (pbk)

Printed in the United States of America

10 9 8 7 6 5 4 3 2 1

to Jack Garfunkel and Angie Garfunkel . . .

Table of Contents

"New":   Addition to COBOL 85 (**compatible** with prior COBOL)
"Change": Current feature changed in COBOL 85
           (**Possible Incompatibility** with prior COBOL)
"Obsolete": Current feature will be deleted in future (Early warning of **eventual potential
           incompatibility** with prior COBOL)

"New":   Addition to COBOL 85 (**compatible** with prior COBOL)

"Change":   Current feature changed in COBOL 85
                  (**Possible Incompatibility** with prior COBOL)

"Obsolete":   Current feature will be deleted in future (Early warning of **eventual potential incompatibility** with prior COBOL)

"New":   Addition to COBOL 85 (**compatible** with prior COBOL)
"Change":   Current feature changed in COBOL 85
            (**Possible Incompatibility** with prior COBOL)
"Obsolete":   Current feature will be deleted in future (Early warning of **eventual potential incompatibility** with prior COBOL)

IV. COBOL 85 Conversion of COBOL 74/68 Programs   147

ALL "literal"   150

New rules have been created for the length of **ALL "literal"**.

A specific use of **ALL "literal"** is made obsolete.

ALPHABET   152

Alphabet-name clause uses the keyword **ALPHABET**.

ALPHABETIC Class   153

New rules have been defined for the **ALPHABETIC** class test.

ALTER   154

The **ALTER** statement has been made obsolete.

"New":   Addition to COBOL 85 (**compatible** with prior COBOL)

"Change":   Current feature changed in COBOL 85
         (**Possible Incompatibility** with prior COBOL)

"Obsolete":   Current feature will be deleted in future (Early warning of **eventual potential incompatibility** with prior COBOL)

The
COBOL 85
Example
Book

I

COBOL 85

Introduction

Structured Trends

The following discussion is presented as a background to the new COBOL 85 language. It is not intended to teach structured methodologies. In order to appreciate the enhancements and changes of COBOL 85, it is helpful to know what was happening in the data-processing industry when COBOL 85 was being developed.

Most textbooks dealing with the evolution of the computer industry over the past 25 years point out the downward trend of hardware costs and the upward trend of software costs. (See graph below.)
The costs for application software (both development and maintenance costs) rose very high and very fast during the sixties and seventies. This growth caused many data-processing managers, responsible for controlling budgets, to look for non-traditional ways of managing application software. One solution was to purchase application packages written by third-party software vendors. But packaged software needs to be maintained just as "homegrown" software does. Packaged software must also go through the same development cycle that any application software does.

During this period, the advice and suggestions of software

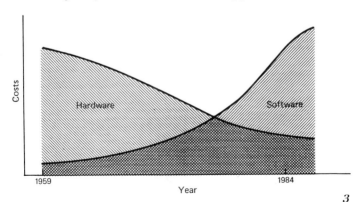

engineers (many from academia) began to receive attention. These engineers presented ways to control the cost of developing and maintaining systems. The most popular concept of software engineers was the design of well-structured systems. This meant different things to different people; common to all structured methodologies, however, was the sense of control and order in a methodical process that replaced the "random" process of systems development. By breaking up the Analysis, Design, Programming, Implementation and Maintenance phases of a system's life cycle, specialists were created. These specialists possess specific skills to match specific technical tasks. Job titles such as Data Base Administrator and Librarian, among many others, appeared.

Another notable problem common to many poorly planned systems was the traditional last-minute panic that occurred when systems went "on-line" for the first time—that is, when all system components were being tested together. (See *Traditional Testing* graph.)

Most experienced COBOL programmers can recount "project burnout" stories of 48-hour shifts with lots of pizza, coke and coffee. Too often, projects needed that eleventh-hour crash effort to meet a deadline. These times in a programmer's career may be rewarding in some ways (the look of accomplishment on their faces upon completion proves that); but it's no way to manage a software-development project.

We had to find out how to test systems' bugs during all stages of systems development, rather than waiting until the

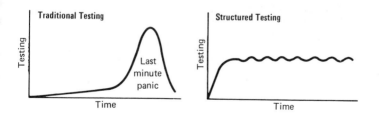

end and discovering them all at once. This led to theories on "structured testing" and "structured walk-throughs."

Having many checkpoints established during the development cycle provides the programmer with many opportunities to discover small problems; having few checkpoints provides few opportunities to discover large problems. Ed Yourdon suggests replacing system-development "milestones" with "inch-pebbles."* (See *Structured Testing* graph.)

It was surprising to some to learn that most of the system errors discovered over the lifetime of a system were more often caused by design flaws than by coding errors. (See *Design vs. Programming Errors* graph.)

This suggested a breakdown in communication between the "end-user" (a business unit within a corporation, for example) and the data-processing department. Somehow the business unit's needs were being misunderstood or inaccurately translated by the computer staff. As a result, end-users needed to become more involved in the development of their own

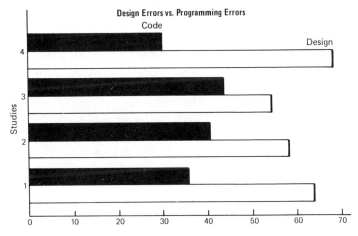

*"Learning to Program in Structured COBOL/Part 2", by Timothy R. Lister and Edward Yourdon.

systems. Structured end-user walkthroughs provided one way to involve the business-unit staff.

One of the most significant trends over the past 25 years has been the growing proportion of resources spent for system maintenance relative to system development. (See *Hardware vs. Software* graph.)

Although software costs in general were rising rapidly during the sixties and seventies, maintenance costs were rising much more rapidly than development costs. System maintenance, which was a fact of life (reluctantly accepted by some data-processing managers), had to be managed and planned for. This led to a new consciousness of the system-maintenance function. It is important to recognize that most systems will require some maintenance (either corrective or perfective) during their life cycle.

> "Changes to computer systems will continue as long as . . . . the business organization continues to evolve. We don't want to treat program specifications as a never-changing oil portrait, but as a single frame of a motion picture. We want to organize our programs in such a way that we don't have to rewrite the entire program when the next frame comes into focus."*

System maintenance is a natural event. Accepting this basic fact, system designers began designing systems with the maintenance function in mind. This was a major change in thinking from earlier development theories. In some of the early systems, we didn't think about the maintenance these systems would require. There are many examples of poorly structured and poorly documented systems, written in assembly language or COBOL (or FORTRAN) in the sixties and early seventies. Often the systems were so out-of-control that they had to be discarded and replaced with completely new systems. In most

*"Learning to Program in Structured COBOL/Part 2", by Timothy R. Lister and Edward Yourdon.

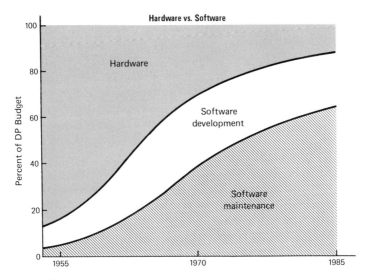

cases the new systems were more "manageable" (maintainable) than the old systems. This basic design principle is best illustrated using the automobile as an example and the most frequent maintenance function that we perform, refueling. Can you imagine if the engineers in Detroit, when designing our cars, had placed the gastank cap underneath the car, behind the transmission (requiring removal of both the transmission and the rear axle), or in any other "hard-to-reach" or "hard-to-find" place? It might take us five hours to put gas in our cars—a maintenance task that now takes us five minutes. (This is assuming we're not waiting on a line at the filling station during an oil embargo.) Furthermore, how many times do you imagine we can dismantle our transmission (or rear axle), and reassemble it without accidentally forgetting to put back a screw (or making some other maintenance error)? We increase the chances of accidentally damaging the transmission (an unconnected function) every time we fill up with gas. Why? Because someone designed our car without anticipating this maintenance function. By isolating the gas cap (and all other features of the car that are required for refueling), in one "easy-to-find" and "easy-to-reach" place, we lower the risk of accidental maintenance error. This same principle applies to computer systems.

During the mid-seventies, the CODASYL COBOL Committee invited software engineers all over the world to suggest improvements in the COBOL language that would make it compatible with state-of-the-art software theory.* One of the most important theories was presented by Larry Constantine:

$$C(\tfrac{1}{2}P) + C(\tfrac{1}{2}P) < C(P)$$

What Constantine said in effect was that if we could somehow measure the complexity of a problem, C(P), and divide the problem in half and measure the complexity of each half, $C(\tfrac{1}{2}P)$, the total complexity of the problem could be reduced (if divided properly). This theory was significant because it suggested to system designers how they could make their systems less complex and more maintainable. Modularization (functional decomposition) became an artful technique in system and program design. Many of the enhancements in COBOL 85 make modular programming easier. Some of these features are nested programming, **GLOBAL**/local data, **CALL . . . BY CONTENT/REFERENCE** and scope terminators. The amount of simplification achieved is of course dependent on how the original problem was broken up. Acceptance of Constantine's theory led to many different suggestions on how to decompose a function (module). Top–down structured design became the rage.

When decomposing a function into component subfunctions, there is some overlapping middle-ground through which one subfunction communicates, or is coupled, with another. Theories of modular coupling and cohesion arose, offering suggestions on how to minimize complexity and maximize

*CODASYL "Proceedings of a Symposium on Structured Programming in COBOL — Future and Present", edited by Henry P. Stevenson, Los Angeles, California, April 7, 1975, published by ACM.

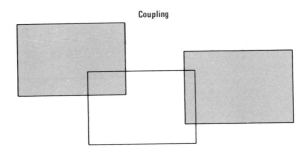

Coupling

efficiency wherever modules needed to "talk to" one another. This resulted in COBOL 85 enhancements such as **CALL . . . BY CONTENT, COMMON** programs and other new features.

The CODASYL symposium produced other suggested improvements to COBOL. Most of these enhancements were eventually incorporated into COBOL 85. One such suggestion was a new "case" statement (**EVALUATE**), the absence of which has been a major deficiency in COBOL until now; also suggested and incorporated into COBOL 85 were significant improvements to the **PERFORM** statement, including an "in-line" version of **PERFORM** and variations of **PERFORM** that allow "do-while" and "do-until" logic. COBOL 85 is clearly a product of the times it grew up in.

The COBOL 85 Controversy

The "Caesarean" Birth of COBOL 85

The new COBOL 85 language has been embroiled in a controversy the likes of which the language-standards community had not seen before. Some feel that it is inevitable for any language that survives as long as COBOL to gain inertia and thus resistance to any change. Evidence of this resistance can also be seen in the revision efforts of the BASIC and FORTRAN languages.

There are many who feel that COBOL is developing too slowly and is becoming—if it has not already become—out of touch with the real needs of the computing community. Application development tools such as "4th Generation languages," Application code generators, report writers, etc., are available. Many software-development installations are turning to these "shortcuts" as alternatives to traditional COBOL application development. Many believe that COBOL has been too slow in responding to the changing needs of the data-processing industry. Lacking high-level syntax and other facilities, COBOL has been rejected in favor of some of the more "modern" application generators. (See the section in this book on COBOL's future.)

This criticism is heard as much outside the United States (where COBOL is just as popular) as in the United States. The international computing community has for many years used the American version of COBOL as its (international) version. They are concerned, however, that COBOL is evolving too slowly.

There are those who believe instead that COBOL should be made more static. Each revision, or "improvement", costs the business community a lot of unnecessary money just to stay current with state-of-the-art technology. They see few benefits in upgrading to the new language in relation to the cost of such a conversion. For them, COBOL is "good enough" as is for solving their programming needs.

> "Good data processing managers never produce 'most efficient' programs. They don't even produce 'very good' programs. They should and do produce 'good enough' programs . . . . The data processing manager is wasting the resources given if he or she has programs written better than 'good enough.' The work spent purifying a 'good enough' program is better spent writing more 'good enough' programs."*

This last group of critics has received most of the public's and the media's attention over the past few years. This is due in large part to the efforts of Joseph Brophy of Travelers Insurance Company who in 1981 stated:

> "...for the (ANSI COBOL) committee to vote in favor of the COBOL-80 standard . . . . would be irresponsible, tantamount to deriliction, and a reflection of its business immaturity . . . . Travelers is willing to take it to court by beginning a class action suit against each individual member of the committee supporting a COBOL-80 standard that is incompatible with COBOL-74."**

A Point-by-Point Rebuke of Revision Efforts on COBOL Standards by Ardyn E. Dubnow, *Data Management*, December, 1981. (Note: In a rebuttal of the above article entitled *COBOL-80 A Feature by Feature Explanation* by Jerome Garfunkel, *Data Management*, July, 1983, I asked the question:

   Is this good enough?

          ADD X Y GIVING Z

   or is this good enough?

          ADD   THIS-WEEKS-SALARY
          TO   YTD-SALARY
          GIVING   NEW-YTD-SALARY

**COMPUTER LAW AND TAX REPORT, Volume 7, Number 6, January 1981.

As discussed elsewhere in this book, the COBOL standardization process includes and encourages public participation.
The first draft proposed revision of the COBOL 74 language
was released to the public for review and comment in September 1981. Travelers Insurance, via a computerized direct-mail
campaign, launched a successful lobbying effort against the
proposed new COBOL language. This resulted in an overwhelmingly negative response. The ANSI COBOL committee
(X3J4) responsible for the revised COBOL received nearly 2,300
comments from the public, most of them form letters and most
of them negative. As a result, the ANSI COBOL committee
went back into deliberation and made new modifications to
COBOL. In June 1983, they published the second proposed
revision of the COBOL language for further public review and
comment. The changes it included were often in direct response to the heightened sensitivity to "unnecessary incompatibilities." Mr. Brophy was indeed being heeded. Feeling that
the ANSI COBOL committee had not gone far enough in solving potential incompatibilities, Travelers Insurance launched
another computerized lobbying effort. This second campaign,
although less impressive than the first, resulted in another
overwhelmingly negative response. This time about 925 public
comments were received, mostly form letters, and again mostly
negative. As a result of this latest public response, the ANSI
COBOL committee was obliged to make still further changes to
COBOL.

    At exactly this time, some interesting things were happen-
ing in the international COBOL community. These events provided the final push to the new COBOL language, both here in
the United States and abroad. In February 1984, the International COBOL Committee met in Vienna. Many issues were
discussed, and two important resolutions were passed. The
Vienna group decided to recommend the adoption of the then-
current version of the draft proposed American Standard
COBOL language as the new International Standard COBOL.
The committee also agreed to a proposal (originated by this

author) for procedural changes that will speed up the intro-
duction of new high level facilities into the COBOL language.
Both these actions were later endorsed (without unanimity) by
the American COBOL committee.*

In May 1984, the third proposed revision of the COBOL
language was published in the United States for public review
and comment. As a result of a third lobbying compaign, 24
comments were sent to the ANSI COBOL committee. Only
minor changes to the new COBOL language were required
after this third public review period. In early 1985, the ANSI
COBOL committee forwarded this latest version of the proposed revision of the COBOL language to the ANSI review committees for official approval as the new standard. On September
10, 1985, final approval was given, and the draft proposed
COBOL language became the new American National Standard COBOL 85.

Portability vs. Compatibility

The issue at the heart of the controversy is the relative
importance of language portability between two different systems and language compatibility with a previous version of a
particular implementor's complier.

The following two examples illustrate language portability.

```
COMPUTE NUMERIC-RESULT = 1 / 3 * 3.
```

```
01  NUMERIC-ITEM PICTURE 999 USAGE IS COMPUTATIONAL-1.
```

A standard-conforming COBOL program containing either of

---

*See *Computer World,* March 12, 1984, ''A Report from Vienna: Which Way
COBOL'' by Ken Meyer. Ken has written an excellent account of the historic
COBOL meeting held in Vienna, Austria. The International COBOL Commit-
tee (ISO TC77/ SC22/WG4) adjourned on February 14, 1984. Some anti-
COBOLists referred to the significant actions taken by the Vienna group as the
Valentine's Day Massacre, 1984.

the statements above may behave differently from one system to another.

In the **COMPUTE** statement, there is no standard for the precision of intermediate data items in arithmetic calculations and expressions. Therefore, this **COMPUTE** statement may behave differently from one system to another.

USAGE IS COMPUTATIONAL-1 is a nonstandard COBOL phrase. It may indicate **BINARY** data on one system and **PACKED-DECIMAL** on another.

Consider the following examples illustrating program compatibility:

```
IF "John Smith" IS ALPHABETIC . . .

ALTER PROCESS-INDICATOR TO PROCEED TO LAST-PROCESS
```

In the examples above, a program may behave differently if compiled with a COBOL 85 compiler rather than with the COBOL 74 or COBOL 68 compiler for which it was written. These features were ambiguous or obsolete in earlier versions of COBOL. In COBOL 85, such features have been either cleanly defined or marked for deletion.

Joseph Brophy estimated that converting Travelers' (mostly) COBOL 68 programs to COBOL 85 would cost his company between 20 and 30 million dollars. Travelers said relatively little about any potential benefits it might derive from such a conversion.

In March 1983, the National Bureau of Standards of the United States Department of Commerce published the 84-page *Cost-Benefit Impact Study on the Adoption of the Draft Proposed Revised X3.23 American National Standard Programming Language COBOL.** The government concluded here that

---

Cost-Benefit Impact Study on the Adoption of the Draft Proposed Revised X3.23 American National Standard Programming Language COBOL, Marco Fiorello and John Cugini
U.S. Department of Commerce, National Bureau of Standards
Publication Number NBSIR 83-2639

over a ten-year period, COBOL 85 will save five dollars in increased productivity for every one dollar of conversion cost. In reviewing the COBOL source programs that were included in the U.S. government study, it is clear that the conclusions of that study can be applied equally to the commercial data-processing community.

Some advice can be drawn from Grace Hopper, who, in September 1984, said:

> "Continually look ahead to absorb the new concepts and implement the new things. Don't ever say, 'Well, we have always done it that way.' That is the deadly thing that kills systems and managers. Just as in the automobile industry or aircraft industry, it's a changing industry. You can't sit back. Imagine what happened to the people when the Model T Ford came out—some people said, 'Get a horse.' And when the telephones first appeared, there were people who wouldn't touch them for fear that they would get electrocuted. And when refrigerators first appeared there were people who wouldn't use them because the only way to keep lettuce and carrots fresh for them was on ice. There were always people who wouldn't change their minds and move forward with the new things."

The CODASYL, ANSI and ISO COBOL Committees

COBOL 85 is the latest version of the COBOL language, whose origin can be traced to a meeting held at the University of Pennsylvania Computing Center in Philadelphia on April 8, 1959. The purpose of the meeting was to lay the groundwork for the COBOL language. There were computer users and representatives from computer manufacturers and universities. The participants suggested to the Department of Defense that a conference be held to discuss the possible development of a "common business language."* This eventually led to the creation of the COnference on DAta SYstems Languages (CODASYL). (See Appendix F.1 and F.2.) The first officially published version of COBOL was COBOL 60. The CODASYL committee followed this with COBOL 61, COBOL 61 Extended and COBOL 65. In the early sixties, the United States of America Standards Institute (USASI—later known as ANSI) made an agreement with CODASYL to jointly develop the American Standard COBOL language. Although challenged over the years, this relationship still exists today. CODASYL develops the "experimental COBOL model" in its *Journal of Development* (JOD); ANSI selects from this model features to be incorporated in the American National Standard (ANS) COBOL. This joint venture has resulted in USAS COBOL 68, ANS COBOL 74 and ANS COBOL 85. Furthermore, the International Standards Organization (ISO) has traditionally specified the American (ANS) COBOL Language as the International (ISO) COBOL language. (See Appendix F.4.)

The ANSI COBOL Committee (X3J4) (See Appendix F.3) began the process of updating COBOL 74 by establishing June

---

*For an excellent examination of the early history of the COBOL language see AFIPS, *Annals of the History of Computing:* v. 7, no. 4, Oct. 85.

1978 as the deadline for selecting features for ANS COBOL 85 from the CODASYL COBOL model published in the JOD.

The procedures required to establish the new COBOL language as the new American National Standard COBOL are lengthy and complex. The process includes and encourages public participation. As mentioned, the "birth" of the new COBOL 85 language began in June 1978; the COBOL 85 language was born (by "Caesarean" operation) in September 1985.

The Future of COBOL

Some very interesting trends are developing in the computer industry today that are certain to affect the future development of the COBOL language as well as that of other application languages.

First, there has been a sharp increase in the number of "end-users" working with computers within large corporations as well as small businesses. By definition, these people are not programmers, yet they very often perform programming tasks. They frequently perform these tasks with the aid of microcomputers along with very "user-friendly" programming languages (Application generators), powerful behind-the-scenes Data Base Management Systems and equally powerful Screen Management Systems. These "programming languages" are often disguised as end-user applications such as "VisiCalc," "JAZZ," "Lotus 1-2-3," to name a few. These new "programming languages," also called "end-user" languages, generally use nonprocedural syntax.

These new programming tools are being used at every level within the business community. The microcomputer applications available in retail outlets indicate just who the audience is.

Software development tools (including COBOL) are evolving in quite a natural way, analogous perhaps to the evolution of nothing less than civilization. As the world's population increases, civilization becomes more complex. There simply are more people to share the work. Thus, the work gets divided further (i.e., into more detail), creating the likelihood of more complexity. Just as our increasingly complex society has led to more and more specialization in job functions, end-user languages are being created for specific applications. The syntax is useful for, but limited to, solving specific kinds of problems; however, it solves those specific problems (i.e., it creates an application program) more quickly and more accurately than the "generalist" programming languages (like COBOL, FORTRAN and PASCAL). And best of all, the learning time required in order for noncomputer personnel to be productive on the computer is minimal. This of course appeals to corporate management because of the tremendous new pool of talented personnel (including themselves) who are now computer literate. It is estimated that by the end of the present decade, nearly 80% of all computer application programs will be written by noncomputer personnel using some form of a "natural" language.*

While it is true that these specialized end-user languages represent a real challenge to the traditional "generalist" languages, their strength lies primarily in program development. However, of at least equal importance today is software maintenance. A 1984 study estimated that nearly 75% of software costs are spent for system and programming maintenance. It took a long time for the data-processing community to accept the fact that system maintenance is a natural phase of every system and therefore must be planned for in the original design.

Program maintenance requires that one generation of programmers understand (decipher) and make changes to the programs produced by an earlier generation of programmers. The program maintenance function requires from a programming language a different set of priorities from those of the program development function. In program development, speed of accurate and efficient coding is the highest priority; but in program maintenance, speed of understanding (deciphering) programs is the highest priority. The importance of system/program *readability* is at the heart of every structured methodology. If a program's functions, which might be modified, are coded in independent (easy-to-find, easy-to-change) modules

---

*An interesting prediction made in 1981 when the first draft of this paper was written. It seemed like a high figure in 1981; in 1985 it seems low. (jg 3/1/85)

in a source program, maintenance is safer and quicker. More-over, when a maintenance programmer is assigned a program that is written with a familiar structure as well as a familiar language, the time required to understand that program is reduced greatly.

I see no other language around today (including Ada, C, Modula2, DIBOL, PL/1, etc.) that is likely to replace COBOL. Even if past versions of COBOL have been behind the times, as some critics have claimed, COBOL 85 will do much to change that perception—but only for a short time. The rapid evolution of COBOL is necessary in order for it to remain the leading application-software development language. This rapid evolu-tion has begun. The procedures by which the COBOL language is developed and standardized are being streamlined.

The continued use of the COBOL language is assured for numerous reasons. First, COBOL is still an excellent ap-plication-development tool. COBOL excels in many areas. Some of its unique strengths include its file-updating and merging facilities; its easy linkage to other COBOL (and non-COBOL) programs; and its industrywide portability (of both programs and programmers). COBOL's future is as-sured because of the importance of program maintenance in today's (and tomorrow's) data-processing environment. In addition, one cannot ignore the large investment already made by the business community in existing COBOL program libraries.

I expect that the microsoftware-development community will increasingly turn to COBOL as their development lan-guage. They will do so for all the same reasons that the "main-frame" world turned to COBOL 25 years ago. In addition to the micro-application world, the corporate mainframe world is increasingly turning to COBOL on micros to develop mainframe COBOL applications. As of this writing (in 1985), there are at least eight GSA certified high-level ANS COBOL 74 compilers running on various microcomputers. It is likely that there will be several COBOL 85 compilers in the near future.

Two Directions for COBOL

The COBOL programming language is evolving simultaneously in two directions. On the one hand, COBOL is becoming more "nonprocedural"; that is, some COBOL syntax allows programmers to specify what functions are to be performed on files and data items, without describing in detail the step-by-step procedures to be carried out to accomplish those functions. Instead, it is left to the complier to determine what procedures must be executed in order to perform those functions. Examples of nonprocedural COBOL features included in the language now are the Report Writer facility, **SORT** and **MERGE**. Other nonprocedural features that may appear in future versions of COBOL include **VALIDATE** and **UPDATE** (see below).

The other direction that COBOL is taking is completely opposite from that described above. COBOL 85 includes features that allow programmers to manipulate files and data items in fine detail (incorporating features often found in assembly languages), and therefore, COBOL is becoming more "procedural." Examples of these features are Reference Modification and the **STRING** and **UNSTRING** statements. Other features that may appear in future versions of COBOL are Boolean data items (bit manipulation) and sign-sensitive **PICTURE** editing characters (see below).

The CODASYL COBOL model (described in the CODASYL COBOL *Journal of Development*) provides compiler writers with a protoype of specifications of advanced functions that they may consider implementing. It is likely that some of the features listed below will appear as "implementor-extensions" to COBOL 85 compilers during the next few years. As various complier writers develop the translators for features that are likely to appear in subsequent versions of COBOL (COBOL 95, perhaps ?), it is often an easy task to add these as extensions to their current COBOL products. It is for this reason that the following potential COBOL features are significant.

Intrinsic Functions*

Over thirty intrinsic functions have been added to the CODA-SYL COBOL model. When provided with specific arguments, these functions return specific results. These intrinsic functions (see figure below) were considered for inclusion in the COBOL 85 language, but unfortunately they were not included. It is likely that these intrinsic functions (and others perhaps) will be an early addition to the updated COBOL language. Numerous proposals have been made to add specific functions to the current list and to create a mechanism for user-defined functions. (It is interesting to note that a similar feature, the **DEFINE** statement, was included in the original COBOL 60 language and deleted in 1968.)** It is likely that these intrinsic functions will be included in an early update to the COBOL 85 language. See table on following pages.

VALIDATE Facility*

The **VALIDATE** Facility was created by a group within the British Computer Society, and is sometimes referred to as a "reverse Report Writer" facility. In the same way that the **GENERATE** statement causes much macro-generated procedural code to be executed, so does the **VALIDATE** statement. All Validation criteria affecting the chosen records are described in the **DATA DIVISION**. All the data relationships and values are verified with a single **VALIDATE** statement in the **PROCEDURE DIVISION**. A proposal has been presented recently in the international programming languages community to create a similar **VALIDATE** facility that can be used by all programming languages.

**Sammet JE, Garfunkel J: "Summary of Changes in COBOL, 1960−1985. AFIPS, "Annals of the History of Computing: v. 7, no. 4, Oct. 85.

Intrinsic Functions

Name	Arguments	Type	Value Returned
ACOS	N1	N	Arccosine of N1
ANNUITY	N1, N2	N	Ratio or annuity paid for N2 periods to investments at interest of N1
ASIN	N1	N	Arcsine of N1
ATAN	N1	N	Arctangent of N1
CHAR	N1	X	Character in position N1 of program collating sequence
COS	N1	N	Cosine of N1
CURRENT-DATE	none	X	Current date and time, and difference from Greenwich Mean Time
DATE-OF-INTEGER	I1	I	Standard date equivalent (YYYYMMDD) of integer date
DAY-OF-INTEGER	I1	I	Julian date equivalent (YYYYDDD) of integer date
FACTORIAL	I1	I	Factorial of I1
INTEGER	N1	I	The largest integer not larger than N1.
INTEGER-OF-DATE	I1	I	Integer date equivalent of Standard date (YYYYMMDD)
INTEGER-OF-DAY	I1	I	Integer date equivalent of Julian date (YYYYDDD)
INTEGER-PART	N1	I	Integer part of N1
LN	N1	N	Natural logarithm of N1
LOG	N1	N	Logarithm to base 10 of N1
LOWER-CASE	X1 or A1	X	All letters in X1 or A1 set lower-case
MAX	A1 ... or X1 ... or I1 ... or N1 ... or	Same as Argument	Value of maximum argument

Name	Arguments	Type	Value Returned
MIN	A1 ... or X1 ... or I1 ... or N1 ...	Same as Argument	Value of minimum argument
MOD	I1, I2	I	I1 modulo I2
NUMVAL	X1	N	Numeric value of simple numeric string
NUMVAL-C	X1, X2	N	Numeric value of numeric string with optional commas and currency sign
NUMVAL-F	X1	N	Numeric value of floating-point string
ORD	X1	I	Ordinal of X1 in collating sequence
ORD-MAX	A1 ... or I1 ... or X1 ... or N1 ...	I	Ordinal of maximum argument
ORD-MIN	A1 ... or I1 ... or X1 ... or N1 ...	I	Ordinal of minimum argument
RANDOM	N1	N	Random number
REM	N1, N2	N	Remainder of N1/N2
REVERSE	X1 or A1	X	Reverse order of the characters of the argument
SIN	N1	N	Sine of N1
SQRT	N1	N	Square root of N1
SUM	I1, ... or N1, ... or	Same as Argument	Sum of arguments
TAN	N1	N	Tangent of N1
UPPER-CASE	X1 or A1	X	All letters in X1 or A1 set uppercase
WHEN-COMPILED	none	X	Date and time program was compiled

UPDATE and ANALYSE

Recently proposed in Great Britain, these two macro facilities use nonprocedural statements to replace the procedural logic of file matching and file updating. (Note the British spelling of what Americans would call the *ANALYZE* Facility).

User-defined COBOL Syntax

A facility called CLEF (COBOL Language Extension Facility) has been proposed. It allows programmers to create their own COBOL syntax for specific functions. A prototype of such a system was developed under the direction of John Triance at the University of Manchester Institute of Science and Technology (UMIST) in England. Its potential impact on COBOL is enormous.

Boolean (bit) Manipulation Facility*

The **USAGE IS BIT** phrase and the **PICTURE** symbol **1** are included in the CODASYL COBOL model. Together they allow a single bit to be defined and accessed. Allowable values are **0** or **1**. New Boolean operators have also been added: **B-AND, B-OR, B-EXOR, B-NOT.** The Boolean (bit) Manipulation Facility may be in an early update to the COBOL 85 language.

Free-Form Coding*

The present reference format for COBOL

Sequence	1−6
Continuation	7
Margin A	8−11
Margin B	12−72
Identification	73−80

is of course based on the 80-column punch card.
Free-form coding puts an end to the punch card tradition.

DELETE File Statement*

This allows a programmer to effectively de**SELECT** a file and
return it to the operating system (**DELETE "Important-File"**
may make its file space available to be written over.)

Enhanced PICTURE String Editing

Enhanced **PICTURE** string editing, such as sign-sensitive editing, has been defined in the CODASYL COBOL model. Also
proposed is user-defined floating and fixed insertion characters.

Other possible future enhancements include:

Deletion of level-77 items*

In-line comments in Source program*

60-character data-names*

Floating-Point data items*

---

*Features that are indicated with * are included in the current CODASYL COBOL
Journal of Development and are already candidates for inclusion into the
next COBOL standard by the ANSI COBOL Committee.

II

COBOL 85

Syntax Skeleton

General Format For Identification Division

<u>IDENTIFICATION</u> <u>DIVISION</u>.

<u>PROGRAM-ID</u>. program-name $\left[\text{IS} \left\{ \left| \begin{array}{c} \underline{\text{COMMON}} \\ \underline{\text{INITIAL}} \end{array} \right| \right\} \text{PROGRAM} \right]$.

[<u>AUTHOR</u>. [comment-entry] . . .]

[<u>INSTALLATION</u>. [comment-entry] . . .]

[<u>DATE-WRITTEN</u>. [comment-entry] . . .]

[<u>DATE-COMPILED</u>. [comment-entry] . . .]

[<u>SECURITY</u>. [comment-entry] . . .]

General Format For Environment Division

[ENVIRONMENT DIVISION.

[CONFIGURATION SECTION.

[SOURCE-COMPUTER. [computer-name [WITH DEBUGGING MODE] .]]

[OBJECT-COMPUTER. [computer-name

$$
\left[\underline{MEMORY} \text{ SIZE integer-1} \left\{ \begin{array}{l} \underline{WORDS} \\ \underline{CHARACTERS} \\ \underline{MODULES} \end{array} \right\} \right]
$$

[PROGRAM COLLATING SEQUENCE IS alphabet-name-1]

[SEGMENT-LIMIT IS segment-number] .]]

[SPECIAL-NAMES. [[implementor-name-1

$$
\left[\begin{array}{l} \text{IS mnemonic-name-1}\quad [\underline{ON} \text{ STATUS IS condition-name-1}\quad [\underline{OFF} \text{ STATUS IS condition-name-2}]] \\ \text{IS mnemonic-name-2}\quad [\underline{OFF} \text{ STATUS IS condition-name-2}\quad [\underline{ON} \text{ STATUS IS condition-name-1}]] \\ \underline{ON} \text{ STATUS IS condition-name-1}\quad [\underline{OFF} \text{ STATUS IS condition-name-2}] \\ \underline{OFF} \text{ STATUS IS condition-name-2}\quad [\underline{ON} \text{ STATUS IS condition-name-1}] \end{array} \right] \right\} \ldots
$$

[ALPHABET alphabet-name-1 IS

$$
\left\{ \begin{array}{l} \underline{STANDARD-1} \\ \underline{STANDARD-2} \\ \underline{NATIVE} \\ \text{implementor-name-2} \\ \left\{ \text{literal-1} \quad \left[\left\{ \begin{array}{l} \underline{THROUGH} \\ \underline{THRU} \end{array} \right\} \text{literal-2} \right] \right\} \ldots \\ \qquad\qquad \{ \underline{ALSO} \text{ literal-3} \} \ldots \end{array} \right\} \ldots \right]
$$

$$
\left[\underline{SYMBOLIC} \text{ CHARACTERS} \left\{ \{ \text{symbolic-character-1} \} \ldots \left\{ \begin{array}{l} \text{IS} \\ \text{ARE} \end{array} \right\} \{\text{integer-1}\} \ldots \right\} \ldots \right.
$$
$$
\left. [\underline{IN} \text{ alphabet-name-2}] \right\} \ldots
$$

$$
\left[\underline{CLASS} \text{ class-name IS} \left\{ \text{literal-4} \left[\left\{ \begin{array}{l} \underline{THROUGH} \\ \underline{THRU} \end{array} \right\} \text{literal-5} \right] \right\} \ldots \right] \ldots
$$

[CURRENCY SIGN IS literal-6]

[DECIMAL-POINT IS COMMA] .]]

[INPUT-OUTPUT SECTION.

FILE-CONTROL.

{file-control-entry} . . .

[I-O-CONTROL.

$$
\left[\left[\underline{RERUN} \left[\underline{ON} \left\{ \begin{array}{l} \text{file-name-1} \\ \text{implementor-name-1} \end{array} \right\} \right] \text{EVERY} \left\{ \begin{array}{l} [\underline{END} \text{ OF}] \left\{ \begin{array}{l} \underline{REEL} \\ \underline{UNIT} \end{array} \right\} \text{OF file-name-2} \\ \text{integer-1} \ \underline{RECORDS} \\ \text{integer-2} \ \underline{CLOCK-UNITS} \\ \text{condition-name-1} \end{array} \right\} \right] \ldots
$$

$$
\left[\left[\underline{SAME} \left[\begin{array}{l} \underline{RECORD} \\ \underline{SORT} \\ \underline{SORT-MERGE} \end{array} \right] \text{AREA FOR file-name-3} \ \{\text{file-name-4}\} \ldots \right] \ldots
$$

[MULTIPLE FILE TAPE CONTAINS

{file-name-5 [POSITION integer-3] } . . .] . . . .]]]]

General Format For File Control Entry

SEQUENTIAL FILE:

<u>SELECT</u> [<u>OPTIONAL</u>] file-name-1

    <u>ASSIGN</u> TO $\left\{ \begin{array}{l} \text{implementor-name-1} \\ \text{literal-1} \end{array} \right\}$ ...

    $\left[\underline{\text{RESERVE}} \text{ integer-1} \left[\begin{array}{l} \text{AREA} \\ \text{AREAS} \end{array} \right] \right]$

    [[<u>ORGANIZATION</u> IS] <u>SEQUENTIAL</u>]

    $\left[\underline{\text{PADDING}} \text{ CHARACTER IS} \left\{ \begin{array}{l} \text{data-name-1} \\ \text{literal-2} \end{array} \right\} \right]$

    $\left[\underline{\text{RECORD}} \text{ } \underline{\text{DELIMITER}} \text{ IS} \left\{ \begin{array}{l} \underline{\text{STANDARD-1}} \\ \text{implementor-name-2} \end{array} \right\} \right]$

    [<u>ACCESS</u> MODE IS <u>SEQUENTIAL</u>]

    [FILE <u>STATUS</u> IS data-name-2].

RELATIVE FILE:

<u>SELECT</u> [<u>OPTIONAL</u>] file-name-1

    <u>ASSIGN</u> TO $\left\{ \begin{array}{l} \text{implementor-name-1} \\ \text{literal-1} \end{array} \right\}$ ...

    $\left[\underline{\text{RESERVE}} \text{ integer-1} \left[\begin{array}{l} \text{AREA} \\ \text{AREAS} \end{array} \right] \right]$

    [<u>ORGANIZATION</u> IS] <u>RELATIVE</u>

$$\left[\underline{\text{ACCESS}} \text{ MODE IS} \left\{ \begin{array}{ll} \underline{\text{SEQUENTIAL}} & [\underline{\text{RELATIVE}} \text{ KEY IS data-name-1} \\ \left\{ \begin{array}{l} \underline{\text{RANDOM}} \\ \underline{\text{DYNAMIC}} \end{array} \right\} & \underline{\text{RELATIVE}} \text{ KEY IS data-name-1} \end{array} \right\} \right]$$

    [FILE <u>STATUS</u> IS data-name-2].

General Format For File-Control Entry

INDEXED FILE:

SELECT [OPTIONAL] file-name-1

    ASSIGN TO $\left\{ \begin{array}{l} \text{implementor-name-1} \\ \text{literal-1} \end{array} \right\}$ ...

    $\left[\text{RESERVE integer-1} \left[\begin{array}{l} \text{AREA} \\ \text{AREAS} \end{array} \right] \right]$

    [ORGANIZATION IS] INDEXED

    $\left[\text{ACCESS MODE IS} \left\{ \begin{array}{l} \underline{\text{SEQUENTIAL}} \\ \underline{\text{RANDOM}} \\ \underline{\text{DYNAMIC}} \end{array} \right\} \right]$

    RECORD KEY IS data-name-1

    [ALTERNATE RECORD KEY IS data-name-2 [WITH DUPLICATES]] ...

    [FILE STATUS IS data-name-3].

REPORT FILE:

SELECT [OPTIONAL] file-name-1

    ASSIGN TO $\left\{ \begin{array}{l} \text{implementor-name-1} \\ \text{literal-1} \end{array} \right\}$ ...

    $\left[\text{RESERVE integer-1} \left[\begin{array}{l} \text{AREA} \\ \text{AREAS} \end{array} \right] \right]$

    [[ORGANIZATION IS] SEQUENTIAL]

    $\left[\text{PADDING CHARACTER IS} \left\{ \begin{array}{l} \text{data-name-1} \\ \text{literal-1} \end{array} \right\} \right]$

    $\left[\text{RECORD DELIMITER IS} \left\{ \begin{array}{l} \underline{\text{STANDARD-1}} \\ \text{implementor-name-2} \end{array} \right\} \right]$

    [ACCESS MODE IS SEQUENTIAL]

    [FILE STATUS IS data-name-2].

SORT OR MERGE FILE:

SELECT file-name-1 ASSIGN TO $\left\{ \begin{array}{l} \text{implementor-name-1} \\ \text{literal-1} \end{array} \right\}$ ...

General Format For Data Division

[<u>DATA</u> <u>DIVISION</u>.

[<u>FILE</u> <u>SECTION</u>.

$$\begin{bmatrix} \text{file-description-entry \{record-description-entry\}} \dots \\ \text{sort-merge-file-description-entry \{record-description-entry\}} \dots \\ \text{report-file-description-entry]} \end{bmatrix} \dots \end{bmatrix}$$

[<u>WORKING-STORAGE</u> <u>SECTION</u>.

$$\begin{bmatrix} \text{77-level-description-entry} \\ \text{record-description-entry} \end{bmatrix} \dots \end{bmatrix}$$

[<u>LINKAGE</u> <u>SECTION</u>.

$$\begin{bmatrix} \text{77-level-description-entry} \\ \text{record-description-entry} \end{bmatrix} \dots \end{bmatrix}$$

[<u>COMMUNICATION</u> <u>SECTION</u>.

[communication-description-entry {record-description-entry} ...] ...]

[<u>REPORT</u> <u>SECTION</u>.

[report-description-entry

{report-group-description-entry} ...] ...]]

General Format For File Description Entry

FD file-name-1

    [IS <u>EXTERNAL</u>]

    [IS <u>GLOBAL</u>]

$$\left[\; \underline{BLOCK}\; \text{CONTAINS}\;\; [\text{integer-1}\; \underline{TO}]\;\; \text{integer-2}\; \left\{ \begin{array}{l} \underline{RECORDS} \\ \text{CHARACTERS} \end{array} \right\} \right]$$

$$\left[\; \underline{RECORD} \left\{ \begin{array}{l} \text{CONTAINS integer-3 CHARACTERS} \\ \text{IS} \; \underline{VARYING}\; \text{IN SIZE [[FROM integer-4]} \;\; [\underline{TO}\; \text{integer-5] CHARACTERS]} \\ \qquad [\underline{DEPENDING}\; \text{ON data-name-1} \\ \text{CONTAINS integer-6}\; \underline{TO}\; \text{integer-7 CHARACTERS} \end{array} \right\} \right]$$

$$\left[\; \underline{LABEL} \left\{ \begin{array}{l} \underline{RECORD}\; \text{IS} \\ \underline{RECORDS}\; \text{ARE} \end{array} \right\} \left\{ \begin{array}{l} \underline{STANDARD} \\ \underline{OMITTED} \end{array} \right\} \right]$$

$$\left[\; \underline{VALUE}\; \underline{OF} \left\{ \text{implementor-name-1 IS} \left\{ \begin{array}{l} \text{data-name-2} \\ \text{literal-1} \end{array} \right\} \right\} \cdots \right]$$

$$\left[\; \underline{DATA} \left\{ \begin{array}{l} \underline{RECORD}\; \text{IS} \\ \underline{RECORDS}\; \text{ARE} \end{array} \right\} \{\text{data-name-3}\} \cdots \right]$$

$$\left[\; \underline{LINAGE}\; \text{IS} \left\{ \begin{array}{l} \text{data-name-4} \\ \text{integer-8} \end{array} \right\} \text{LINES} \left[\text{WITH}\; \underline{FOOTING}\; \text{AT} \left\{ \begin{array}{l} \text{data-name-5} \\ \text{integer-9} \end{array} \right\} \right] \right.$$

$$\left. \left[\text{LINES AT}\; \underline{TOP} \left\{ \begin{array}{l} \text{data-name-6} \\ \text{integer-10} \end{array} \right\} \right] \left[\text{LINES AT}\; \underline{BOTTOM} \left\{ \begin{array}{l} \text{data-name-7} \\ \text{integer-11} \end{array} \right\} \right] \right]$$

[<u>CODE-SET</u> IS alphabet-name-1] .

General Format For File Description Entry

RELATIVE FILE:

<u>FD</u> file-name-1

    [IS <u>EXTERNAL</u>]

    [IS <u>GLOBAL</u>]

    $\left[\underline{BLOCK} \text{ CONTAINS } [\text{integer-1 } \underline{TO}] \text{ integer-2} \left\{ \begin{array}{l} \underline{RECORDS} \\ \underline{CHARACTERS} \end{array} \right\} \right]$

    $\left[\underline{RECORD} \left\{ \begin{array}{l} \text{CONTAINS integer-3 CHARACTERS} \\ \text{IS } \underline{VARYING} \text{ IN SIZE } [\text{ [FROM integer-4]} \text{ } [\underline{TO} \text{ integer-5}] \text{ CHARACTERS]} \\ \text{\hspace{1.5em} [\underline{DEPENDING} ON data-name-1]} \\ \text{CONTAINS integer-6 } \underline{TO} \text{ integer-7 CHARACTERS} \end{array} \right\} \right]$

    $\left[\underline{LABEL} \left\{ \begin{array}{l} \underline{RECORD} \text{ IS} \\ \underline{RECORDS} \text{ ARE} \end{array} \right\} \left\{ \begin{array}{l} \underline{STANDARD} \\ \underline{OMITTED} \end{array} \right\} \right]$

    $\left[\underline{VALUE} \text{ } \underline{OF} \left\{ \text{implementor-name-1 IS} \left\{ \begin{array}{l} \text{data-name-2} \\ \text{literal-1} \end{array} \right\} \right\} \cdots \right]$

    $\left[\underline{DATA} \left\{ \begin{array}{l} \underline{RECORD} \text{ IS} \\ \underline{RECORDS} \text{ ARE} \end{array} \right\} \{\text{data-name-3}\} \cdots \right]$.

General Format For File Description Entry

INDEXED FILE:

<u>FD</u> file-name-1

[IS <u>EXTERNAL</u>]

[IS <u>GLOBAL</u>]

$$\left[\underline{\text{BLOCK}} \text{ CONTAINS } [\text{integer-1 } \underline{\text{TO}}] \text{ integer-2 } \left\{ \begin{array}{l} \underline{\text{RECORDS}} \\ \text{CHARACTERS} \end{array} \right\} \right]$$

$$\left[\underline{\text{RECORD}} \left\{ \begin{array}{l} \text{CONTAINS integer-3 CHARACTERS} \\ \text{IS } \underline{\text{VARYING}} \text{ IN SIZE } [[\text{FROM integer-4}] \quad [\underline{\text{TO}} \text{ integer-5}] \text{ CHARACTERS}] \\ \quad\quad [\underline{\text{DEPENDING}} \text{ ON data-name-1}] \\ \text{CONTAINS integer-6 } \underline{\text{TO}} \text{ integer-7 CHARACTERS} \end{array} \right\} \right]$$

$$\left[\underline{\text{LABEL}} \left\{ \begin{array}{l} \underline{\text{RECORD}} \text{ IS} \\ \underline{\text{RECORDS}} \text{ ARE} \end{array} \right\} \left\{ \begin{array}{l} \underline{\text{STANDARD}} \\ \underline{\text{OMITTED}} \end{array} \right\} \right]$$

$$\left[\underline{\text{VALUE}} \ \underline{\text{OF}} \left\{ \text{implementor-name-1 IS} \left\{ \begin{array}{l} \text{data-name-2} \\ \text{literal-1} \end{array} \right\} \right\} \cdots \right]$$

$$\left[\underline{\text{DATA}} \left\{ \begin{array}{l} \underline{\text{RECORD}} \text{ IS} \\ \underline{\text{RECORDS}} \text{ ARE} \end{array} \right\} \{\text{data-name-3}\} \cdots \right].$$

General Format For File Description Entry

REPORT FILE:

FD file-name-1

  [IS EXTERNAL]

  [IS GLOBAL]

$$\left[\underline{BLOCK}\text{ CONTAINS }[\text{integer-1 }\underline{TO}]\text{ integer-2 }\left\{\begin{array}{l}\underline{RECORDS}\\\underline{CHARACTERS}\end{array}\right\}\right]$$

$$\left[\underline{RECORD}\left\{\begin{array}{l}\text{CONTAINS integer-3 CHARACTERS}\\\text{CONTAINS integer-4 }\underline{TO}\text{ integer-5 CHARACTERS}\end{array}\right\}\right]$$

$$\left[\underline{LABEL}\left\{\begin{array}{l}\underline{RECORD}\text{ IS}\\\underline{RECORDS}\text{ ARE}\end{array}\right\}\left\{\begin{array}{l}\underline{STANDARD}\\\underline{OMITTED}\end{array}\right\}\right]$$

$$\left[\underline{VALUE}\ \underline{OF}\left\{\text{implementor-name-1 IS }\left\{\begin{array}{l}\text{data-name-2}\\\text{literal-1}\end{array}\right\}\right\}\ ...\ \right]$$

[CODE-SET IS alphabet-name-1] .

$$\left\{\begin{array}{l}\underline{REPORT}\text{ IS}\\\underline{REPORTS}\text{ ARE}\end{array}\right\}\{\text{report-name-1}\}\ ...\ .$$

SORT-MERGE FILE:

SD file-name-1

$$\left[\underline{RECORD}\left\{\begin{array}{l}\text{CONTAINS integer-1 CHARACTERS}\\\text{IS }\underline{VARYING}\text{ IN SIZE }[\ [\text{FROM integer-2}]\ \ [\underline{TO}\text{ integer-3}]\text{ CHARACTERS}]\\\quad[\underline{DEPENDING}\text{ ON data-name-1}]\\\text{CONTAINS integer-4 }\underline{TO}\text{ integer-5 CHARACTERS}\end{array}\right\}\right]$$

$$\left[\underline{DATA}\left\{\begin{array}{l}\underline{RECORD}\text{ is}\\\underline{RECORDS}\text{ ARE}\end{array}\right\}\{\text{data-name-2}\}\ ...\ \right].$$

General Format For Data Description Entry

FORMAT 1:

level-number $\left[\begin{array}{l}\text{data-name-1} \\ \text{FILLER}\end{array}\right]$

    [REDEFINES data-name-2]

    [IS EXTERNAL]

    [IS GLOBAL]

    $\cdot\left[\left\{\begin{array}{l}\text{PICTURE} \\ \text{PIC}\end{array}\right\} \text{IS character-string}\right]$

$\left[\text{[USAGE IS]}\left\{\begin{array}{l}\text{BINARY} \\ \text{COMPUTATIONAL} \\ \text{COMP} \\ \text{DISPLAY} \\ \text{INDEX} \\ \text{PACKED-DECIMAL}\end{array}\right\}\right]$

$\left[\text{[SIGN IS]}\left\{\begin{array}{l}\text{LEADING} \\ \text{TRAILING}\end{array}\right\} \text{[SEPARATE CHARACTER]}\right]$

$\left[\begin{array}{l}\text{OCCURS integer-2 TIMES} \\ \quad\left[\left\{\begin{array}{l}\text{ASCENDING} \\ \text{DESCENDING}\end{array}\right\} \text{KEY IS \{data-name-3\} ...}\right]\text{...} \\ \quad\quad\text{[INDEXED BY \{index-name-1\} ...]} \\ \text{OCCURS integer-1 TO integer-2 TIMES DEPENDING ON data-name-4} \\ \quad\left[\left\{\begin{array}{l}\text{ASCENDING} \\ \text{DESCENDING}\end{array}\right\} \text{KEY IS \{data-name-3\} ...}\right]\text{...} \\ \quad\quad\text{[INDEXED BY \{index-name-1\} ...]}\end{array}\right]$

$\left[\left\{\begin{array}{l}\text{SYNCHRONIZED} \\ \text{SYNC}\end{array}\right\}\left[\begin{array}{l}\text{LEFT} \\ \text{RIGHT}\end{array}\right]\right]$

$\left[\left\{\begin{array}{l}\text{JUSTIFIED} \\ \text{JUST}\end{array}\right\} \text{RIGHT}\right]$

[BLANK WHEN ZERO]

[VALUE IS literal-1] .

General Format For Data Description Entry

FORMAT 2:

66 data-name-1 <u>RENAMES</u> data-name-2 $\left[\ \left\{\begin{matrix} \underline{\text{THROUGH}} \\ \underline{\text{THRU}} \end{matrix}\right\}\ \text{data-name-3}\ \right]$.

FORMAT 3:

88 condition-name-1 $\left\{\begin{matrix} \underline{\text{VALUE}}\ \text{IS} \\ \underline{\text{VALUES}}\ \text{ARE} \end{matrix}\right\}$ $\left\{\ \text{literal-1}\ \left[\ \left\{\begin{matrix} \underline{\text{THROUGH}} \\ \underline{\text{THRU}} \end{matrix}\right\}\ \text{literal-2}\ \right]\ \right\}$ $\cdots$.

General Format For Communication Entry

FORMAT 1:

<u>CD</u> cd-name-1

FOR [<u>INITIAL</u>] <u>INPUT</u>

[[SYMBOLIC <u>QUEUE</u> IS data-name-1]

[SYMBOLIC <u>SUB-QUEUE-1</u> IS data-name-2]

[SYMBOLIC <u>SUB-QUEUE-2</u> IS data-name-3]

[SYMBOLIC <u>SUB-QUEUE-3</u> IS data-name-4]

[<u>MESSAGE</u> <u>DATE</u> IS data-name-5]

[<u>MESSAGE</u> <u>TIME</u> IS data-name-6]

[SYMBOLIC <u>SOURCE</u> IS data-name-7]

[<u>TEXT</u> <u>LENGTH</u> IS data-name-8]

[<u>END</u> <u>KEY</u> IS data-name-9]

[<u>STATUS</u> <u>KEY</u> IS data-name-10]

[<u>MESSAGE</u> <u>COUNT</u> IS data-name-11]]

[data-name-1, data-name-2, data-name-3,

data-name-4, data-name-5, data-name-6,

data-name-7, data-name-8, data-name-9,

data-name-10, data-name-11]

General Format For Communication Description Entry

CD cd-name-1 **FOR OUTPUT**

    [DESTINATION COUNT IS data-name-1]

    [TEXT LENGTH IS data-name-2]

    [STATUS KEY IS data-name-3]

    [DESTINATION TABLE OCCURS integer-1 TIMES

        [INDEXED BY {index-name-1} ...]]

    [ERROR KEY IS data-name-4]

    [SYMBOLIC DESTINATION IS data-name-5] .

CD cd-name-1

FOR [INITIAL] I-O

$$\begin{bmatrix} [\text{[MESSAGE DATE IS data-name-1]} \\ \text{[MESSAGE TIME IS data-name-2]} \\ \text{[SYMBOLIC TERMINAL IS data-name-3]} \\ \text{[TEXT LENGTH IS data-name-4]} \\ \text{[END KEY IS data-name-5]} \\ \text{[STATUS KEY IS data-name-6]]} \\ \text{[data-name-1, data-name-2, data-name-3,} \\ \text{data-name-4, data-name-5, data-name-6]} \end{bmatrix}$$

General Format For Report Description Entry

RD   report-name-1

    [IS GLOBAL]

    [CODE literal-1]

$$\left[\left\{\begin{array}{l}\underline{\text{CONTROL}}\ \ \text{IS}\\ \underline{\text{CONTROLS}}\ \ \text{ARE}\end{array}\right\}\ \left\{\begin{array}{l}\{\text{data- name-1}\}\ \ldots\\ \underline{\text{FINAL}}\ \ [\text{data-name-1}]\ \ldots\end{array}\right\}\right]$$

$$\left[\underline{\text{PAGE}}\ \left[\begin{array}{l}\text{LIMIT IS}\\ \text{LIMITS ARE}\end{array}\right]\ \text{integer-1}\ \left[\begin{array}{l}\text{LINE}\\ \text{LINES}\end{array}\right]\ [\underline{\text{HEADING}}\ \text{integer-2}]\right.$$

        [FIRST DETAIL integer-3]   [LAST DETAIL integer-4]

$$\left.[\underline{\text{FOOTING}}\ \text{integer-5}]\ \right]\ .$$

General Format For Report Group Description Entry

FORMAT 1:

01 [data-name-1]

$$\left[\underline{\text{LINE}} \text{ NUMBER IS} \left\{ \begin{array}{l} \text{integer-1} \quad [\text{ON } \underline{\text{NEXT}} \ \underline{\text{PAGE}}] \\ \underline{\text{PLUS}} \text{ integer-2} \end{array} \right\} \right]$$

$$\left[\underline{\text{NEXT}} \ \underline{\text{GROUP}} \text{ IS} \left\{ \begin{array}{l} \text{integer-3} \\ \underline{\text{PLUS}} \text{ integer-4} \\ \underline{\text{NEXT}} \ \underline{\text{PAGE}} \end{array} \right\} \right]$$

$$\underline{\text{TYPE}} \text{ IS} \left\{ \begin{array}{l} \left\{ \begin{array}{l} \underline{\text{REPORT}} \ \underline{\text{HEADING}} \\ \underline{\text{RH}} \end{array} \right\} \\ \left\{ \begin{array}{l} \underline{\text{PAGE}} \ \underline{\text{HEADING}} \\ \underline{\text{PH}} \end{array} \right\} \\ \left\{ \begin{array}{l} \underline{\text{CONTROL}} \ \underline{\text{HEADING}} \\ \underline{\text{CH}} \end{array} \right\} \left\{ \begin{array}{l} \text{data-name-2} \\ \underline{\text{FINAL}} \end{array} \right\} \\ \left\{ \begin{array}{l} \underline{\text{DETAIL}} \\ \underline{\text{DE}} \end{array} \right\} \\ \left\{ \begin{array}{l} \underline{\text{CONTROL}} \ \underline{\text{FOOTING}} \\ \underline{\text{CF}} \end{array} \right\} \left\{ \begin{array}{l} \text{data-name-3} \\ \underline{\text{FINAL}} \end{array} \right\} \\ \left\{ \begin{array}{l} \underline{\text{PAGE}} \ \underline{\text{FOOTING}} \\ \underline{\text{PF}} \end{array} \right\} \\ \left\{ \begin{array}{l} \underline{\text{REPORT}} \ \underline{\text{FOOTING}} \\ \underline{\text{RF}} \end{array} \right\} \end{array} \right\}$$

[[[USAGE] IS] DISPLAY]] .

General Format For Report Group Description Entry

FORMAT 2:

level-number [data-name-1]

$$\left[\underline{\text{LINE}} \text{ NUMBER IS} \left\{ \begin{array}{l} \text{integer-1} \quad [\text{ON } \underline{\text{NEXT}} \ \underline{\text{PAGE}}] \\ \underline{\text{PLUS}} \text{ integer-2} \end{array} \right\} \right]$$

[[\underline{\text{USAGE}} IS]   \underline{\text{DISPLAY}}] .

FORMAT 3:

level-number [data-name-1]

$$\left\{ \begin{array}{l} \underline{\text{PICTURE}} \\ \underline{\text{PIC}} \end{array} \right\} \text{ IS character-string}$$

[[\underline{\text{USAGE}} IS]   \underline{\text{DISPLAY}}]

$$\left[[\underline{\text{SIGN}} \text{ IS}]\left\{ \begin{array}{l} \underline{\text{LEADING}} \\ \underline{\text{TRAILING}} \end{array} \right\} \underline{\text{SEPARATE}} \text{ CHARACTER} \right]$$

$$\left[\left\{ \begin{array}{l} \underline{\text{JUSTIFIED}} \\ \underline{\text{JUST}} \end{array} \right\} \text{ RIGHT} \right]$$

[\underline{\text{BLANK}} WHEN \underline{\text{ZERO}}]

$$\left[\underline{\text{LINE}} \text{ NUMBER IS} \left\{ \begin{array}{l} \text{integer-1} \quad [\text{ON } \underline{\text{NEXT}} \ \underline{\text{PAGE}}] \\ \underline{\text{PLUS}} \text{ integer-2} \end{array} \right\} \right]$$

[\underline{\text{COLUMN}} NUMBER IS integer-3]

$$\left\{ \begin{array}{l} \underline{\text{SOURCE}} \text{ IS identifier-1} \\ \underline{\text{VALUE}} \text{ IS literal-1} \\ \{\underline{\text{SUM}} \ \{\text{identifier-2}\} \ \ldots \ [\underline{\text{UPON}} \ \{\text{data-name-2}\} \ \ldots \ ] \} \ \ldots \\ \qquad \left[\underline{\text{RESET}} \text{ ON } \left\{ \begin{array}{l} \text{data-name-3} \\ \underline{\text{FINAL}} \end{array} \right\} \right] \end{array} \right\}$$

[\underline{\text{GROUP}} INDICATE] .

General Format For Procedure Division

FORMAT 1:

[<u>PROCEDURE</u> <u>DIVISION</u>   [<u>USING</u> {data-name-1} ...] .

[<u>DECLARATIVES</u>.

{section-name <u>SECTION</u> [segment-number] .

    USE statement.

[paragraph-name.

    [sentence] ...] ... } ...

   <u>END</u> <u>DECLARATIVES</u>.]

{section-name <u>SECTION</u> [segment-number] .

[paragraph-name.

    [sentence] ...] ... } ...]

FORMAT 2:

[<u>PROCEDURE</u> <u>DIVISION</u>   [<u>USING</u>   {data-name-1} ...] .

{paragraph-name.

    [sentence] ... } ...]

General Format For COBOL Verbs

ACCEPT identifier-1 [FROM mnemonic-name-1]

ACCEPT identifier-2 FROM $\left\{\begin{array}{l}\text{DATE}\\\text{DAY}\\\text{DAY-OF-WEEK}\\\text{TIME}\end{array}\right\}$

ACCEPT cd-name-1 MESSAGE COUNT

ADD $\left\{\begin{array}{l}\text{identifier-1}\\\text{literal-1}\end{array}\right\}$ ... TO {identifier-2 [ROUNDED]} ...

   [ON SIZE ERROR imperative-statement-1]

   [NOT ON SIZE ERROR imperative-statement-2]

   [END-ADD]

ADD $\left\{\begin{array}{l}\text{identifier-1}\\\text{literal-1}\end{array}\right\}$ ... TO $\left\{\begin{array}{l}\text{identifier-2}\\\text{literal-2}\end{array}\right\}$

   GIVING {identifier-3 [ROUNDED] } ...

   [ON SIZE ERROR imperative-statement-1]

   [NOT ON SIZE ERROR imperative-statement-2]

   [END-ADD]

ADD $\left\{\begin{array}{l}\text{CORRESPONDING}\\\text{CORR}\end{array}\right\}$ identifier-1 TO identifier-2 [ROUNDED]

   [ON SIZE ERROR imperative-statement-1]

   [NOT ON SIZE ERROR imperative-statement-2]

   [END-ADD]

ALTER {procedure-name-1 TO [PROCEED TO] procedure-name-2} ...

CALL $\left\{\begin{array}{l}\text{identifier-1}\\\text{literal-1}\end{array}\right\}$ $\left[\text{USING} \left\{\begin{array}{l}\text{[BY REFERENCE]} \quad \text{{identifier-2} ..}\\\text{BY CONTENT} \quad \text{{identifier-2} ...}\end{array}\right\}...\right]$

   [ON OVERFLOW imperative-statement-1] [END-CALL]

General Format For COBOL Verbs

$$\underline{CALL} \left\{ \begin{matrix} \text{identifier-1} \\ \text{literal-1} \end{matrix} \right\} \left[\underline{USING} \left\{ \begin{matrix} [\text{BY } \underline{REFERENCE}] \quad \{\text{identifier-2}\} \ldots \\ \text{BY } \underline{CONTENT} \quad \{\text{identifier-2}\} \ldots \end{matrix} \right\} \ldots \right]$$

    [ON <u>EXCEPTION</u> imperative-statement-1]

    [<u>NOT</u> ON <u>EXCEPTION</u> imperative-statement-2]

    [<u>END-CALL</u>]

$$\underline{CANCEL} \left\{ \begin{matrix} \text{identifier-1} \\ \text{literal-1} \end{matrix} \right\} \ldots$$

$$\underline{CLOSE} \left\{ \text{file-name-1} \left[\begin{matrix} \left\{ \begin{matrix} \underline{REEL} \\ \underline{UNIT} \end{matrix} \right\} [\text{FOR } \underline{REMOVAL}] \\ \text{WITH } \left\{ \begin{matrix} \underline{NO} \ \underline{REWIND} \\ \underline{LOCK} \end{matrix} \right\} \end{matrix} \right] \right\} \ldots$$

<u>CLOSE</u> {file-name-1 [WITH <u>LOCK</u>] } ...

<u>COMPUTE</u> {identifier-1 [<u>ROUNDED</u>] } ... = arithmetic-expression-1

    [ON <u>SIZE</u> <u>ERROR</u> imperative-statement-1]

    [<u>NOT</u> ON <u>SIZE</u> <u>ERROR</u> imperative-statement-2]

    [<u>END-COMPUTE</u>]

<u>CONTINUE</u>

<u>DELETE</u> file-name-1 RECORD

    [<u>INVALID</u> KEY imperative-statement-1]

    [<u>NOT</u> <u>INVALID</u> KEY imperative-statement-2]

    [<u>END-DELETE</u>]

$$\underline{DISABLE} \left\{ \begin{matrix} \underline{INPUT} \ [\underline{TERMINAL}] \\ \underline{I\text{-}O} \ \underline{TERMINAL} \\ \underline{OUTPUT} \end{matrix} \right\} \text{cd-name-1} \left[\text{WITH } \underline{KEY} \left\{ \begin{matrix} \text{identifier-1} \\ \text{literal-1} \end{matrix} \right\} \right]$$

General Format For COBOL Verbs

DISPLAY $\left\{ \begin{array}{l} \text{identifier-1} \\ \text{literal-1} \end{array} \right\}$ ... [UPON mnemonic-name-1]   [WITH NO ADVANCING]

DIVIDE $\left\{ \begin{array}{l} \text{identifier-1} \\ \text{literal-1} \end{array} \right\}$ INTO {identifier-2 [ROUNDED] } ...

   [ON SIZE ERROR imperative-statement-1]

   [NOT ON SIZE ERROR imperative-statement-2]

   [END-DIVIDE]

DIVIDE $\left\{ \begin{array}{l} \text{identifier-1} \\ \text{literal-1} \end{array} \right\}$ INTO $\left\{ \begin{array}{l} \text{identifier-2} \\ \text{literal-2} \end{array} \right\}$

   GIVING {identifier-3 [ROUNDED] } ...

   [ON SIZE ERROR imperative-statement-1]

   [NOT ON SIZE ERROR imperative-statement-2]

   [END-DIVIDE]

DIVIDE $\left\{ \begin{array}{l} \text{identifier-1} \\ \text{literal-1} \end{array} \right\}$ BY $\left\{ \begin{array}{l} \text{identifier-2} \\ \text{literal-2} \end{array} \right\}$

   GIVING {identifier-3 [ROUNDED] } ...

   [ON SIZE ERROR imperative-statement-1]

   [NOT ON SIZE ERROR imperative-statement-2]

   [END-DIVIDE]

DIVIDE $\left\{ \begin{array}{l} \text{identifier-1} \\ \text{literal-1} \end{array} \right\}$ INTO $\left\{ \begin{array}{l} \text{identifier-2} \\ \text{literal-2} \end{array} \right\}$ GIVING identifier-3   [ROUNDED]

   REMAINDER identifier-4

   [ON SIZE ERROR imperative-statement-1]

   [NOT ON SIZE ERROR imperative-statement-2]

   [END-DIVIDE]

General Format For COBOL Verbs

<u>DIVIDE</u> $\left\{ \begin{array}{l} \text{identifier-1} \\ \text{literal-1} \end{array} \right\}$ <u>BY</u> $\left\{ \begin{array}{l} \text{identifier-2} \\ \text{literal-2} \end{array} \right\}$ <u>GIVING</u> identifier-3 [<u>ROUNDED</u>]

    <u>REMAINDER</u> identifier-4

    [ON <u>SIZE</u> <u>ERROR</u> imperative-statement-1]

    [<u>NOT</u> ON <u>SIZE</u> <u>ERROR</u> imperative-statement-2]

    [<u>END-DIVIDE</u>]

<u>ENABLE</u> $\left\{ \begin{array}{l} \text{[INPUT [TERMINAL]} \\ \text{I-O TERMINAL} \\ \text{OUTPUT} \end{array} \right\}$ cd-name-1 $\left[\text{WITH } \underline{\text{KEY}} \left\{ \begin{array}{l} \text{identifier-1} \\ \text{literal-1} \end{array} \right\} \right]$

<u>ENTER</u> language-name-1 [routine-name-1].

<u>EVALUATE</u> $\left\{ \begin{array}{l} \text{identifier-1} \\ \text{literal-1} \\ \text{expression-1} \\ \underline{\text{TRUE}} \\ \underline{\text{FALSE}} \end{array} \right\}$ $\left[\underline{\text{ALSO}} \left\{ \begin{array}{l} \text{identifier-2} \\ \text{literal-2} \\ \text{expression-2} \\ \underline{\text{TRUE}} \\ \underline{\text{FALSE}} \end{array} \right\} \right]$ ...

$\left\{ \begin{array}{l} \underline{\text{WHEN}} \left\{ \begin{array}{l} \underline{\text{ANY}} \\ \text{condition-1} \\ \underline{\text{TRUE}} \\ \underline{\text{FALSE}} \\ [\underline{\text{NOT}}] \left\{ \begin{array}{l} \text{identifier-3} \\ \text{literal-3} \\ \text{arithmetic-expression-1} \end{array} \right\} \left[\left\{ \begin{array}{l} \underline{\text{THROUGH}} \\ \underline{\text{THRU}} \end{array} \right\} \left\{ \begin{array}{l} \text{identifier-4} \\ \text{literal-4} \\ \text{arithmetic-expression-2} \end{array} \right\} \right] \right\} \\ \quad [\underline{\text{ALSO}} \left\{ \begin{array}{l} \underline{\text{ANY}} \\ \text{condition-2} \\ \underline{\text{TRUE}} \\ \underline{\text{FALSE}} \\ [\underline{\text{NOT}}] \left\{ \begin{array}{l} \text{identifier-5} \\ \text{literal-5} \\ \text{arithmetic-expression-3} \end{array} \right\} \left[\left\{ \begin{array}{l} \underline{\text{THROUGH}} \\ \underline{\text{THRU}} \end{array} \right\} \left\{ \begin{array}{l} \text{identifier-6} \\ \text{literal-6} \\ \text{arithmetic-expression-4} \end{array} \right\} \right] \right\} ... \\ \quad \text{imperative-statement-1} \end{array} \right\}$ ...

    [<u>WHEN</u> <u>OTHER</u> imperative-statement-2]

    [<u>END-EVALUATE</u>]

<u>EXIT</u>

<u>EXIT</u> <u>PROGRAM</u>

General Format For COBOL Verbs

GENERATE $\left\{ \begin{array}{l} \text{data-name-1} \\ \text{report-name-1} \end{array} \right\}$

GO TO [procedure-name-1]

GO TO {procedure-name-1} ... DEPENDING ON identifier-1

IF condition-1 THEN $\left\{ \begin{array}{l} \text{\{statement-1\} ...} \\ \underline{\text{NEXT}}\ \underline{\text{SENTENCE}} \end{array} \right\}$ $\left\{ \begin{array}{l} \underline{\text{ELSE}}\ \text{\{statement-2\} ... [\underline{\text{END-IF}}]} \\ \underline{\text{ELSE}}\ \underline{\text{NEXT}}\ \underline{\text{SENTENCE}} \\ \underline{\text{END-IF}} \end{array} \right\}$

INITIALIZE   {identifier-1} ...

$\left[\text{REPLACING} \left\{ \left\{ \begin{array}{l} \underline{\text{ALPHABETIC}} \\ \underline{\text{ALPHANUMERIC}} \\ \underline{\text{NUMERIC}} \\ \underline{\text{ALLPHANUMERIC-EDITED}} \\ \underline{\text{NUMERIC-EDITED}} \end{array} \right\} \text{DATA}\ \underline{\text{BY}} \left\{ \begin{array}{l} \text{identifier-2} \\ \text{literal-1} \end{array} \right\} \right\} ... \right]$

INITIATE   {report-name-1} ...

INSPECT   identifier-1 TALLYING

$\left\{ \text{identifier-2}\ \underline{\text{FOR}} \left[\begin{array}{l} \underline{\text{CHARACTERS}} \left[\left\{ \begin{array}{l} \underline{\text{BEFORE}} \\ \underline{\text{AFTER}} \end{array} \right\} \text{INITIAL} \left\{ \begin{array}{l} \text{identifier-4} \\ \text{literal-2} \end{array} \right\} \right] ... \\ \left\{ \begin{array}{l} \underline{\text{ALL}} \\ \underline{\text{LEADING}} \end{array} \right\} \left\{ \left\{ \begin{array}{l} \text{identifier-3} \\ \text{literal-1} \end{array} \right\} \left[\left\{ \begin{array}{l} \underline{\text{BEFORE}} \\ \underline{\text{AFTER}} \end{array} \right\} \text{INITIAL} \left\{ \begin{array}{l} \text{identifier-4} \\ \text{literal-2} \end{array} \right\} \right] \right\} ... \end{array} \right] ... \right\} ...$

INSPECT   identifier-1 REPLACING

$\left\{ \begin{array}{l} \underline{\text{CHARACTERS}}\ \underline{\text{BY}} \left\{ \begin{array}{l} \text{identifier-5} \\ \text{literal-3} \end{array} \right\} \left[\left\{ \begin{array}{l} \underline{\text{BEFORE}} \\ \underline{\text{AFTER}} \end{array} \right\} \text{INITIAL} \left\{ \begin{array}{l} \text{identifier-4} \\ \text{literal-2} \end{array} \right\} \right] ... \\ \\ \left\{ \begin{array}{l} \underline{\text{ALL}} \\ \underline{\text{LEADING}} \\ \underline{\text{FIRST}} \end{array} \right\} \left\{ \left\{ \begin{array}{l} \text{identifier-3} \\ \text{literal-1} \end{array} \right\} \underline{\text{BY}} \left\{ \begin{array}{l} \text{identifier-5} \\ \text{literal-3} \end{array} \right\} \left[\left\{ \begin{array}{l} \underline{\text{BEFORE}} \\ \underline{\text{AFTER}} \end{array} \right\} \text{INITIAL} \left\{ \begin{array}{l} \text{identifier-4} \\ \text{literal-2} \end{array} \right\} \right] ... \right\} ... \end{array} \right\} ...$

General Format For COBOL Verbs

```
INSPECT identifier-1 TALLYING

       ┌                                                                              ┐
       │              ┌ CHARACTERS [{ BEFORE / AFTER } INITIAL { identifier-4 / literal-2 }] ...        ┐ │
       │ identifier-2 FOR │                                                                       │ │ ...
       │              │ { ALL / LEADING } {{ identifier-3 / literal-1 }} [{ BEFORE / AFTER } INITIAL { identifier-4 / literal-2 }] ... │ │
       └              └                                                                       ┘ ┘

       REPLACING

              ┌ CHARACTERS BY { identifier-5 / literal-3 } [{ BEFORE / AFTER } INITIAL { identifier-4 / literal-2 }] ...         ┐
              │                                                                                        │
              │ { ALL / LEADING / FIRST } { identifier-3 / literal-1 } BY { identifier-5 / literal-3 } [{ BEFORE / AFTER } INITIAL { identifier-4 / literal-2 }] ... │
              └                                                                                        ┘

INSPECT identifier-1 CONVERTING { identifier-6 / literal-4 } TO { identifier-7 / literal-5 }

    [{ BEFORE / AFTER } INITIAL { identifier-4 / literal-2 }] ...

MERGE file-name-1 { ON { ASCENDING / DESCENDING } KEY {data-name-1} ... } ...

    [COLLATING SEQUENCE IS alphabet-name-1]

    USING file-name-2 {file-name-3} ...

    { OUTPUT PROCEDURE IS procedure-name-1 [{ THROUGH / THRU } procedure-name-2] }
    { GIVING {file-name-4} ... }

MOVE { identifier-1 / literal-1 } TO {identifier-2} ...

MOVE { CORRESPONDING / CORR } identifier-1 TO identifier-2

MULTIPLY { identifier-1 / literal-1 } BY { identifier-2 [ROUNDED]) ...

    [ON SIZE ERROR imperative-statement-1]

    [NOT ON SIZE ERROR imperative-statement-2]

    [END-MULTIPLY]
```

General Format For COBOL Verbs

MULTIPLY $\left\{ \begin{matrix} \text{identifier-1} \\ \text{literal-1} \end{matrix} \right\}$ BY $\left\{ \begin{matrix} \text{identifier-2} \\ \text{literal-2} \end{matrix} \right\}$

    GIVING {identifier-3 [ROUNDED]} . . .

    [ON SIZE ERROR imperative-statement-1]

    [NOT ON SIZE ERROR imperative-statement-2]

    [END-MULTIPLY]

OPEN $\left\{ \begin{matrix} \text{INPUT} \left\{ \text{file-name-1} \left[\begin{matrix} \text{REVERSED} \\ \text{WITH NO REWIND} \end{matrix} \right] \right\} \cdots \\ \text{OUTPUT \{file-name-2 \quad [WITH NO REWIND]\}} \quad \cdots \\ \text{I-O \{file-name-3\} } \cdots \\ \text{EXTEND \{file-name-4\} } \cdots \end{matrix} \right\} \cdots$

OPEN $\left\{ \begin{matrix} \text{INPUT \{file-name-1\} } \cdots \\ \text{OUTPUT \{file-name-2\} } \cdots \\ \text{I-O \{file-name-3\} } \cdots \\ \text{EXTEND \{file-name-4\} } \cdots \end{matrix} \right\} \cdots$

OPEN $\left\{ \begin{matrix} \text{OUTPUT \{file-name-1} \quad \text{[WITH NO REWIND]\} } \cdots \\ \text{EXTEND \{file-name-2\} } \cdots \end{matrix} \right\} \cdots$

PERFORM $\left[\text{procedure-name-1} \left[\left\{ \begin{matrix} \text{THROUGH} \\ \text{THRU} \end{matrix} \right\} \text{procedure-name-2} \right] \right]$

    [imperative-statement-1 END-PERFORM]

PERFORM $\left[\text{procedure-name-1} \left[\left\{ \begin{matrix} \text{THROUGH} \\ \text{THRU} \end{matrix} \right\} \text{procedure-name-2} \right] \right]$

$\left\{ \begin{matrix} \text{identifier-1} \\ \text{integer-1} \end{matrix} \right\}$ TIMES [imperative-statement-1 END-PERFORM]

PERFORM $\left[\text{procedure-name-1} \left[\left\{ \begin{matrix} \text{THROUGH} \\ \text{THRU} \end{matrix} \right\} \text{procedure-name-2} \right] \right]$

$\left[\text{WITH TEST} \left\{ \begin{matrix} \text{BEFORE} \\ \text{AFTER} \end{matrix} \right\} \right]$ UNTIL condition-1

    [imperative-statement-1 END-PERFORM]

General Format For COBOL Verbs

PERFORM [procedure-name-1 [{ THROUGH / THRU } procedure-name-2]]

   [WITH TEST { BEFORE / AFTER }]

   VARYING { identifier-2 / index-name-1 } FROM { identifier-3 / index-name-2 / literal-1 }

      BY { identifier-4 / literal-2 } UNTIL condition-1

   [AFTER { identifier-5 / literal-3 } FROM { identifier-6 / index-name-4 / literal-3 }

      BY { identifier-7 / literal-4 } UNTIL condition-2] . . .

   [imperative-statement-1 END-PERFORM]

PURGE cd-name-1

READ file-name-1 [NEXT] RECORD [INTO identifier-1]

   [AT END imperative-statement-1]

   [NOT AT END imperative-statement-2]

   [END-READ]

READ file-name-1 RECORD [INTO identifier-1]

   [INVALID KEY imperative-statement-3]

   [NOT INVALID KEY imperative-statement-4]

   [END-READ]

General Format For COBOL Verbs

READ file-name-1 RECORD   [INTO identifier-1]

   [KEY IS data-name-1]

   [INVALID KEY imperative-statement-3]

   [NOT INVALID KEY imperative-statement-4]

   [END-READ]

RECEIVE cd-name-1 $\left\{ \begin{array}{l} \underline{\text{MESSAGE}} \\ \underline{\text{SEGMENT}} \end{array} \right\}$ INTO identifier-1

   [NO DATA imperative-statement-1]

   [WITH DATA imperative-statement-2]

   [END-RECEIVE]

RELEASE record-name-1   [FROM identifier-1]

RETURN file-name-1 RECORD   [INTO identifier-1]

   AT END imperative-statement-1

   [NOT AT END imperative-statement-2]

   [END-RETURN]

REWRITE record-name-1   [FROM identifier-1]

REWRITE record-name-1   [FROM identifier-1]

   [INVALID KEY imperative-statement-1]

   [NOT INVALID KEY imperative-statement-2]

   [END-REWRITE]

General Format For COBOL Verbs

$$\underline{\text{SEARCH}} \text{ identifier-1} \left[\underline{\text{VARYING}} \left\{ \begin{array}{l} \text{identifier-2} \\ \text{index-name-1} \end{array} \right\} \right]$$

[AT __END__ imperative-statement-1]

$$\left\{ \underline{\text{WHEN}} \text{ condition-1} \left\{ \begin{array}{l} \text{imperative-statement-2} \\ \underline{\text{NEXT}} \ \underline{\text{SENTENCE}} \end{array} \right\} \right\} \dots$$

[END-SEARCH]

$$\underline{\text{SEARCH}} \ \underline{\text{ALL}} \text{ identifier-1} \quad [\text{AT} \ \underline{\text{END}} \text{ imperative-statement-1}]$$

$$\underline{\text{WHEN}} \left\{ \begin{array}{l} \text{data-name-1} \left\{ \begin{array}{l} \text{IS} \ \underline{\text{EQUAL}} \ \text{TO} \\ \text{IS} = \end{array} \right\} \left\{ \begin{array}{l} \text{identifier-3} \\ \text{literal-1} \\ \text{arithmetic-expression-1} \end{array} \right\} \\ \text{condition-name-1} \end{array} \right\}$$

$$\left[\underline{\text{AND}} \left\{ \begin{array}{l} \text{data-name-2} \left\{ \begin{array}{l} \text{IS} \ \underline{\text{EQUAL}} \ \text{TO} \\ \text{IS} = \end{array} \right\} \left\{ \begin{array}{l} \text{identifier-4} \\ \text{literal-2} \\ \text{arithmetic-expression-2} \end{array} \right\} \\ \text{condition-name-2} \end{array} \right\} \right] \dots$$

$$\left\{ \begin{array}{l} \text{imperative-statement-2} \\ \underline{\text{NEXT}} \ \underline{\text{SENTENCE}} \end{array} \right\}$$

[END-SEARCH]

$$\underline{\text{SEND}} \text{ cd-name-1} \ \underline{\text{FROM}} \text{ identifier-1}$$

$$\underline{\text{SEND}} \text{ cd-name-1} \ [\underline{\text{FROM}} \text{ identifier-1}] \left\{ \begin{array}{l} \text{WITH identifier-2} \\ \text{WITH } \underline{\text{ESI}} \\ \text{WITH } \underline{\text{EMI}} \\ \text{WITH } \underline{\text{EGI}} \end{array} \right\}$$

$$\left[\left\{ \begin{array}{l} \underline{\text{BEFORE}} \\ \underline{\text{AFTER}} \end{array} \right\} \text{ADVANCING} \left\{ \begin{array}{l} \left\{ \begin{array}{l} \text{identifier-3} \\ \text{integer-1} \end{array} \right\} \left[\begin{array}{l} \text{LINE} \\ \text{LINES} \end{array} \right] \\ \left\{ \begin{array}{l} \text{mnemonic-name-1} \\ \underline{\text{PAGE}} \end{array} \right\} \end{array} \right\} \right]$$

[REPLACING LINE]

$$\underline{\text{SET}} \left\{ \begin{array}{l} \text{index-name-1} \\ \text{identifier-1} \end{array} \right\} \dots \ \underline{\text{TO}} \left\{ \begin{array}{l} \text{index-name-2} \\ \text{identifier-2} \\ \text{integer-1} \end{array} \right\}$$

General Format For COBOL Verbs

$\underline{\text{SET}}$ {index-name-3} ... $\left\{ \begin{array}{l} \underline{\text{UP}} \ \underline{\text{BY}} \\ \underline{\text{DOWN}} \ \underline{\text{BY}} \end{array} \right\} \left\{ \begin{array}{l} \text{identifier-2} \\ \text{integer-2} \end{array} \right\}$

$\underline{\text{SET}}$ $\left\{ \text{{MNEMONIC-NAME-1}} \ ... \ \underline{\text{TO}} \left\{ \begin{array}{l} \underline{\text{ON}} \\ \underline{\text{OFF}} \end{array} \right\} \right\}$ ...

$\underline{\text{SET}}$ {condition-name-1} ... $\underline{\text{TO}}$ $\underline{\text{TRUE}}$

$\underline{\text{SORT}}$ file-name-1 $\left\{ \text{ON} \left\{ \begin{array}{l} \underline{\text{ASCENDING}} \\ \underline{\text{DESCENDING}} \end{array} \right\} \text{KEY} \ \text{{data-name-1}} \ ... \right\}$ ...

    [WITH $\underline{\text{DUPLICATES}}$ IN ORDER]

    [COLLATING $\underline{\text{SEQUENCE}}$ IS alphabet-name-1]

$\left\{ \begin{array}{l} \underline{\text{INPUT}} \ \underline{\text{PROCEDURE}} \text{ IS procedure-name-1} \left[\left\{ \begin{array}{l} \underline{\text{THROUGH}} \\ \underline{\text{THRU}} \end{array} \right\} \text{procedure-name-2} \right] \\ \underline{\text{USING}} \ \text{{file-name-2}} \ ... \end{array} \right\}$

$\left\{ \begin{array}{l} \underline{\text{OUTPUT}} \ \underline{\text{PROCEDURE}} \text{ IS procedure-name-3} \left[\left\{ \begin{array}{l} \underline{\text{THROUGH}} \\ \underline{\text{THRU}} \end{array} \right\} \text{procedure-name-4} \right] \\ \underline{\text{GIVING}} \ \text{{file-name-3}} \ ... \end{array} \right\}$

$\underline{\text{START}}$ file-name-1 $\left[\underline{\text{KEY}} \text{ IS} \left\{ \begin{array}{l} \underline{\text{EQUAL}} \text{ TO} \\ = \\ \underline{\text{GREATER}} \text{ THAN} \\ > \\ \underline{\text{NOT}} \ \underline{\text{LESS}} \text{ THAN} \\ \underline{\text{NOT}} < \\ \underline{\text{GREATER}} \text{ THAN OR } \underline{\text{EQUAL}} \text{ TO} \\ >= \end{array} \right\} \text{data-name-1} \right]$

    [$\underline{\text{INVALID}}$ KEY imperative-statement-1]

    [$\underline{\text{NOT}}$ $\underline{\text{INVALID}}$ KEY imperative-statement-2]

    [$\underline{\text{END-START}}$]

$\underline{\text{STOP}}$ $\left\{ \begin{array}{l} \underline{\text{RUN}} \\ \text{literal-1} \end{array} \right\}$

General Format For COBOL Verbs

STRING $\left\{ \left\{ \begin{matrix} \text{identifier-1} \\ \text{literal-1} \end{matrix} \right\} \dots \text{DELIMITED BY} \left\{ \begin{matrix} \text{identifier-2} \\ \text{literal-2} \\ \underline{\text{SIZE}} \end{matrix} \right\} \right\} \dots$

    INTO identifier-3

    [WITH POINTER identifier-4]

    [ON OVERFLOW imperative-statement-1]

    [NOT ON OVERFLOW imperative-statement-2]

    [END-STRING]

SUBTRACT $\left\{ \begin{matrix} \text{identifier-1} \\ \text{literal-1} \end{matrix} \right\} \dots$ FROM {identifier-3 [ROUNDED]} ...

    [ON SIZE ERROR imperative-statement-1]

    [NOT ON SIZE ERROR imperative-statement-2]

    [END-SUBTRACT]

SUBTRACT $\left\{ \begin{matrix} \text{identifier-1} \\ \text{literal-1} \end{matrix} \right\} \dots$ FROM $\left\{ \begin{matrix} \text{identifier-2} \\ \text{literal-2} \end{matrix} \right\}$

    GIVING {identifier-3 [ROUNDED]} ...

    [ON SIZE ERROR imperative-statement-1]

    [NOT ON SIZE ERROR imperative-statement-2]

    [END-SUBTRACT]

SUBTRACT $\left\{ \begin{matrix} \underline{\text{CORRESPONDING}} \\ \underline{\text{CORR}} \end{matrix} \right\}$ identifier-1 FROM identifier-2 [ROUNDED]

    [ON SIZE ERROR imperative-statement-1]

    [NOT ON SIZE ERROR imperative-statement-2]

    [END-SUBTRACT]

SUPPRESS PRINTING

TERMINATE {report-name-1} ...

General Format For COBOL Verbs

UNSTRING identifier-1

$$\left[\underline{\text{DELIMITED}} \text{ BY } [\underline{\text{ALL}}] \left\{ \begin{array}{l} \text{identifier-2} \\ \text{literal-1} \end{array} \right\} \left[\underline{\text{OR}} \ [\underline{\text{ALL}}] \left\{ \begin{array}{l} \text{identifier-3} \\ \text{literal-2} \end{array} \right\} \right] \dots \right]$$

INTO {identifier-4 [DELIMITER IN identifier-5] [COUNT IN identifier-6] } ...

[WITH POINTER identifier-7]

[TALLYING IN identifier-8]

[ON OVERFLOW imperative-statement-1]

[NOT ON OVERFLOW imperative-statement-2]

[END-UNSTRING]

$$\text{USE } [\underline{\text{GLOBAL}}] \ \underline{\text{AFTER}} \ \text{STANDARD} \left\{ \begin{array}{l} \underline{\text{EXCEPTION}} \\ \underline{\text{ERROR}} \end{array} \right\} \underline{\text{PROCEDURE}} \text{ ON} \left\{ \begin{array}{l} \{\text{file-name-1}\} \dots \\ \underline{\text{INPUT}} \\ \underline{\text{OUTPUT}} \\ \underline{\text{I-O}} \\ \underline{\text{EXTEND}} \end{array} \right\}$$

$$\underline{\text{USE}} \ \underline{\text{AFTER}} \ \text{STANDARD} \left\{ \begin{array}{l} \underline{\text{EXCEPTION}} \\ \underline{\text{ERROR}} \end{array} \right\} \underline{\text{PROCEDURE}} \text{ ON} \left\{ \begin{array}{l} \{\text{file-name-3}\} \dots \\ \underline{\text{OUTPUT}} \\ \underline{\text{EXTEND}} \end{array} \right\}$$

USE [GLOBAL] BEFORE REPORTING identifier-1

$$\underline{\text{USE}} \ \text{FOR} \ \underline{\text{DEBUGGING}} \text{ ON} \left\{ \begin{array}{l} \text{cd-name-1} \\ [\underline{\text{ALL}} \ \text{REFERENCES OF}] \ \text{identifier-1} \\ \text{file-name-1} \\ \text{procedure-name-1} \\ \underline{\text{ALL}} \ \underline{\text{PROCEDURES}} \end{array} \right\} \dots$$

WRITE record-name-1 [FROM identifier-1]

$$\left[\left\{ \begin{array}{l} \underline{\text{BEFORE}} \\ \underline{\text{AFTER}} \end{array} \right\} \text{ADVANCING} \left\{ \begin{array}{l} \left\{ \begin{array}{l} \text{identifier-2} \\ \text{integer-1} \end{array} \right\} \left[\begin{array}{l} \text{LINE} \\ \text{LINES} \end{array} \right] \\ \left\{ \begin{array}{l} \text{mnemonic-name-1} \\ \underline{\text{PAGE}} \end{array} \right\} \end{array} \right\} \right]$$

$$\left[\text{AT} \left\{ \begin{array}{l} \underline{\text{END-OF-PAGE}} \\ \underline{\text{EOP}} \end{array} \right\} \text{imperative-statement-1} \right]$$

$$\left[\underline{\text{NOT}} \text{ AT} \left\{ \begin{array}{l} \underline{\text{END-OF-PAGE}} \\ \underline{\text{EOP}} \end{array} \right\} \text{imperative-statement-2} \right]$$

[END-WRITE]

WRITE record-name-1 [FROM identifier-1]

[INVALID KEY imperative-statement-1]

[NOT INVALID KEY imperative-statement-2]

[END-WRITE]

General Format For Copy And Replace Statements

COPY text-name-1 $\left[\left\{ \dfrac{OF}{IN} \right\} \text{library-name-1} \right]$

$$\left[\text{REPLACING} \left\{ \left\{ \begin{array}{l} ==\text{pseudo-text-1}== \\ \text{identifier-1} \\ \text{literal-1} \\ \text{word-1} \end{array} \right\} \text{BY} \left\{ \begin{array}{l} ==\text{pseudo-text-2}== \\ \text{identifier-2} \\ \text{literal-2} \\ \text{word-2} \end{array} \right\} \right\} \ldots \right]$$

REPLACE   {==pseudo-text-1== BY ==pseudo-text-2==} . . .

REPLACE OFF

General Format For Conditions

RELATION CONDITION

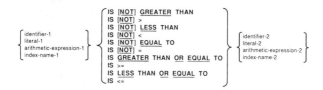

$$\left\{\begin{array}{l}\text{identifier-1}\\\text{literal-1}\\\text{arithmetic-expression-1}\\\text{index-name-1}\end{array}\right\}\left\{\begin{array}{l}\text{IS [\underline{NOT}] \underline{GREATER} THAN}\\\text{IS [\underline{NOT}] >}\\\text{IS [\underline{NOT}] \underline{LESS} THAN}\\\text{IS [\underline{NOT}] <}\\\text{IS [\underline{NOT}] \underline{EQUAL} TO}\\\text{IS [\underline{NOT}] =}\\\text{IS \underline{GREATER} THAN \underline{OR} \underline{EQUAL} TO}\\\text{IS >=}\\\text{IS \underline{LESS} THAN \underline{OR} \underline{EQUAL} TO}\\\text{IS <=}\end{array}\right\}\left\{\begin{array}{l}\text{identifier-2}\\\text{literal-2}\\\text{arithmetic-expression-2}\\\text{index-name-2}\end{array}\right\}$$

CLASS CONDITION

$$\text{identifier-1 IS [\underline{NOT}] }\left\{\begin{array}{l}\underline{\text{NUMERIC}}\\\underline{\text{ALPHABETIC}}\\\underline{\text{ALPHABETIC-LOWER}}\\\underline{\text{ALPHABETIC-UPPER}}\\\text{class-name}\end{array}\right\}$$

CONDITION-NAME CONDITION

condition-name-1

SWITCH-STATUS CONDITION

condition-name-1

SIGN CONDITION

$$\text{arithmetic-expression-1 IS [\underline{NOT}] }\left\{\begin{array}{l}\underline{\text{POSITIVE}}\\\underline{\text{NEGATIVE}}\\\underline{\text{ZERO}}\end{array}\right\}$$

NEGATED CONDITION

<u>NOT</u> condition-1

COMBINED CONDITION

$$\text{condition-1 }\left\{\left\{\begin{array}{l}\underline{\text{AND}}\\\underline{\text{OR}}\end{array}\right\}\text{ condition-2}\right\}\cdots$$

General Format For Conditions

ABBREVIATED COMBINED RELATION CONDITION:

relation-condition $\left\{ \left\{ \begin{array}{c} \underline{AND} \\ \underline{OR} \end{array} \right\} \right.$ [<u>NOT</u>] [relational-operator] object $\left. \right\} \cdots$

Qualification

FORMAT 1:

$$\left\{ \begin{matrix} \text{data-name-1} \\ \text{condition-name} \end{matrix} \right\} \left[\begin{matrix} \left\{ \left\{ \begin{matrix} \underline{\text{IN}} \\ \underline{\text{OF}} \end{matrix} \right\} \text{data-name-2} \right\} \cdots \left[\left\{ \begin{matrix} \underline{\text{IN}} \\ \underline{\text{OF}} \end{matrix} \right\} \left\{ \begin{matrix} \text{file-name} \\ \text{cd-name} \end{matrix} \right\} \right] \\ \left\{ \begin{matrix} \underline{\text{IN}} \\ \underline{\text{OF}} \end{matrix} \right\} \left\{ \begin{matrix} \text{file-name} \\ \text{cd-name} \end{matrix} \right\} \end{matrix} \right]$$

FORMAT 2:

$$\text{paragraph-name} \left\{ \begin{matrix} \underline{\text{IN}} \\ \underline{\text{OF}} \end{matrix} \right\} \text{section-name}$$

FORMAT 3:

$$\text{text-name} \left\{ \begin{matrix} \underline{\text{IN}} \\ \underline{\text{OF}} \end{matrix} \right\} \text{library-name}$$

FORMAT 4:

$$\underline{\text{LINAGE-COUNTER}} \left\{ \begin{matrix} \underline{\text{IN}} \\ \underline{\text{OF}} \end{matrix} \right\} \text{report-name}$$

FORMAT 5:

$$\left\{ \begin{matrix} \underline{\text{PAGE-COUNTER}} \\ \underline{\text{LINE-COUNTER}} \end{matrix} \right\} \left\{ \begin{matrix} \underline{\text{IN}} \\ \underline{\text{OF}} \end{matrix} \right\} \text{report-name}$$

FORMAT 6:

$$\text{data-name-3} \left\{ \begin{matrix} \left\{ \begin{matrix} \underline{\text{IN}} \\ \underline{\text{OF}} \end{matrix} \right\} \text{data-name-4} \left[\left\{ \begin{matrix} \underline{\text{IN}} \\ \underline{\text{OF}} \end{matrix} \right\} \text{report-name} \right] \\ \left\{ \begin{matrix} \underline{\text{IN}} \\ \underline{\text{OF}} \end{matrix} \right\} \text{report-name} \end{matrix} \right\}$$

Miscellaneous Formats

SUBSCRIPTING:

$$\left\{ \begin{array}{l} \text{condition-name-1} \\ \text{data-name-1} \end{array} \right\} \ (\ \left\{ \begin{array}{ll} \text{integer-1} & \\ \text{data-name-2} & [\{\pm\} \ \text{integer-2}] \\ \text{index-name-1} & [\{\pm\} \ \text{integer-3}] \end{array} \right\} \ \dots \ )$$

REFERENCE MODIFICATION:

data-name-1   (leftmost-character-position: [length])

IDENTIFIER:

$$\text{data-name-1} \ \left[\left\{ \begin{array}{l} \textbf{IN} \\ \textbf{OF} \end{array} \right\} \text{data-name-2} \right] \ \dots \ \left[\left\{ \begin{array}{l} \textbf{IN} \\ \textbf{OF} \end{array} \right\} \left\{ \begin{array}{l} \text{cd-name} \\ \text{file-name} \\ \text{report-name} \end{array} \right\} \right]$$

[({subscript} ...)]   [(leftmost-character-position: [length])]

General Format For Nested Source Programs

IDENTIFICATION DIVISION.

PROGRAM-ID. program-name-1 [IS INITIAL PROGRAM].

[ENVIRONMENT DIVISION. environment-division-content]

[DATA DIVISION. data-division-content]

[PROCEDURE DIVISION. procedure-division-content]

[[nested-source-program] . . .

END PROGRAM program-name-1.]

General Format For Nested-Source-Program

IDENTIFICATION DIVISION.

PROGRAM-ID. program-name-2 $\left[\text{IS} \left\{ \left| \frac{\text{COMMON}}{\text{INITIAL}} \right| \right\} \text{PROGRAM} \right]$.

[ENVIRONMENT DIVISION. environment-division-content]

[DATA DIVISION. data-division-content]

[PROCEDURE DIVISION. procedure-division-content]

[nested-source-program] . . .

END PROGRAM program-name-2.

General Format For Multiple Source Programs

{**IDENTIFICATION DIVISION**.

PROGRAM-ID. program-name-3 [IS **INITIAL** PROGRAM].

[**ENVIRONMENT DIVISION**. environment-division-content]

[**DATA DIVISION**. data-division-content]

[**PROCEDURE DIVISION**. procedure-division-content]

[nested-source-program] . . .

END PROGRAM program-name-3} . . .

IDENTIFICATION DIVISION.

PROGRAM-ID. program-name-4 [IS **INITITAL** PROGRAM].

[**ENVIRONMENT DIVISION**. environment-division-content]

[**DATA DIVISION**. data-division-content]

[**PROCEDURE DIVISION**. procedure-division-content]

[[nested-source-program] . . .

END PROGRAM program-name-4.]

III

COBOL 85

Examples

ALL "literal"   (Change, Obsolete)

When the figurative constant **ALL "literal"** is not associated with another data item, as in the following example,

```
SPECIAL-NAMES.

        ALPHABET COLAT-SEQUENCE IS ALL "9876543210".
```

in COBOL 85, the length of the string is the length of the literal (ten characters). In COBOL 74, the length of this literal is one (the leftmost character **9**).

This makes the rules for the figurative constant **ALL "literal"** consistent wherever it appears in a COBOL program. In the following example, **ALL "( ) ( )"** is associated with another data item.

```
        MOVE ALL "( )    (   )" TO SCREEN-FIELD-FORMAT
```

The length of the literal **"( ) ( )"** is seven, and the number of characters **MOVE**d is determined by the size of the receiving data item **SCREEN-FIELD-FORMAT**.

The figurative constant **ALL "literal"**, when associated with a numeric or numeric-edited item, and when the length of the literal is greater than one character, is an obsolete language element. In the following example, the figurative constant **ALL "123"** (where the size of the literal is greater than one character) is **MOVE**d to three different numeric (numeric-edited) data items. Each **MOVE** statement produces a different result as indicated in the following example.

RESULT AFTER MOVE

```
01  THREE-POINT-TWO-ITEM              PIC 999.99
    . . . MOVE ALL "123" TO THREE-POINT-TWO-ITEM.
           123123                                123.00


01  THREE-PLUS-TWO-ITEM               PIC 999V99.
    . . . MOVE ALL "123" TO THREE-PLUS-TWO-ITEM.
           12312                                 31200


01  AMOUNT-FIELD                      PIC $999.99.
    . . . MOVE ALL "123" TO AMOUNT-FIELD.
           1231231                             $231.00
```

ALPHABET   (New; Change)

In the **ALPHABET**-name clause of the **SPECIAL-NAMES** paragraph, **STANDARD-2** represents the (ISO) International Standard 7-Bit ASCII variant character set.
    In the following example,

```
SPECIAL-NAMES.

    ALPHABET INTERNATIONAL-CHARACTERS IS STANDARD-2.
```

INTERNATIONAL-CHARACTERS is a user-defined name, and
STANDARD-2 is a reserved word that represents the International Standard 7-Bit ASCII variant character set.
    NOTE: The new reserved word **ALPHABET** is now required
in the **ALPHABET**-name clause. COBOL 74 does not require it.
(See *COBOL 85 Conversion*, page 152.)

ALPHABETIC Class   (New, Change)

As the chart below indicates, the class condition test for
ALPHABETIC contains all uppercase and lowercase letters (**A**
through **Z** and **a** through **z**) and the space character. The new
reserved word **ALPHABETIC-UPPER** represents only the upper-

case letters (**A** through **Z**) and a space character. The new reserved word **ALPHABETIC-LOWER** represents only the lowercase letters (**a** through **z**) and a space character.

	A through Z	a through z	space character
ALPHABETIC	yes	yes	yes
ALPHABETIC-UPPER	yes		yes
ALPHABETIC-LOWER		yes	yes

This change affects COBOL 74/68 programs whose **ALPHABETIC** class test includes only uppercase letters and the space character. (See *COBOL 85 Conversion*, page 153.)

ALTER   (Obsolete)

The **ALTER** statement, which changes the procedure referenced in a **GO TO** statement, is an obsolete language element. The **ALTER** statement is a nemesis for maintenance programmers.

```
. . . ALTER CONTROL-POINTER
      TO PROCEED TO LAST-PROCESS.

CONTROL-POINTER. GO TO FIRST-PROCESS.
```

NOTE: An understanding of the unpopularity of the **ALTER** statement is essential to understanding the essence of maintenance programming. (See *COBOL 85 Conversion*, page 154.)

CALL   (New)

The **CALL** statement—the mechanism by which one COBOL program **CALL**s in other programs—has been enhanced.

One of the most important theories suggested by software engineers regarding structured system design is the notion of system modularization. The interaction between modules is referred to as "coupling." The aim is to keep functional modules as independent from one another as possible. This is important for numerous reasons. First, it minimizes the accidental effect one module may have on another; that is, if one module is in error, the bad results should stay localized and affect few other modules.

Second, independent modules provide the maintenance programmer an easier recognition of system functions. This becomes important when a system function needs to be changed, because the corresponding code, if isolated, can be identified and changed without having to change small pieces of code in many other modules.

To aid the programmer in module decoupling (i.e., to make the modules more independent), the **USING BY CONTENT** phrase has been added to the **CALL** statement. This allows **MODULE-A** to **CALL MODULE-B**, and to pass data to that module with an assurance that the original values of the passed data will be restored when control is returned to **MODULE-A** later. Thus, in the following example,

```
CALL MODULE-B USING BY CONTENT ITEM-X
```

the original **CALL**ing program **(MODULE-A)** will have the value of **ITEM-X** restored when control is returned from **MODULE-B**. This occurs despite any changes **MODULE-B** may make to **ITEM-X** (via its corresponding linked data item).

The alternative to the **USING BY CONTENT** phrase is the **USING BY REFERENCE** phrase. In the following example,

```
CALL MODULE-B USING BY REFERENCE ITEM-Y
```

the original **CALL**ing module will receive **ITEM-Y** with whatever value it presently has when control is returned from **MODULE-B**. This, of course, is precisely how the current COBOL 74 **CALL** statement works. In fact, when neither the **BY CONTENT** nor **BY REFERENCE** phrase is specified as in

```
CALL MODULE-B USING ITEM-Z
```

the results are the same as if **BY REFERENCE** (default) had been specified.

It is permissible to alternate between the two modes **(BY CONTENT** and **BY REFERENCE)** in the same **CALL** statement. In the following example,

```
┌─────────────────────────────────────────────┐
│                 PROGRAM A                     │
├─────────────────────────────────────────────┤
│        •                                      │
│        •                                      │
│        •                                      │
│    DATA DIVISION.                             │
│        •                                      │
│        •                                      │
│        •                                      │
│    01  ITEM-1  . . .                          │
│    01  ITEM-2  . . .                          │
│    01  ITEM-3  . . .                          │
│    01  Q.                                     │
│        03  ITEM-A  . . .                      │
│                                               │
│    PROCEDURE DIVISION.                        │
│        •                                      │
│        •                                      │
│        •                                      │
│        CALL   PROGRAM-B                        │
│               USING        ITEM-1             │
│               BY CONTENT   ITEM-2             │
│               BY REFERENCE ITEM-3             │
│                            ITEM-4.            │
│                                               │
└─────────────────────────────────────────────┘
```

(Example continues on page 76)

```
┌────────────────────────────────────────────────────────┐
│                      PROGRAM  B                          │
├────────────────────────────────────────────────────────┤
│                .                                         │
│                .                                         │
│                .                                         │
│      LINKAGE  SECTION.                                   │
│                .                                         │
│                .                                         │
│                .                                         │
│      01   FIELD-A   . . .                                │
│      01   FIELD-B   REDEFINES  FIELD-A   . . .           │
│      01   FIELD-C   . . .                                │
│      01   FIELD-D   . . .                                │
│      01   FIELD-E   . . .                                │
│                .                                         │
│                .                                         │
│                .                                         │
│                                                          │
│                .                                         │
│      PROCEDURE  DIVISION   USING   FIELD-A               │
│                                    FIELD-C               │
│                                    FIELD-D               │
│                                    FIELD-E.              │
└────────────────────────────────────────────────────────┘
```

the contents of **ITEM-2** are protected from being changed (even though **PROGRAM-B** may change its corresponding **FIELD-C**); however, **ITEM-1, ITEM-3** and **ITEM-4** will (perhaps) have new values placed in them, based on what is left in **FIELD-A, FIELD-D** and **FIELD-E**, respectively, when control is returned from **PROGRAM-B**.

Note also, in the above example, that passed parameters are no longer restricted to level-**01** or level-**77** items (see for instance, **ITEM-4** in **PROGRAM-A**). In addition, a level-**01** data item (**FIELD-E**) may be linked to a level-**03** data item (**ITEM-4**). Neither of these features is permitted in previous versions of COBOL.

CANCEL   (Change)

There are some subtle changes to the behavior of COBOL programs containing a **CANCEL** (or **STOP RUN** or **EXIT PRO-**

GRAM) statement. In COBOL 85, a **CANCEL** statement causes any files that were left in the **OPEN** mode (in the program being **CANCEL**ed) to be implicitly **CLOSE**d.

Furthermore, an implicit **EXIT PROGRAM** will be executed in a **CALL**ed program when there is no more code to execute. (See *COBOL 85 Conversion*, page 155.)

Character Substitution   (Obsolete)

Some early implementations of COBOL were designed to work on limited hardware systems, where the character set available included fewer than 51 characters. The substitution of double characters for a single COBOL character is now an obsolete language element. Programs containing statements like the following, where **GT** is to be substituted for **>**,

```
IF AGE-OF-DEBT GT 120 PERFORM COLLECTIONS-ROUTINE.
```

are affected by this change. It is unlikely that this will affect many programs in use today. (See *COBOL 85 Conversion*, page 156.)

CLASS   (New)

A user-defined **CLASS** may be defined in the **SPECIAL-NAMES** paragraph. In the following example,

```
SPECIAL-NAMES.
    CLASS SPECIAL-ALPHABETIC IS
        "A" THRU "Z",
        "å  β  ∂  ∫  Δ  œ  Σ  Ø  π".
```

thirty-five individual characters are defined as belonging to the **CLASS SPECIAL-ALPHABETIC**. This user-defined **CLASS**-name (**SPECIAL-ALPHABETIC**) can be used in a condition statement the same way that the **ALPHABETIC** class condition is used.

```
IF LAST-NAME IS NOT SPECIAL-ALPHABETIC PERFORM ERROR-ROUTINE.
```

CLOSE   (New, Change)

The **FOR REMOVAL** phase of the **CLOSE** statement is allowed for a **SEQUENTIAL** single **REEL/UNIT** file. In addition, the **REEL/UNIT** phase of the **CLOSE** statement can be used with a single **REEL/UNIT** file. The **REEL/UNIT** phrase can also be specified for a **REPORT** file. In COBOL 74/68, neither of these features is permitted.

```
      CLOSE     SOMETIME-MULTIPLE-REEL-FILE
        FOR REMOVAL. . .

      CLOSE     RELATIVE-FILE,
                REPORT-FILE,
                SOMETIME-MULTI-VOLUME-FILE
        UNIT. . .
```

There is also a subtle change in the **CLOSE** statement. In COBOL 85, the **NO REWIND** and **REEL/UNIT** phrases cannot be specified together in a **CLOSE** statement. (See *COBOL 85 Conversion*, page 157.)

Communication Description(New, Change)

In the following example,

```
  CD   MESSAGE-CONTROL-AREA      FOR I-O.
       SYMBOLIC TERMINAL IS NAME-OF-TERMINAL
       MESSAGE DATE IS DATE-OF-MESSAGE
       MESSAGE TIME IS TIME-OF-MESSAGE
       TEXT LENGTH  IS SIZE-OF-MESSAGE
       END KEY      IS TYPE-OF-MESSAGE
       STATUS KEY   IS STATUS-OF-MESSAGE.
```

the **FOR I-0** phrase in the **CD** entry allows both input and output functions to and from the **MESSAGE-CONTROL-AREA** (for nondisk devices only, e.g., terminals).

NOTE: The order of clauses in the **CD** entry (**SYMBOLIC TERMINAL, MESSAGE DATE**, etc.) is immaterial. In COBOL 74, this order is specified.

COBOL 85 has added new status-key values, which may affect some COBOL 74/68 programs. (See *COBOL 85 Conversion*, page 158.)

Conditional Expressions   (Change)

The order of evaluating multiple conditions in a complex conditional expression is from left to right. The evaluation terminates as soon as the truth value of the entire conditional expression can be determined. COBOL 74 does not define this order of evaluation.

In the following example,

```
IF              AMOUNT-ONE  >  0
      AND       AMOUNT-TWO  <  100
      AND       AMOUNT-THREE  GREATER  THAN  OR  EQUAL  1000
   THEN         PERFORM  SUMMARY-ROUTINE
   END-IF
```

the truth value of the conditional expression

```
              AMOUNT-ONE  >  0
      AND     AMOUNT-TWO  <  100
      AND     AMOUNT-THREE  GREATER  THAN  OR  EQUAL  1000
```

may be determined after evaluating the first condition **AMOUNT-ONE > 0**. If in fact **AMOUNT-ONE** is not greater than **ZERO**, the other two conditions (**AMOUNT-TWO < 100** and **AMOUNT-THREE GREATER THAN OR EQUAL 1000**) will not be evaluated, since the truth value of the entire conditional expression has already been determined to be **FALSE**. (See *COBOL 85 Conversion*, page 160.)

CURRENCY SIGN   (Change)

The literal specified in the **CURRENCY SIGN** clause in the
SPECIAL-NAMES paragraph must be a one-character nonnumeric literal, as in the following example.

```
SPECIAL-NAMES.  CURRENCY SIGN IS "L".
```

COBOL 74/68 permits the literal in the **CURRENCY SIGN**
clause to be a figurative constant **ALL "literal"**. Thus, the
following example, which is *invalid* in COBOL 85,

```
SPECIAL-NAMES.  CURRENCY SIGN IS ALL "DOL$".
```

is valid in COBOL 74. Its meaning is unclear, and it is doubtful
that any COBOL 74/68 programs contain such a statement.
(See *COBOL 85 Conversion*, page 162.)

DAY-OF-WEEK   (New)

The new reserved word **DAY-OF-WEEK** represents a one-digit
character that stands for:

```
1 IS  MONDAY
2 IS  TUESDAY
3 IS  WEDNESDAY
4 IS  THURSDAY
5 IS  FRIDAY
6 IS  SATURDAY
7 IS  SUNDAY
```

This one-digit value is returned by the operating system to the
program via the **ACCEPT** statement. It is particularly useful as a
subscript value as the following example illustrates.

```
WORKING-STORAGE SECTION.
01  DAYS.
   03   PIC X(9)   VALUE "MONDAY    ".
   03   PIC X(9)   VALUE "TUESDAY   ".
   03   PIC X(9)   VALUE "WEDNESDAY".
   03   PIC X(9)   VALUE "THURSDAY ".
   03   PIC X(9)   VALUE "FRIDAY    ".
   03   PIC X(9)   VALUE "SATURDAY ".
   03   PIC X(9)   VALUE "SUNDAY    ".
01  DAY-TABLE REDEFINES DAYS.
   03   NAME-OF-DAY    PICTURE X(9) OCCURS 7 TIMES.
01  DAY-CODE          PICTURE 9.


     . . .ACCEPT DAY-CODE
           FROM DAY-OF-WEEK.

DISPLAY  "TODAY IS",  NAME-OF-DAY (DAY-CODE)
```

Debug   (Obsolete)

The Debug facility is an obsolete language element. Therefore, the "compile-time" **DEBUGGING** switch, **WITH DEBUG-GING MODE,** which is in the **SOURCE-COMPUTER** paragraph of the **ENVIRONMENT DIVISION**, is obsolete.

```
SOURCE-COMPUTER.  SYT-VX WITH DEBUGGING MODE.
```

The **USE FOR DEBUGGING** procedure in the **DECLARA-TIVES** is also obsolete.

```
DECLARATIVES.
DEBUG-PROCESS SECTION.
    USE FOR DEBUGGING ON FILE-A.
    . . .
```

NOTE: The feature for handling debug-lines, indicated by a **D** in column 7 of a COBOL source line, is technically not considered part of the Debug facility and is *not* an obsolete language element. (See *COBOL 85 Conversion*, page 163.)

De-editing (New)

De-editing allows programmers to move numeric-edited data items to purely numeric data items. This results in the pure numeric value being stored in the receiving field. The following example illustrates this process.

```
01          NUMERIC-EDITED-GROUP.
            05  FIRST-FIELD                     PIC ZZ..
            05  SECOND-FIELD                     PIC Z,ZZZ,
                                                     ZZZ.99.
            05  THIRD-FIELD                      PIC ZZ.ZZ.

01  NUMERIC-GROUP.
    03  FIRST-NUMERIC            PIC 99V99.
    03  SECOND-NUMERIC           PIC S9(7)V99.
                                 SIGN IS SEPARATE.
    03  THIRD-NUMERIC            PIC S9(4)V99
                                 SIGN IS SEPARATE.
    03  THIRD-NUMERIC-VARIATION  PIC S99
                                 SIGN IS LEADING SEPARATE.


    . . .MOVE FIRST-FIELD TO FIRST-NUMERIC
    . . .MOVE SECOND-FIELD TO SECOND-NUMERIC
    . . .MOVE THIRD-FIELD TO THIRD-NUMERIC
    . . .MOVE THIRD-FIELD TO THIRD-NUMERIC-VARIATION
    . . .MOVE FIRST-FIELD TO SECOND-FIELD
```

Each numeric-edited data item in **NUMERIC-EDITED-GROUP** is moved respectively to a corresponding numeric data item in **NUMERIC-GROUP**. The starting values of each sending item, as well as the resulting values of each receiving item, are indicated in the table that follows.

	Starting Value	Ending Value
FIRST-FIELD	"12."	"12"
SECOND-FIELD	"12,345.67"	"12,345.67"
THIRD-FIELD	"12.34"	"12.34"
FIRST-NUMERIC	–	1200
SECOND-NUMERIC	–	001234567+
THIRD-NUMERIC	–	001234+
THIRD-NUMERIC-VARIATION	–	+12

NOTE: **PICTURE** clauses in COBOL 85 may be continued over multiple lines and may now end with (..) and (,.). These are minor features not permitted in COBOL 74.

DISABLE ... WITH KEY   (Obsolete)

In the Communications module of COBOL, the **WITH KEY** phrase of both the **DISABLE** and **ENABLE** statements is an obsolete language element. The **WITH KEY** phrase specifies a ''password'' for the operating system to verify for terminal access. (See *COBOL 85 Conversion,* page 164.)

```
. . . ENABLE OUTPUT TERMINAL-CD WITH KEY "SESAME"

. . . DISABLE OUTPUT TERMINAL-CD WITH KEY "SESAME"
```


DISPLAY   (New)

The figurative constant **ALL ''literal''** as in

```
DISPLAY ALL "*" WITH NO ADVANCING
```

is permitted in a **DISPLAY** statement. COBOL 74/68 do not permit **ALL ''literal''** to be **DISPLAY**ed.

In addition, the **WITH NO ADVANCING** phrase of the **DISPLAY** statement ensures that the vertical position of the **DISPLAY** device will not be changed.

NOTE: Omission of the **WITH NO ADVANCING** phrase causes the position of the **DISPLAY** device, after executing a **DISPLAY** statement, to be set to the leftmost position of the next line. COBOL 74/68 do not specify what the position will be after the execution of a **DISPLAY** statement.

DIVIDE   (Change)

As with the **INSPECT, STRING, UNSTRING** and **PERFORM** statements, the order of evaluation of subscripts of the **RE-**

MAINDER data item of the **DIVIDE** statement is specified in COBOL 85 but is not in COBOL 74/68.

In the following example,

```
. . . DIVIDE A INTO B GIVING C REMAINDER D(C)
```

the subscript of the **REMAINDER** data item, **D(C)**, is evaluated after the result of the **DIVIDE** operation is stored in the **GIVING** data item, **C**. (See *COBOL 85 Conversion*, page 166.)

ENABLE ... WITH KEY   (Obsolete)

In the Communications module of COBOL, the **WITH KEY** phrase of both the **ENABLE** and **DISABLE** statements is an obsolete language element. The **WITH KEY** phrase specifies a "password" for the operating system to verify for terminal access. (See *COBOL 85 Conversion*, page 167.)

```
. . . ENABLE OUTPUT TERMINAL-CD WITH KEY "SESAME"

. . . DISABLE OUTPUT TERMINAL-CD WITH KEY "SESAME"
```

ENTER   (Obsolete)

The **ENTER** statement, which permits the coding of non-COBOL instructions in the midst of a COBOL **PROCEDURE DIVISION**, is an obsolete language element. (See *COBOL 85 Conversion*, page 168.)

```
PERFORM SCIENTIFIC-PREPARATION
ENTER FORTRAN.
   . . . DIMENSION NAME (5), TOTALS (2)
100   FORMAT (5A6, 4X, 1A6, 1A3)
      IF (GROSS-SALES .GT. 1000) GOTO 500
ENTER COBOL.
MOVE SCIENTIFIC-RESULTS TO COBOL-AREA. . .
```

EVALUATE   (New)

One limitation of previous versions of COBOL has been the absence of a well-structured case statement, which provides multijoin and multibranch selection. The new **EVALUATE** statement corrects this deficiency.

Traditionally, there have been two forms of control selection in COBOL. These are the **IF** statement and the computed **GO TO . . . DEPENDING ON . . .** statement. Each of these selection statements, however, is limited in its own way.

The **IF** statement simply provides only two branching alternatives and therefore is a very special (limited) case statement.

```
IF        AGE-OF-DEBT > 90
  THEN    PERFORM COLLECTIONS
  ELSE    CONTINUE
END-IF
```

The computed **GO TO . . . DEPENDING ON . . .** statement, while providing the only true multibranch case construct in COBOL until now, is poor for other reasons.

```
GO TO     PROCESS-NEW-DEBT
          PROCESS-DEBT-30
          PROCESS-DEBT-60
          NOTIFY-COLLECTIONS
DEPENDING ON N
```

To use this case statement, programmers must use the "dreaded" **GO TO** statement. For many structured programmers, this is a cardinal sin (although total avoidance of this statement may make some programs harder to follow rather than easier).

The more severe problem with the **GO TO . . . DEPENDING ON . . .** statement is with the variable that controls which path of logic is taken. In the figure above, the variable **N** controls which one of four control branches will be taken. The value of **N** must be in a range of one to four. Often the variable **N** has nothing to do with the data-processing problem at hand

and is therefore an artificial control. Clearly, it is the **AGE-OF-DEBT** that would logically determine which procedure should be executed. But we are forced to use a symbolic representation of the problem instead.

The **EVALUATE** statement combines the strengths of both selection statements (**IF** and **GO TO . . . DEPENDING ON . . .**) and eliminates the restrictions of each.

In its simplest form, the **EVALUATE** statement can be used to duplicate the effect of an **IF** statement:

```
EVALUATE   AGE-OF-DEBT  >= 90
     WHEN   TRUE   PERFORM NOTIFY-COLLECTIONS.
```

In the example above, **AGE-OF-DEBT > = 90** is referred to as the subject of the **EVALUATE** statement, and **TRUE** is the object of the statement. When the subject and the object of the **EVALUATE** statement match, the subsequent imperative statement(s), such as **PERFORM NOTIFY-COLLECTIONS**, is executed.

Note the new relational operators: **> =** , **GREATER THAN OR EQUAL** and **< =** , **LESS THAN OR EQUAL**.

In the example above, the subject, **AGE-OF-DEBT > = 90**, is a conditional expression. Therefore, the object must also be conditional. The word **TRUE** used in this case is a new conditional constant in COBOL 85. **TRUE** and **FALSE** are two new reserved words and can be used whenever a conditional value is required.

Conditional expressions are not the only subjects that can be evaluated. Consider the example that follows.

```
EVALUATE AGE-OF-DEBT
    WHEN  0 THROUGH 30   PERFORM NO-NOTICE
END-EVALUATE
```

In this example, the subject is a numeric data item. Therefore, the object must be numeric. (Note that in the example presented, we could *not* have said: *"WHEN LESS THAN THIRTY-ONE PERFORM NO-NOTICE".*)

So far we have seen the **EVALUATE** statement in its simplest form. The real value of **EVALUATE** is its use as a multi-branch case statement.

```
EVALUATE AGE-OF-DEBT
    WHEN  Ø                 PERFORM ACKNOWLEDGE-PREPAYMENT-THANKS
    WHEN  Ø   THRU 30       PERFORM SEND-FIRST-LETTER
    WHEN  31  THRU 60       PERFORM SEND-SECOND-LETTER
    WHEN  61  THRU 90       PERFORM SEND-THIRD-LETTER
    WHEN  OTHER             PERFORM NOTIFY-COLLECTIONS
END-EVALUATE
```

In the example above, the subject **AGE-OF-DEBT** is tested against each object (**0, 0 THRU 30, 31 THRU 60,** etc.) in order. As soon as a match occurs, the subsequent imperative statement(s) is executed, and control resumes after the scope-terminator **END-EVALUATE**. In other words, only one **WHEN** path—the first one that matches—can ever be taken.

Each **WHEN** phrase (except the last) is terminated by the beginning of the next **WHEN** phrase. The final **WHEN** phrase can be terminated by either a period (.) or the scope-terminator **END-EVALUATE**.

The optional use of the "catchall" object **OTHER** (a new reserved word) assures that at least one **WHEN** phrase will be chosen. The next two examples illustrate identical logic using two different **EVALUATE** statements.

```
EVALUATE  MONTH
    WHEN  1             PERFORM JANUARY-PROC
    WHEN  4 THRU 6      PERFORM SECOND-QTR
    WHEN  12            PERFORM YEAR-END
    WHEN  OTHER         PERFORM NORMAL-MONTH
END-EVALUATE
```

```
EVALUATE  TRUE
    WHEN  MONTH = 1              PERFORM JANUARY-PROC
    WHEN  MONTH > 3 AND < 7      PERFORM SECOND-QTR
    WHEN  MONTH = 12             PERFORM YEAR-END
    WHEN  OTHER                  PERFORM NORMAL-MONTH
END-EVALUATE
```

The first example above uses a numeric subject and object. The second example uses a conditional subject and object (i.e., **MONTH > 3 AND < 7** is a conditional expression whose value is either **TRUE** or **FALSE**).

There are numerous rules for matching subjects and objects; simply stated, the subject and object must be of the same category and capable of matching, as the following table of permissible pairs illustrates.

SUBJECT	OBJECT
NUMERIC	
NUM-X	NUM-RESULT
12	14
X + Y * Z	16 THRU 35
ZERO	A / 5 - 3
NONNUMERIC	
LAST-NAME	ALPH-NAME
SPACES	"SMITH"
"JONES"	SPACES
CONDITIONAL	
A > B	TRUE
TRUE	FALSE
FALSE	X < Y
HIGH-USAGE	
SWITCH-1-ON	
ITEM-A IS NUMERIC	

The **EVALUATE** statement can be used to test multiple subjects against corresponding multiple objects. In this format, the **EVALUATE** statement resembles a truth table transposed into COBOL code.

```
EVALUATE   AGE-OF-DEBT   ALSO          TRUE
    WHEN    0 THRU 30    ALSO   CREDIT-RATING = "A" OR "B"   PERFORM SEND-NO-NOTICE
    WHEN    0 THRU 30    ALSO   CREDIT RATING = "C"          PERFORM SEND-MILD-NOTICE
    WHEN   31 THRU 60    ALSO   CREDIT-RATING = "A"          PERFORM SEND-MILD-NOTICE
    WHEN   31 THRU 60    ALSO   CREDIT-RATING = "B"          PERFORM SEND-NORMAL-NOTICE
    WHEN   31 THRU 60    ALSO   CREDIT-RATING = "C"          PERFORM SEND-FIRM-NOTICE
    WHEN   61 THRU 90    ALSO   CREDIT-RATING = "A"          PERFORM SEND-NORMAL-NOTICE
    WHEN   61 THRU 90    ALSO   CREDIT-RATING = "B"          PERFORM SEND-FIRM-NOTICE
    WHEN   61 THRU 90    ALSO   CREDIT-RATING = "C"          PERFORM NOTIFY-COLLECTIONS
    WHEN   91 THRU 999   ALSO   CREDIT-RATING = "A"          PERFORM SEND-FIRM-NOTICE
    WHEN   91 THRU 999   ALSO   CREDIT-RATING = "B" OR "C"   PERFORM NOTIFY-COLLECTIONS
END-EVALUATE
```

In the example above, the reserved word **ALSO** separates multiple subjects from each other and multiple objects from each other. There is no limit to the number of subjects and objects allowed in the **EVALUATE** statement (horizontally or vertically). It is permissible in one statement to **EVALUATE** different categories of subjects (**AGE-OF-DEBT** is numeric, **TRUE** is conditional) as long as their corresponding objects belong to the same category (**31 THRU 60** is numeric, **CREDIT-RATING = "A"** is conditional).

There are times, when **EVALUATE**ing multiple subjects, that a **WHEN** phrase need not match all subjects and objects to determine which specific action is to be taken. For example, when **EVALUATE**ing three subjects, if two of them match their corresponding objects, **ANY** value for the third object is acceptable for the desired action to occur. This is illustrated in the following example. (Note the new reserved word **ANY**.)

```
EVALUATE   QTY-ON-HAND   ALSO   LOCAL-VENDOR   ALSO   WEEKLY-USE
    WHEN   50 THRU 100   ALSO      ANY         ALSO     ANY      PERFORM NO-REORDER
    WHEN   10 THRU 49    ALSO      TRUE        ALSO    "HIGH"    PERFORM RUSH-ORDER
    WHEN   10 THRU 49    ALSO      TRUE        ALSO    "LOW"     PERFORM NORMAL-ORDER
    WHEN   10 THRU 49    ALSO      FALSE       ALSO    "HIGH"    PERFORM RUSH-ORDER
    WHEN    0 THRU 9     ALSO      ANY         ALSO    "HIGH"    PERFORM RUSH-ORDER
    WHEN    0 THRU 9     ALSO      FALSE       ALSO     ANY      PERFORM RUSH-ORDER
    WHEN   OTHER                                                 PERFORM SPECIAL-ACTION
END-EVALUATE
```

EXIT PROGRAM   (New, Change)

The **EXIT PROGRAM** statement in a **CALL**ed program need not be in a separate paragraph. (COBOL 74 requires that it be in a paragraph by itself.)

In the following example,

```
IF        TIME-TO-GO
          EXIT PROGRAM
ELSE
          GO TO FINAL-ROUTINE.
   .
   .
   .


FINAL-ROUTINE.
          DISPLAY "PROGRAM WILL EXIT NOW".
```

if the level-**88** condition-name **TIME-TO-GO** is true, the program will return control to its **CALL**ing program.

There are some subtle changes to the behavior of COBOL programs that contain an **EXIT PROGRAM** (or **CANCEL** or **STOP RUN**) statement. The **EXIT PROGRAM** statement will close all "left-opened" **PERFORM** loops in the program that is **EXIT**ing. That is, if any **PERFORM**ed procedure is interrupted while the paragraph is being executed (thereby leaving a stray implicit return instruction at the end of that procedure), that implicit return instruction will be canceled by the execution of an **EXIT PROGRAM** statement. This prevents accidental branching to an unwanted point in the program the next time that program is **CALL**ed and that procedure is executed in a "fall through" fashion.

Further, if a **CALL**ed program "runs out of code" while executing (as in **FINAL-ROUTINE**), an implicit **EXIT PROGRAM** will be executed. (See *COBOL 85 Conversion*, page 168.)

FD   (New, Obsolete)

In the **FD** clause shown in the following example,

```
FD    VARIABLE-LENGTH-FILE-A
      RECORD IS VARYING IN SIZE
                  FROM 100 TO 400 CHARACTERS
                  DEPENDING ON RECORD-LENGTH-VALUE.
```

the **RECORD IS VARYING IN SIZE** clause specifies variable-length records. In the **DEPENDING ON** phrase, the user-defined data item **RECORD-LENGTH-VALUE** contains the number of character positions in the record. In INPUT mode, the actual length of the record **READ** or **RETURN**ed is placed in **RECORD-LENGTH-VALUE**. In OUTPUT mode, the program uses **RECORD-LENGTH-VALUE** to determine the number of characters in the record to **WRITE, REWRITE** or **RELEASE**. When in OUTPUT mode, the programmer is responsible for placing the proper value in **RECORD-LENGTH-VALUE**.

The following example contains the minimum specifications for variable-length records. The actual number of characters in the record determines the record size.

```
FD    VARIABLE-LENGTH-FILE-B
      RECORD VARYING 100 TO 400.
```

In the following example,

```
FD    VARIABLE-LENGTH-FILE-C
      RECORD IS VARYING IN SIZE
                  FROM 100 CHARACTERS.
```

the maximum length of the record is determined by the largest **01** record description for the file.

Likewise, in this example,

```
FD    VARIABLE-LENGTH-FILE-D
      RECORD IS VARYING IN SIZE
                  TO 400 CHARACTERS
                  DEPENDING ON RECORD-LENGTH-VALUE.
```

the minimum length of the record is determined by the smallest **01** record description for this file.

The **RECORD IS VARYING IN SIZE** clause can be specified for any file organization and type (**SEQUENTIAL, RELATIVE, INDEXED, SORT/MERGE, REPORT**).

NOTE: The **RECORD CONTAINS** clause in the following example,

```
FD    COBOL-74-VARIABLE-LENGTH-FILE
      RECORD CONTAINS 100 TO 400 CHARACTERS.
```

which is valid in COBOL 74, is also valid in COBOL 85. It is equivalent to specifying, as follows:

```
FD    COBOL-74-85-VAR-LEN-FILE
      RECORD IS VARYING IN SIZE
                  FROM 100
                  TO   400  CHARACTERS.
```

In the following example, the **CODE-SET** clause can be specified for any **SEQUENTIAL** file (COBOL 74 restricts the **CODE-SET** clause to nondisk files).

Furthermore, the **LABEL RECORDS** clause is now optional.

```
FD    SEQUENTIAL-DISK-FILE-A
      BLOCK CONTANS 5 RECORDS
      LABEL RECORDS ARE STANDARD
      VALUE OF IDENTIFICATION IS "MASTERFILE"
      CODE-SET IS ISO-7-BIT.


FD    SEQUENTIAL-DISK-FILE-B.
```

Omission of the **LABEL RECORDS** clause implies by default that **LABEL RECORDS ARE STANDARD**.

Omission of the **BLOCK CONTAINS** clause is permitted when the block size is specified by the operating environment (e.g., via Job Control Language).

NOTE: The **LABEL RECORD, VALUE OF, DATA RECORD** clauses of the **FD** are all obsolete language elements. (See *COBOL 85 Conversion,* page 171.)

```
FD   COBOL-74-FILE
     LABEL RECORD IS STANDARD
     VALUE OF IDENTIFICATION IS "COBOL-74"
     DATA RECORD IS COBOL-74-RECORD.
01   COBOL-74-RECORD.
```

FILLER (New)

The word **FILLER** may now be used at a group level. COBOL 74 does not allow this.

```
01      FILLER.
        03  PERIOD-AMT    PIC X(6)V99
                          OCCURS 4 TIMES.
```

The word **FILLER** (at any level) is optional. Since data items defined as **FILLER** in the **DATA DIVISION** are not "reference-able" by statements in the **PROCEDURE DIVISION**, the optional word **FILLER** will be inferred if omitted, as the following example shows.

```
01   HEADING-LINE.
     03              PIC X(20)   VALUE SPACES.
     03   TITLE      PIC X(30)   VALUE SPACES.
     03              PIC X(20)   VALUE SPACES.
     03   PGE-NBR    PIC X(15)   VALUE SPACES.
     03   FILLER REDEFINES PGE-NBR.
       05            PIC X(5).
       05   PAGEE    PIC 999.
       05            PIC XXXX.
       05   MAX-PG   PIC 999.
     03   FILLER     PIC X(23)   VALUE SPACES.
```

By combining both new features of **FILLER** presented above, the following code is now permissible.

```
01.
   03 A   PIC XXX.
   03 B   PIC 999.
   03 C   PIC XXX.
```

FOOTING (Change)

If a **WRITE** statement includes an **END-OF-PAGE** phrase, the **FD** for the file being written must specify a **FOOTING** phrase in its **LINAGE** clause.

The following example is invalid in COBOL 85 but is valid in COBOL 74.

```
FD PRINT-FILE
01 PRINT RECORD


          WRITE      PRINT-RECORD
          AT         END-OF-PAGE PERFORM HEADING-ROUTINE.
```

If a COBOL 74 compiler does permit the statements in the example above, it is likely that some default **FOOTING** has been assigned. (See *COBOL 85 Conversion*, page 173.)

GO TO ... DEPENDING ON ...   (New)

In the following example,

```
          GO TO           END-OF-MONTH-ROUTINE
            DEPENDING ON   END-OF-MONTH-FLAG.
```

the number of procedure-names in the **DEPENDING ON** phrase may be one. COBOL 74/68 require at least two procedure-names. In this example, **END-OF-MONTH-FLAG** is a conditional variable.

```
          01     END-OF-MONTH-FLAG     PICTURE 9.
            88   END-OF-MONTH          VALUE 1.
```

The previous **GO TO** statement is equivalent to the following.

```
          IF       END-OF-MONTH
            GO TO   END-OF-MONTH-ROUTINE.
```

In both statements (**GO TO** and **IF**), if the value of **END-OF-MONTH-FLAG** is other than 1, control falls through to the next statement.

IDENTIFICATION DIVISION—Comment entries

(Obsolete)

The five comment entries in the **IDENTIFICATION DIVISION** (**AUTHOR, INSTALLATION, DATE-WRITTEN, DATE-COMPILED** and **SECURITY**) are obsolete language elements. (See *COBOL 85 Conversion*, page 174.)

```
IDENTIFICATION DIVISION.
PROGRAM-ID.      TEST-EDIT.
AUTHOR.          R. KNIGHTS.
INSTALLATION.    PIGGOTT ET AL.
DATE-WRITTEN.    JANUARY 1, 1985.
DATE-COMPILED.   JULY 24, 1985.
SECURITY.        FOR ROBERT AND JANET ONLY.
```

INITIALIZE

(New)

The **INITIALIZE** statement allows the programmer to set initial values for a whole group of elementary data items at one "fell swoop".

```
01  GROUP-ITEM.
    03  ALPHA-NUMERIC-ITEM                  PIC XXX.
    03  ALPHABETIC-ITEM                     PIC AAA.
    03  NUMERIC-ITEM                        PIC 999.
    03  SUBGROUP-ITEM.
        05  NUMERIC-EDITED-ITEM             PIC $$9.
        05  ALPHANUMERIC-EDITED-ITEM        PIC XX/XX/XX.
        05  NUMERIC-TABLE.
            07  TABLE-ITEM OCCURS 100 TIMES PIC 999.


    . . . INITIALIZE GROUP-ITEM.
```

In its simplest form, as in the following example, each elementary data item, either numeric (pure numeric and numeric-edited) or nonnumeric (alphabetic, alphanumeric and alphanumeric-edited), is reset to **ZERO** or to **SPACES**, whichever is appropriate (i.e., numeric items are reset to **ZERO**;

nonnumeric items are reset to **SPACES**). The effect is as though the programmer had written:

```
MOVE ZERO TO NUMERIC-ITEM.
MOVE ZERO TO NUMERIC-EDITED-ITEM.
MOVE SPACES TO ALPHA-NUMERIC-ITEM.
MOVE SPACES TO ALPHABETIC-ITEM.
MOVE SPACES TO ALPHA-NUMERIC-EDITED-ITEM.
PERFORM   VARYING X
            FROM 1
            BY 1
            UNTIL X > 100
        MOVE ZERO TO TABLE-ITEM (X)
END-PERFORM
```

In the following example, specific categories of data items are **INITIALIZE**d without affecting any others.

```
INITIALIZE GROUP-ITEM REPLACING NUMERIC DATA BY ZERO.
```

Categories of data items may be reset to values other than **ZERO** or **SPACES**, as the following example illustrates.

```
INITIALIZE    GROUP-ITEM
              REPLACING   NUMERIC DATA BY 10
                          ALPHANUMERIC DATA BY "*".
```

The table below shows resulting values of the corresponding data items after executing the above **INITIALIZE** statement.

DATA ITEM	CONTENTS
ALPHANUMERIC-ITEM	*
ALPHABETIC-ITEM	spaces
NUMERIC-ITEM	10
NUMERIC-EDITED-ITEM	0
ALPHANUMERIC-EDITED-ITEM	/ /
TABLE-ITEM elements (each of 100 occurences)	10

INSPECT   (New, Change)

The **CONVERTING** phrase of the **INSPECT** statement gives the programmer a form of shorthand for performing multiple replacements in one **INSPECT** statement. (It also provides an occasional miracle, as we shall see.)

   In the following examples, "WATER" is turned into "WINE" using a COBOL 74 **INSPECT** statement (still perfectly valid in a COBOL 85 program).

```
01  BOTTLE                  PIC X(5) VALUE "WATER".


        . . . INSPECT BOTTLE
              REPLACING    ALL "A" BY "I"
                           ALL "T" BY "N"
                           ALL "R" BY " ".
```

   In the following example, an alternative format of the **INSPECT** statement using the new **CONVERTING** phrase allows the programmer to perform the same miracle (turning "WATER" into "WINE"), but with less effort.

```
INSPECT BOTTLE CONVERTING "ATR" TO "IN ".
```

   Both the **BEFORE** and **AFTER** phrases of the **INSPECT** statement may now appear together in the same **INSPECT** statement.

   In the following example,

```
01  INPUT-BUFFER   PIC  X(13)   VALUE  "A*B*C*D*E*F*G".


INSPECT          INPUT-BUFFER
    REPLACING ALL "*"
    BY               "-"
    AFTER            "B"
    BEFORE           "F".
```

only the "middle" portion of **INPUT-BUFFER** is changed. The new value of **INPUT-BUFFER** is "A*B-C-D-E-F*G."

NOTE: COBOL 74 does not permit **BEFORE** and **AFTER** phrases to be used in the same **INSPECT** statement.

As the following example illustrates, the **ALL** and **LEADING** adjectives of the **INSPECT** statement can be distributed over multiple identifiers. There can also be multiple **REPLACING** phrases in one **INSPECT** statement.

```
INSPECT          INPUT-DATA-ITEM
   REPLACING ALL      "("        ")"
   BY        SPACES
   REPLACING LEADING ZEROS,   "$"
   BY        SPACES.
```

In the above example, **ALL** "("   ")" is equivalent to **ALL** "(" , **ALL** ")".

As with the **DIVIDE, PERFORM, STRING** and **UNSTRING** statements, the order of evaluating subscripts in the **INSPECT** statement is specified in COBOL 85. This order is not specified in COBOL 74/68.

In the following example,

```
INSPECT FIELD(X) TALLYING X FOR ALL CHARACTERS
```

the subscript in **FIELD (X)** is evaluated once prior to the **INSPECT** operation. (See *COBOL 85 Conversion*, page 176.)

LINAGE   (New, Change)

Data-names in the **LINAGE** clause of an **FD** may now be qualified. In COBOL 74, they may not be qualified.

Files that contain a **LINAGE** clause in their **FD** may not be **OPEN**ed in the **EXTEND** mode. The following COBOL 74 example is *invalid* in COBOL 85.

```
FD    NON-EXTENDED-PRINT-FILE
      LINAGE IS 66 LINES
      WITH FOOTING AT 60.


OPEN EXTEND NON-EXTENDED-PRINT-FILE
```

The action resulting from the above example is undefined but permitted in COBOL 74. (See *COBOL 85 Conversion,* page 183.)

Line-Reference "Numbers"   (New)

The optional line-reference numbers of a COBOL program need not be numbers at all. They can contain any characters in the COBOL character set. COBOL 74 requires that they be digits. The following excerpt from the **ENVIRONMENT DIVISION** illustrates the use of nonnumeric sequence "numbers."

```
ED0100    SELECT    SOMETIME-MULTIPLE-REEL-FILE
ED0200              ASSIGN TO DEVICE-AA.
ED0300    SELECT    SOMETIME-MULTI-VOLUME-FILE
ED0400              ASSIGN TO DISK-BB.
ED0500    SELECT    RELATIVE-FILE
ED0600              ASSIGN TO DISK-CC
ED0700              ACCESS IS SEQUENTIAL.
ED0800    SELECT    REPORT-FILE
ED0900              ASSIGN TO TAPE-DD.
ED1000    SELECT    OPTIONAL SOMETIMES-FILE
ED1100              ASSIGN TO DISK-A.
```

Literals   (New)

The maximum size of a nonnumeric literal (e.g., "**JOHN SMITH**") is 160 characters. In COBOL 74/68, the maximum size is 120.

Lowercase letters (New)

As the following example illustrates, lowercase letters may be used in a COBOL source program. Except when used in a nonnumeric literal ("**John Smith**"), lowercase letters are equivalent to uppercase letters.

```
ADD        This-Week-Salary
TO         Old-Ytd-Salary
GIVING     New-Ytd-Salary
```

NOTE: The optional word **TO** is now allowed in the **ADD** statement with the **GIVING** phrase. (It's about time.)

MEMORY SIZE (Obsolete)

In the **OBJECT-COMPUTER** paragraph of the **ENVIRONMENT DIVISION**, the **MEMORY SIZE** clause that specifies to the operating system the amount of memory available for object program execution is an obsolete language element. (See *COBOL 85 Conversion*, page 184.)

```
OBJECT-COMPUTER.    SYSTEM-VX
                    MEMORY SIZE IS 96000 CHARACTERS.
```

MERGE and SORT (New, Change)

For an explanation of new features of the **MERGE** statement, see **SORT and MERGE** on page 137.

For a discussion of new restrictions on the **MERGE** statement, possibly affecting COBOL 74/68 programs, see *COBOL 85 Conversion* on page 184.

MULTIPLE FILE TAPE (Obsolete)

The **MULTIPLE FILE TAPE** clause of the **I-O-CONTROL** paragraph is an obsolete language element. (See *COBOL 85 Conversion*, page 185.)

```
FILE-CONTROL.
    SELECT THIRD-LARGE-FILE ASSIGN TO TAPE.
    SELECT FOURTH-LARGE-FILE ASSIGN TO TAPE.
I-O-CONTROL.
    MULTIPLE FILE TAPE CONTAINS   THIRD-LARGE-FILE POSITION 3
                                  FOURTH-LARGE-FILE POSITION 4.
```

Nested Programs (New)

An important addition to COBOL 85 is the ability to nest complete COBOL programs within other COBOL programs. This adds greatly to the versatility with which programs and systems can be developed and tested. This ability is especially useful in team programming environments.

In the example on the following page, three levels of nested programs are presented. Each program (outer and inner) begins with an **IDENTIFICATION DIVISION** header and **PROGRAM-ID**. All inner programs end with an

```
IDENTIFICATION DIVISION.
PROGRAM-ID.  OUTER-PROGRAM.
   .
   .
   .
   IDENTIFICATION DIVISION.
   PROGRAM-ID.  FIRST-LEVEL-PROGRAM.
      .
      .
      .
      IDENTIFICATION DIVISION.
      PROGRAM-ID.  SECOND-LEVEL-PROGRAM.
         .
         .
         .
      END PROGRAM  SECOND-LEVEL-PROGRAM.
      IDENTIFICATION DIVISION.
      PROGRAM-ID.  ANOTHER-SECOND-LEVEL-PROGRAM.
         .
         .
         .
      END PROGRAM  ANOTHER-SECOND-LEVEL-PROGRAM.
   END PROGRAM  FIRST-LEVEL-PROGRAM.
   IDENTIFICATION DIVISION.
   PROGRAM-ID.  ANOTHER-FIRST-LEVEL-PROGRAM.
      .
      .
      .
   END PROGRAM  ANOTHER-FIRST-LEVEL-PROGRAM.
END PROGRAM  OUTER-PROGRAM.
```

END PROGRAM header. ("Header" seems an odd name for the **END PROGRAM** statement, but that is what it is called technically.) As the following example shows, programs can be written without a **PROCEDURE DIVISION**, purely for abbreviated compilations and syntax checking of the other divisions.

```
IDENTIFICATION DIVISION.
PROGRAM-ID.  OPTIONAL-DIVISION-PROG.

ENVIRONMENT DIVISION.
CONFIGURATION SECTION.

SOURCE-COMPUTER.  MODEL-VX.
OBJECT-COMPUTER.  MODEL-VX.
INPUT-OUTPUT SECTION.
FILE-CONTROL.
     SELECT FILE-A ASSIGN TO TAPE.
     SELECT FILE-B ASSIGN TO DISK.
I-O-CONTROL.
     SAME RECORD AREA FOR FILE-A, FILE-B.

DATA DIVISION.
     .
     .
     .
     .
     .
     .
     .
END PROGRAM  OPTIONAL-DIVISION-PROG.
```

Nested programs also allow outer programs to define files and data items that can be shared by all inner programs. This is accomplished by the **GLOBAL** clause, as shown in the example on the following page.

```
IDENTIFICATION DIVISION.
PROGRAM-ID.              OUTER-PROGRAM.
DATA DIVISION.
FILE SECTION.
FD    IN-FILE . . .   IS GLOBAL . . .
01    IN-RECORD . . .
WORKING-STORAGE SECTION.
01    FIELD-A        IS GLOBAL    PICTURE XXX.
01    FIELD-B                     PICTURE XXX.
01    FIELD-C        IS GLOBAL.
        03   FIELD-C1             PICTURE XXX.
        03   FIELD-C2             PICTURE XXX.
        03   FIELD-C3.
          05    FIELD-C4          PICTURE XXX.
          05    FIELD-C4          PICTURE XXX.
01    RA                          PICTURE X(100).
01    GLOB-REC    REDEFINES RA IS GLOBAL.
        03   . . .
          .
          .
          .
PROCEDURE DIVISION.
DECLARATIVES.
A SECTION.
      USE GLOBAL AFTER ERROR PROCEDURE ON INPUT.
          .
          .
B SECTION.
      USE GLOBAL AFTER ERROR PROCEDURE ON OUTPUT.
          .
          .
IDENTIFICATION DIVISION.
PROGRAM-ID.             FIRST-LEVEL-PROGRAM.
PROCEDURE DIVISION.
DECLARATIVES.
A SECTION.
      USE AFTER ERROR PROCEDURE ON INPUT.
          .
          .
B SECTION.
      USE GLOBAL AFTER ERROR PROCEDURE ON I-O.
          .
          .
IDENTIFICATION DIVISION.
PROGRAM-ID.            SECOND-LEVEL-PROGRAM
PROCEDURE DIVISION.
DECLARATIVES.
A SECTION.
      USE AFTER ERROR PROCEDURE ON OUTPUT.
          .
          .
END PROGRAM           SECOND-LEVEL-PROGRAM.
END PROGRAM           FIRST-LEVEL-PROGRAM.
END PROGRAM           OUTER-PROGRAM.
```

IN-FILE is a **GLOBAL** file in the outer program, and therefore references to **IN-FILE** and its **IN-RECORD** can be made by statements in any of the inner programs as well as by statements in the outer program. The same is true for **GLOBAL** data items (including elementary items that are subordinate to a **GLOBAL** group item) appearing in the **WORKING-STORAGE** section of the outer program (i.e., **FIELD-A**, **FIELD-C** and all subordinate items in **FIELD-C**). Note that if a **GLOBAL** item is redefined, only the new name (**GLOB-REC**) is considered **GLOBAL**, not the object of the **REDEFINES** clause (**RA**).

GLOBAL USE PROCEDUREs are in effect for the outer program in which they are specified, as well as for all (inner) programs contained within. A **GLOBAL USE PROCEDURE** in an outer (containing) program, however, will be overridden at any level by a more local **USE PROCEDURE** (**GLOBAL** or not) in the **DECLARATIVE SECTION** of an inner program.

In the example above, errors may occur on three types of files at each level. The **USE PROCEDURE** that will be in effect for each type of file at each level is shown in the table below.

```
SECOND-LEVEL PROGRAM

        File-Type Error        Program Executing USE PROCEDURE
            INPUT                      OUTER-PROGRAM
            I-O                        FIRST-LEVEL-PROGRAM
            OUTPUT                     SECOND-LEVEL PROGRAM


FIRST-LEVEL PROGRAM

        File Type Error        Program Executing USE PROCEDURE
            INPUT                      FIRST-LEVEL PROGRAM
            I-O                        FIRST-LEVEL PROGRAM
            OUTPUT                     OUTER-PROGRAM


OUTER-PROGRAM

        File Type Error        Program Executing USE PROCEDURE
            INPUT                      OUTER-PROGRAM
            I-O                        (none)
            OUTPUT                     OUTER-PROGRAM
```

Note: If there is a conflict between two **USE PROCEDURE**s—one naming a specific file and one specifying a file type—as in

```
USE AFTER ERROR PROCEDURE ON OUTPUT-FILE-A

USE AFTER ERROR PROCEDURE ON OUTPUT
```

the **USE PROCEDURE** naming the specific file (**OUTPUT-FILE-A**) takes precedence.

The **DATA DIVISION** of a COBOL program is optional. Omitting the **DATA DIVISION** from a program may be useful when the procedural statements of an inner program reference only **GLOBAL** data items that are defined in the outer (containing) program.

```
IDENTIFICATION DIVISION.
PROGRAM-ID.  OPTIONAL-DIVISION-PROG.

PROCEDURE DIVISION.
   .
   .
   .
```

While we are "stripping down" our program, it might be useful to note that the **ENVIRONMENT DIVISION** is also optional. In fact, the **CONFIGURATION SECTION** must be omitted in inner programs to avoid contradiction between the **CONFIGURATION SECTION** of the outer program.

```
IDENTIFICATION DIVISION.
PROGRAM-ID.  OPTIONAL-DIVISION-PROG.
   .
   .
   .
DATA DIVISON.
   .
   .
   .
PROCEDURE DIVISION.
   .
   .
   .
```

Moreover, the order of the clauses in the **I-O-CONTROL** paragraph is immaterial. In COBOL 74, the order is specified.

The **CALL** statement is coded identically, regardless of whether the program being **CALL**ed is nested (contained within) or separately compiled.

There are some restrictions, however, regarding **CALL**ing programs that are nested in other programs.

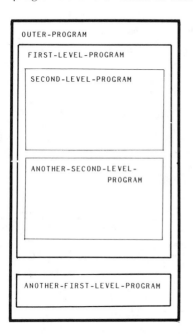

As in COBOL 74, all programs can of course **CALL** any separately compiled program. Thus, in the example above, all five programs (**OUTER-PROGRAM** and the four inner programs) can **CALL SEPARATELY-COMPILED-PROGRAM**.

We will look at an exception to the following rule shortly. However, in order to reach a nested program (one contained within another), it can normally be **CALL**ed only by its "parent" (directly containing program). Thus, **ANOTHER-SECOND-**

LEVEL-PROGRAM can be **CALL**ed only by **FIRST-LEVEL-PRO-GRAM** (its "parent").

One program cannot jump over another; that is, **OUTER-PROGRAM** may *not* **CALL SECOND-LEVEL-PROGRAM** directly.

There are times, however, when we want more flexibility in accessing an inner program from other than its "parent." This can be accomplished by declaring that an inner program is **COMMON**, as in the following example.

```
PROGRAM-ID.  ANOTHER-FIRST-LEVEL-PROGRAM IS COMMON.
```

```
PROGRAM-ID.  SECOND-LEVEL-PROGRAM IS COMMON.
```

Using the two previous examples, the same hierarchy of programs can be viewed from a different perspective.

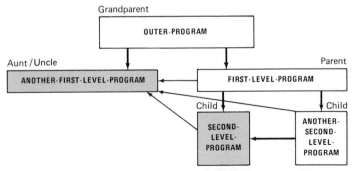

A **COMMON** program may be **CALL**ed from its "parent" (as before); it may also be **CALL**ed from any program descending from its "parent" ("Brother/Sister," "Niece/Nephew," etc., however, not "Aunts/Uncles," "Cousins," etc.). I call these the "incest rules" of nested programming.

Thus, in the example above, **ANOTHER-FIRST-LEVEL-PROGRAM**, which is **COMMON**, can be **CALL**ed not only by its "parent" (**OUTER-PROGRAM**) as before, but now it can also be **CALL**ed by any of the three programs that are descended from its "parent" (i.e., **FIRST-LEVEL-PROGRAM**, **SECOND-LEVEL-PROGRAM** or **ANOTHER-SECOND-LEVEL-PROGRAM**).

Likewise, **SECOND-LEVEL-PROGRAM**, which has been made **COMMON**, can now be **CALL**ed by **ANOTHER-SECOND-LEVEL-PROGRAM** in addition to **FIRST-LEVEL-PROGRAM** (its "parent").

Occasionally, when **CALL**ing a program that has previously been executed, it is desirable to assure that we will start with a "fresh copy" of that **CALL**ed program; that is, we want all data items restored to their original (compiled) values and all **AL-TER**ed **GO TO** statements restored to their original operands. This is accomplished by the **INITIAL** phrase in the **PROGRAM-ID** entry.

In the following example,

```
IDENTIFICATION DIVISION.
PROGRAM-ID.  OUTER-PROGRAM.


  IDENTIFICATION DIVISION.
  PROGRAM-ID.  FIRST-LEVEL-PROGRAM, IS INITIAL.


    IDENTIFICATION DIVISION.
    PROGRAM-ID.  SECOND-LEVEL-PROGRAM IS COMMON.
    END PROGRAM SECOND-LEVEL-PROGRAM.


    IDENTIFICATION DIVISION.
    PROGRAM-ID.  ANOTHER-SECOND-LEVEL-PROGRAM.
    END PROGRAM ANOTHER-SECOND-LEVEL-PROGRAM.

  END PROGRAM  FIRST-LEVEL-PROGRAM.


  IDENTIFICATION DIVISION.
  PROGRAM-ID.  ANOTHER FIRST-LEVEL-PROGRAM IS COMMON.
  END PROGRAM ANOTHER-FIRST-LEVEL-PROGRAM.

END PROGRAM  OUTER-PROGRAM.
```

FIRST-LEVEL-PROGRAM will be **INITIAL**ized before it starts executing, as will all programs nested within it (i.e., contained within, subordinate to, etc.), regardless of whether they are **COMMON** or not. Note: A program can use both **COMMON** and **INITIAL** phrases together.

Another new feature of COBOL 85 is the designation of files and records as **EXTERNAL**. This is similar to the concept of "labeled common" or "block common" data. It is a storage-allocation efficiency device that permits a file or a record area to be created just once and shared by all programs in a single run unit.

In the following example,

```
IDENTIFICATION DIVISION.
PROGRAM-ID.  OUTER-PROGRAM.
        .
        .
        .
DATA DIVISION.
FILE   SECTION.
FD     EXT-FILE                 IS EXTERNAL.
01     EXT-FILE-RECORD          PIC X(30).
        .
        .
        .
WORKING-STORAGE SECTION.
01     EXT-DATA                 IS EXTERNAL.
       03  A                    PIC XXX.
       03  B                    PIC 99V99.
       03  C                    PIC 9(4)V99.
    IDENTIFICATION DIVISION.
    PROGRAM-ID.  FIRST-LEVEL-PROGRAM.
            .
            .
            .
      IDENTIFICATION DIVISION.
      PROGRAM-ID.  SECOND-LEVEL-PROGRAM.
              .
              .
              .
      WORKING-STORAGE SECTION.
      01     EXT-DATA                 IS EXTERNAL.
             03  A                    PIC XXX.
             03  B                    PIC 99V99.
             03  C                    PIC 9(4)V99.
      END PROGRAM SECOND-LEVEL-PROGRAM.
    END PROGRAM FIRST-LEVEL-PROGRAM.
END PROGRAM OUTER-PROGRAM.
```

```
      IDENTIFICATION DIVISION.
      PROGRAM-ID.  SEPARATELY-COMPILED-PROGRAM.
          .
          .
          .
      FILE SECTION.
      FD    EXT-FILE                      IS EXTERNAL.
      01    EXT-FILE-RECORD               PIC X(30).
```

the file named **EXT-FILE** as well as the **WORKING-STORAGE**
record **EXT-DATA** are declared to be **EXTERNAL** items. Each
program that uses **EXT-FILE** or **EXT-DATA** must define these
items in the same way, but only one storage area for each will
be allocated for the entire run unit. Note that items declared as
EXTERNAL cannot be **GLOBAL**, and no **VALUE** clauses can be
included in their **PICTURE** descriptions. Declaring an **01** record
to be **EXTERNAL** includes all subordinate items as well.

OCCURS   (New)

A **VALUE** clause can be specified in the same entry of a data
item that also contains an **OCCURS** clause. COBOL 74 does
not permit this. A programmer can specify initial values for the
elements of a table without having to redefine that table. In the
following example,

```
      01.
         05  YTD-AMT      OCCURS 12 TIMES
                          PIC S9(8)
                          VALUE ZERO.
```

each of the twelve occurrences of **YTD-AMT** is given an initial
value of **ZERO**.
   A variable-length table (one that **OCCURS** from *n1* to *n2*
times) can now have **ZERO** as a minimum number of occurrences, as in the example that follows. COBOL 74 requires at
least one occurrence.

```
01     PRIOR-PERIOD-TABLE.
  05   PERIOD-AMT   PIC 9(6)
                    OCCURS ZERO TO 12 TIMES
                    DEPENDING ON PRIOR-PERIODS.
```

OPEN   (New, Obsolete)

| OPEN EXTEND |

As the following example illustrates, **RELATIVE** and **INDEXED** files (along with **SEQUENTIAL** files) may be **OPEN**ed in the **EXTEND** mode. COBOL 74 allows only **SEQUENTIAL** files to be **OPEN**ed in the **EXTEND** mode.

```
OPEN   EXTEND   RELATIVE-FILE
OPEN   EXTEND   INDEXED-FILE
```

In the following example, the **OPTIONAL** phrase in a **SELECT** clause can be applied to **SEQUENTIAL**, **RELATIVE** and **INDEXED** files that are **OPEN**ed in the **INPUT**, **I-O** or **EXTEND** modes. In COBOL 74, the **OPTIONAL** phrase applies only to **SEQUENTIAL** files **OPEN**ed in the **OUTPUT** mode.

```
SELECT   OPTIONAL   SOMETIMES-FILE-SEQUENTIAL
                    ASSIGN TO DISK-1
                    ORGANIZATION IS SEQUENTIAL.
SELECT              SOMETIMES-FILE-RELATIVE
                    ASSIGN TO "A"
                    ORGANIZATION IS RELATIVE.
SELECT   OPTIONAL   SOMETIMES-FILE-INDEXED
                    ASSIGN TO "XX", "YY"
                    ORGANIZATION IS INDEXED.


OPEN   INPUT    SOMETIMES-FILE-SEQUENTIAL
OPEN   EXTEND   SOMETIMES-FILE-RELATIVE
OPEN   I-O      SOMETIMES-FILE-INDEXED
```

Note in the above example the use of nonnumeric literals

("AA", "XX", "YY") in the **ASSIGN** clause. COBOL 74 does not permit this.

In both COBOL 74 and COBOL 85, an **OPEN** statement in the **OUTPUT** mode for a file (**OPTIONAL** or not **OPTIONAL**) that is not available to the program will cause that file to be created. In addition, in COBOL 85, an **OPEN** statement in either the **I-O** mode or the **EXTEND** mode for an **OPTIONAL** file that is not currently available to the program will cause that file to be created.

The following table illustrates the possible combinations for **OPEN**ing a file that is:

- **OPTIONAL** or not **OPTIONAL,**
- available or not available to the program,
- in either **INPUT**, **I-O**, **OUTPUT** or **EXTEND** modes.

OPEN MODE	FILE IS AVAILABLE	FILE IS UNAVAILABLE
INPUT	Normal open	Open is unsuccessful
INPUT (optional file)	Normal open	Normal open: The first read causes the AT END condition
I-O	Normal open	Open is unsuccessful
I-O (optional file)	Normal open	Open causes the file to be created
OUTPUT	Normal open: The file contains no records	Open causes the file to be created
EXTEND	Normal open	Open is unsuccessful
EXTEND (optional file)	Normal open	Open causes the file to be created

OPEN REVERSED

The **REVERSED** phrase of the **OPEN** statement, which permits the processing of a **SEQUENTIAL** file in **REVERSED** order (from last record to first record), is an obsolete language element. (See *COBOL 85 Conversion*, page 186.)

```
OPEN INPUT SEQUENTIAL-FILE REVERSED
```

PERFORM   (New, Change)

The **PERFORM** statement has been enhanced to allow an optional "in-line" version. That is, the programmer need not create a spearate paragraph (often out of the control sequence) when writing a sub-function to be **PERFORM**ed.

In the following example, note the absence of a procedure name after **PERFORM**.

```
PERFORM 9 TIMES
    ADD AMOUNT (X) TO AMOUNT (X + 1)
    ADD 1 TO X
END-PERFORM


PERFORM UNTIL AMOUNT (X) > 100
    ADD 1 TO X.
    ADD AMOUNT (X) TO AMOUNT (X + 1).
END-PERFORM
```

All imperative statements between the **PERFORM** statement and the **END-PERFORM** scope terminator will be executed in accordance with the specific phrases of the **PERFORM** statement. All regular controlling phrases of the **PERFORM** statement (**TIMES, UNTIL, VARYING, AFTER, WITH TEST AFTER/BEFORE**) are usable with this in-line version of the **PERFORM** statement.

The **PERFORM** statement in COBOL 85 allows the programmer to test a controlling condition either **BEFORE** or **AFTER** each execution of the desired procedure. Software engineers refer to these two different **PERFORM** mechanisms as the "do-while" construct (**PERFORM WITH TEST BEFORE**) and the "do-until" construct (**PERFORM WITH TEST AFTER**). COBOL 74 allows only the "do-while" version; that is, the controlling condition of the **PERFORM** statement is implicitly tested before each cycle is executed.

In the following examples, which are functionally equivalent,

```
PERFORM SOME-ROUTINE WITH TEST AFTER
        VARYING COUNTER
        FROM 1   BY 1
        UNTIL COUNTER = COUNTER-MAXIMUM


PERFORM SOME-ROUTINE WITH TEST BEFORE
        VARYING COUNTER
        FROM 1   BY 1
        UNTIL COUNTER = COUNTER-MAXIMUM-PLUS-1
```

the programmer can explicitly state that the required procedure should be **PERFORM**ed **WITH TEST AFTER** or **WITH TEST BEFORE**. If neither **AFTER** nor **BEFORE** is specified, the procedure will be implicitly **PERFORM**ed **WITH TEST BEFORE** (exactly as in COBOL 74). If a procedure is **PERFORM**ed **WITH TEST AFTER**, the programmer is assured of at least one execution of the (named) procedure.

In COBOL 85, the **PERFORM** statement can now execute up to seven levels of nested **PERFORM** loops (a **PERFORM** within a **PERFORM** within a **PERFORM**, etc.). This is accomplished by up to six **AFTER** phrases of the **PERFORM . . . VARYING** statement, as the following example illustrates. COBOL 74 allows only three levels of nested **PERFORM** loops, that is, only two occurrences of nested **AFTER** phrases.

```
PERFORM   INIT-TABLE VARYING SUB-1 FROM 1 BY 1 UNTIL SUB-1 = 10
                     AFTER   SUB-2 FROM 1 BY 1 UNTIL SUB-2 = 10
                     AFTER   SUB-3 FROM 1 BY 1 UNTIL SUB-3 = 10
                     AFTER   SUB-4 FROM 1 BY 1 UNTIL SUB-4 = 10
                     AFTER   SUB-5 FROM 1 BY 1 UNTIL SUB-5 = 10
                     AFTER   SUB-6 FROM 1 BY 1 UNTIL SUB-6 = 10
                     AFTER   SUB-7 FROM 1 BY 1 UNTIL SUB-7 = 10
END-PERFORM
```

There are some other subtle but significant changes to the behavior of the **PERFORM** statement in COBOL 85. These changes may affect the behavior of some COBOL 74/68 programs when used with a COBOL 85 compiler. Specifically, rules have been added specifying precisely when variables are initialized and augmented in a nested **PERFORM** statement; and a new sequence is specified when evaluating subscripts in a **PERFORM** statement.

The order of initialization of multiple **VARYING** identifiers in the **PERFORM** statement is specified in COBOL 85. The outer identifier is initialized first. This order is unspecified in COBOL 74. In a **PERFORM** statement in COBOL 74, when the setting of one **VARYING** item determines the value of the other, the order in which the compiler chooses to augment the two items becomes critical, and an incompatibility may result if not done in the same order each time. Here is an example.

```
MOVE      2   TO   X
PERFORM
          VARYING    X
              FROM   1
              BY     1
              UNTIL  X  =  3
          AFTER      Y
              FROM   X
              BY     1
              UNTIL  Y  =  3
```

In the **PERFORM** statement, if **Y** is set before **X**, **Y**'s initial value will be **2**; if **X** is set before **Y**, **Y**'s initial value will be **1**.

This change clarifies an ambiguity in COBOL 74. It will increase COBOL program portability. The use of such "clever" coding as in the example above is considered to be limited to "esoteric" programs.

The rules relating to how identifiers are augmented in a nested **PERFORM** statement have also changed.

Given the following **PERFORM** statement,

```
PERFORM            A100-PROCESSING-ROUTINE
      VARYING      COUNTER-1
         FROM      1
         BY        1
         UNTIL     COUNTER-1 = 5
      AFTER        COUNTER-2
         FROM      COUNTER-1
         BY        2
         UNTIL     COUNTER-2 = 6
```

in COBOL 85, **COUNTER-1** is augmented before **COUNTER-2** is set. In COBOL 74, **COUNTER-1** is set before **COUNTER-2** is augmented.

These changed features received much criticism for creating needless incompatibilities between COBOL 74 and COBOL 85. The reason for the change was to provide programmers with a simple mechanism for processing half of a multidimensional table along a bisecting diagonal. The COBOL 74 rules do not produce accurate results; COBOL 85 rules do.

The order of evaluating subscripts in the **PERFORM VARYING** statement is specified in COBOL 85. This order is not defined in COBOL 74.

In COBOL 85, any subscripted identifiers are evaluated for each iteration of the **PERFORM**ed subroutine. They are evaluated at the time the identifier is used either in a setting or augmenting or condition-testing operation.

This change in COBOL 85 may cause incompatibilities *only* if a COBOL 74/68 program:

a. uses subscripted identifiers in a **PERFORM VARYING** statement;
b. changes the value(s) of the subscript(s) while the **PERFORM** statement is active; and
c. runs on an implementation which chose to evaluate subscripts in some other way than defined in COBOL 85.

For further discussion on the impact that these changes to the

PERFORM statement will have on COBOL 74/68 programs, see
COBOL 85 Conversion, page 187.

PICTURE P   (Change)

The **RELATIVE KEY** data item specified for a **RELATIVE** file cannot contain a **P** in the **PICTURE** clause.

In the following COBOL 74 example, which violates the
new rule stated above,

```
ENVIRONMENT DIVISION.
SELECT  RELATIVE-FILE   ASSIGN TO DISK
                        ORGANIZATION IS RELATIVE
                        RELATIVE KEY IS RELATIVE-FILE-KEY.


DATA DIVISION.
WORKING-STORAGE SECTION
01  RELATIVE-FILE-KEY  PIC 9P.
```

the values that **RELATIVE-FILE-KEY** can have are **00**, **10**, **20**,
30, **40**, **50**, **60**, **70**, **80**, **90**. Therefore, it is possible that not all
records in this file are accessible by the program (i.e., the
record with a **RELATIVE KEY** value of **25**, etc.). It is likely that
such a **PICTURE** description for a **RELATIVE-KEY** in a COBOL
74 program is in error. (See *Impact and Conversion*, page   .)

When the **PICTURE** clause of a numeric or numeric-edited
data item contains the scaling symbol **P**, the digit positions
represented by **P** will be considered to contain zero when that
item is **MOVE**d. In COBOL 74/68, those digit positions may
have been ignored in some circumstances (when data conversion is not necessary).

As the following example illustrates,

```
01   NON-NUMERIC-ITEM        PIC    XXX.
01   SCALED-NUMERIC-ITEM     PIC    99P
                             VALUE  320.


     . . . MOVE SCALED-NUMERIC-ITEM TO NON-NUMERIC-ITEM.
```

in COBOL 85, the receiving data item, **NON-NUMERIC-ITEM**
will contain a value of **320**. In COBOL 74, depending on the
COBOL compiler being used, this value may have been **32**.
(See *COBOL 85 Conversion*, page 191.)

Punctuation   (New)

As the following example illustrates, the separators *comma,
semicolon* and *space* are interchangeable in a COBOL source
program.

```
ADD   FIRST-QTR,
      SECOND-QTR;
      THIRD-QTR
TO    FOURTH-QTR
GIVING   YEAR-TOTAL;
         PRINT-TOTAL
```

NOTE: The optional word **TO** is allowed in the format of
the **ADD** statement with the **GIVING** phrase.

PURGE   (New)

The **PURGE** statement in the following example

```
PURGE MESSAGE-CONTROL-AREA
```

causes the Message Control System to eliminate any partial
messages that had been created by previous **SEND** statements.

Qualification   (New)

Up to 50 levels of qualification are permitted to assure uniqueness of reference for data names. COBOL 74/68 provide only
five levels of qualification.

READ and RETURN   (New, Change)

The **NEXT RECORD** phrase of the **READ** statement is permitted for **SEQUENTIAL** (as well as for **RELATIVE** and **INDEXED**) files.

```
READ SEQUENTIAL-FILE NEXT RECORD
```

No new "functionality" is gained by specifying the **NEXT RECORD** phrase in the **READ** statement of a **SEQUENTIAL** file; the **NEXT RECORD** is always retrieved by a **READ** statement for a **SEQUENTIAL** file. COBOL 74 does not permit the **NEXT RECORD** phrase for **SEQUENTIAL** files.

The **INTO** phrase of both the **READ** and **RETURN** statements is now allowed for files with variable-length records. The subsequent **MOVE** to the **INTO** identifier is an implied group **MOVE**, as in the following example.

```
READ       VARIABLE-LENGTH-REC          INTO PROCESS-AREA

RETURN     SORT-VARIABLE-LENGTH-RECORD  INTO SORT-PROCESS-AREA
```

In COBOL 85, the **INTO** phrase of a **READ** and **RETURN** statement can be used if and only if:

1) all data records of the file being **READ** (or **RETURN**ed), as well as the identifier specified in the **INTO** phrase, are either group items or alphanumeric data items (i.e., **PIC X(100)**); or

2) only one data record description is specified for the file being **READ** (or **RETURN**ed).

In the following example,

```
FD    LITTLE-FILE . . .

01    RECORD-A    PIC S9(18).
01    RECORD-B    PIC 9(9)V9(9).
01    RECORD-C    PIC X(18).

WORKING-STORAGE SECTION.

01    PROCESS-AREA    PIC S9(10)V9(9).


     . . . READ LITTLE-FILE INTO PROCESS-AREA . . .
```

the **READ** statement causes an implicit **MOVE** of the data records associated with **LITTLE-FILE** to the **INTO** identifier, **RECEIVING-RECORD**. However, since there are three different data records associated with **LITTLE-FILE** (**RECORD-A**, **RECORD-B**, **RECORD-C**), each with a different data description - **PIC S9(18)**, **PIC S9(9)V9(9)**, **PIC X(18)**, respectively- the compiler cannot determine which data description should be used to implicitly **MOVE** the record to the **RECEIVING-RECORD**. (See *COBOL 85 Conversion*, page 193.)

REDEFINES   (New)

A data item that **REDEFINES** another data item may be smaller than the original data item.

In the following example,

```
01 FIRST-DATA-ITEM                          PICTURE X(30).
01 SECOND-DATA-ITEM REDEFINES FIRST-DATA-ITEM PICTURE X(10).
```

SECOND-DATA-ITEM is smaller than **FIRST-DATA-ITEM**. COBOL 74/68 do not permit this.

Reference Modification   (New)

Reference modification allows a programmer to reference in the **PROCEDURE DIVISION** a portion (substring) of a data item that was not explicitly defined in the **DATA DIVISION**. The reference modifier is a pair of numeric values appended to a data-name. It looks like a subscript, but is not. In the example below, note the colon (:) rather than a comma (,) or space separating the two arguments. The first argument specifies the starting location within the field being referenced; the second argument specifies the length of the new data item. The general format of a reference modified data item is:

data-name-1   (leftmost-character-position: [length])

In the following example,

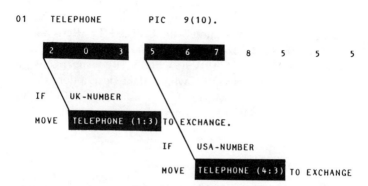

```
01    TELEPHONE          PIC    9(10).
```

the ten-digit **TELEPHONE** item is reference-modified twice. In the first instance, **TELEPHONE (1:3)** refers to positions 1, 2 and 3 of **TELEPHONE** (starting in position **1**: for a length of **3**). In the second instance, **TELEPHONE (4:3)** refers to positions 4, 5 and 6 of **TELEPHONE** (starting in position **4**: for a length of **3**).

If the second argument of a reference modifier is omitted, the length is assumed to be "until the end." Thus **TELEPHONE (7:)** refers to positions 7, 8, 9 and 10 of **TELEPHONE** (starting in position **7**: until the end).

NOTE: the first argument (starting location) cannot be omitted.

Reference modification can be used only with data items whose **USAGE IS DISPLAY** (either implicitly or explicitly). The arguments used as reference modifiers must be numeric (with an integer value), but they need not be literals.

In the following example, the second argument (number of characters) is a numeric identifier, **ALPHA-CODE** (rather than a numeric literal).

```
          MOVE    LAST-NAME (1:ALPHA-CODE)
          TO      ALPHA-KEY.
```

Furthermore, the reference-modifying arguments can contain any expression that has an integer value; that is, they can be numeric literals, numeric identifiers or arithmetic expressions. Reference modification can be applied to subscripted data items, and the arguments themselves can be subscripted data items. Each of these cases is illustrated in the following complex (and horrendous) example. Note the colons (:).

```
MOVE    ADDRESS (NEXT-LINE : LINE-SIZE (LINE-SIZE INDEX))
   TO   ADDRESS-LINE (ADDRESS-INDEX) (2 * LINE-NUMBER : 40 - 2 * LINE-NUMBER).
```

I strongly suggest using caution with reference modification. Although perfectly valid, its overuse (or abuse, as in the above example) may lead to poorly documented programs.

REPLACE
(New)

The **REPLACE** statement is an aid to the programmer generally, and is specifically useful in dealing with possible conflicts over new reserved words in COBOL 85 and user-defined words in COBOL 74/68 programs. The **REPLACE** statement operates on source text and converts the source program before it is compiled.

In the following example,

```
REPLACE   ==END-READ==    BY  ==END-READ-PROCEDURE==
          ==CLASS==        BY  ==DATA-CLASS==
          ==ALPHABETIC==   BY  ==ALPHABETIC-UPPER==.
```

the source program is scanned for occurrences of the COBOL words preceding the reserved word **BY** (**END-READ**, **CLASS**, **ALPHABETIC**). Each such occurrence will be replaced by its corresponding entry following the reserved word **BY** (**END-READ-PROCEDURE**, **DATA-CLASS**, **ALPHABETIC-UPPER**, respectively).

All **REPLACE**ments take place before the program is compiled. Double equal signs (==) are used as delimiters.

Multiple **REPLACE** statements are permitted. They can appear anywhere in the source program. Each new **REPLACE** statement cancels the effect of the previous **REPLACE** statement.

In order to cancel a **REPLACE** statement without introducing a new **REPLACE** statement, simply write:

```
REPLACE OFF.
```

Each **REPLACE** statement, whether **REPLACE**ing one item or many items, must terminate with a period (.).

To delete text from a source program (i.e., **REPLACE** something with nothing), simply enter ==== following the word **BY**.

REPLACEment of source text occurs after all library **COPY**s have been executed; therefore, **REPLACE**d text (following **BY**) cannot contain **COPY** statements (nor can it contain another **REPLACE** statement). Copied library modules may, however, contain a **REPLACE** statement.

The **REPLACE** statement does not act as a character-string (substring) editor; therefore, parts of COBOL words cannot be **REPLACE**d, only whole words. The sequence of the items to be **REPLACE**d within a single **REPLACE** statement is irrelevant.

The **REPLACE** statement will be most useful to COBOL installations that create standard conversion library routines that can be **COPY**ed into individual programs. In such a situation, a programmer might code the following,

```
IDENTIFICATION DIVISION.
PROGRAM-ID   CONVERTED-COBOL-74-PROGRAM.
COPY COBOL-74-85-CONVERSION IN USER-LIBRARY.
```

and the resulting source program (after the library **COPY**) will look like this:

```
IDENTIFICATION DIVISION.
PROGRAM-ID.   CONVERTED-COBOL-74-85-PROGRAM.
REPLACE   ==WITH DEBUGGING MODE==  BY   ====
          ==END-READ==             BY   ==END-OF-READ==
          ==END-WRITE==            BY   ==END-OF-WRITE==
          ==TRUE==                 BY   ==TRUE-STATUS==
          ==FALSE==                BY   ==FALSE-STATUS==
          ==CONTINUE==             BY   ==CONTINUE-ON==
          ==OTHER==                BY   ==ALL-OTHER==
          ==ALPHABETIC==           BY   ==ALPHABETIC-UPPER==
          ==INITIALIZE==           BY   ==INITIALIZE-PROCESS==.

ENVIRONMENT DIVISION.
```

RERUN   (Obsolete)

In the **I-O-CONTROL** paragraph of the **ENVIRONMENT DIVI-SION**, the **RERUN** statement, which specifies checkpoint intervals for recovery, is an obsolete language element. (See *COBOL 85 Conversion*, page 196.)

```
I-O-CONTROL.
    . . . RERUN EVERY 100 RECORDS OF MASTER-FILE.
```

Reserved Words   (New, Change)

New Reserved Words

Forty-nine new reserved words have been added to COBOL 85.

ALPHABET	END-DIVIDE	EXTERNAL
ALPHABETIC-LOWER	END-EVALUATE	FALSE
ALPHABETIC-UPPER	END-IF	GLOBAL
ALPHANUMERIC	END-MULTIPLY	INITIALIZE
ALPHANUMERIC-EDITED	END-PERFORM	NUMERIC-EDITED
ANY	END-READ	ORDER
BINARY	END-RECEIVE	OTHER
CLASS	END-RETURN	PACKED-DECIMAL
COMMON	END-REWRITE	PADDING
CONTENT	END-SEARCH	PURGE
CONTINUE	END-START	REFERENCE
CONVERTING	END-STRING	REPLACE
DAY-OF-WEEK	END-SUBTRACT	STANDARD-2
END-ADD	END-UNSTRING	TEST
END-CALL	END-WRITE	THEN
END-COMPUTE	EVALUATE	TRUE
END-DELETE		

Conflicts may occur where COBOL 74/68 programs used these words as user-defined names.

To reduce this problem in future COBOL revisions, the following rules were created to provide a "safety zone" for user-defined data-names and procedure-names:

1) Future reserved words will not begin with the digits **0** through **9** or the letters **X**, **Y** or **Z** (except the words **ZERO**, **ZEROS**, **ZEROES**).

2) Reserved words will not consist of a single letter.

3) Reserved words will not start with one or two characters, followed by a dash, except:

the word **I-O-CONTROL**,

words that begin with **B-**, such as **B-AND**, **B-OR**, **B-EXOR**, and **B-LESS** (used for Boolean operators in the CODASYL COBOL *Journal of Development*), and

words that begin with **DB-**.

4) Reserved words will not have two hyphens (--) together. (See *COBOL 85 Conversion*, page 196.)

User-Defined Words

A user-defined word need not be unique in a program unless it is referenced. In COBOL 74, a user-defined word must always be unique.

In addition, user-defined words (referenced or not) can be the same as system-names (i.e., implementor-names), as in the **SPECIAL-NAMES** entry that follows.

```
SPECIAL-NAMES.

    SWITCH-21 IS SWITCH-21.
```

The first occurrence of **SWITCH-21** is an implementor-name; the second occurrence is a user-defined word.

RETURN   (New, Change)

For an explanation of new features of the **RETURN** (and **READ**) statement in COBOL 85, see page 120.

For a discussion of new restrictions on the **RETURN** (and **READ**) statement possibly affecting COBOL 74/68 programs, see *COBOL 85 Conversion*, page 199.

REWRITE   (New)

The record in a **REWRITE** statement may be of a different length
from the record retrieved by the previous **READ** (or **RETURN**)
statement. The size of the record in the **REWRITE** statement
must, however, be in the range of the minimum and maximum
values specified in the **FD** for that file.

Scope Terminators   (New)

Scope terminators are used mainly to delimit the scope of
conditional statements. Basically, they serve a purpose similar
to that of the period (.). They can also be used to code nested
conditional statements (a conditional statement within a conditional statement). As we shall see shortly, periods cannot be
used within nested conditional statements.

In their simplest use, scope terminators can be used in
place of a period in any conditional statement. (They should
not be used together, however, unless the period ends the
sentence.)

```
IF      AGE-OF-DEBT >= 120  PERFORM  CALL-COLLECTION-DEPARTMENT
END-IF


READ    INPUT-FILE
AT END  PERFORM WRAP-UP-PROCEDURE
        EXIT PROGRAM
END-READ


ADD     THIS-WEEKS-SALARY
 TO     YTD-SALARY
 GIVING NEW-YTD-SALARY
 ON SIZE ERROR
        DISPLAY "ARITHMETIC ERROR"
        PERFORM RESTORE-PROCEDURE
END-ADD
```

Scope terminators are also used to delimit the scope of the
last **WHEN** phrase in **SEARCH** and **EVALUATE** statements. (See
EVALUATE.)

```
SEARCH    ALL CODE-TABLE
    WHEN  CODE-TABLE-ENTRY = "S" PERFORM SHIPPING-PROCEDURE
    WHEN  CODE-TABLE-ENTRY = "P" PERFORM PURCHASE-PROCEDURE
    WHEN  CODE-TABLE-ENTRY = "R" PERFORM RETURN-PROCEDURE
END-SEARCH
```

In the example above, each subsequent **WHEN** phrase delimits the scope of the previous **WHEN** phrase: the **END-SEARCH** delimits the final **WHEN** phrase.

The scope terminator **END-PERFORM** is used to delimit the scope of any imperative statements within the new "in-line" version of the **PERFORM** statement. (See **PERFORM**.)

```
PERFORM    UNTIL X >= 100
        ADD  1 TO X
        MOVE TABLE-ITEM (X) TO TABLE-ITEM (X + 1)
END-PERFORM
```

There are a total of 19 scope terminators (each is a new reserved word in COBOL 85).

ADD	NUMBER-1 TO NUMBER-2	(NOT) ON SIZE ERROR	PERFORM ERROR-PROCEDURE	END-ADD
SUBTRACT		(NOT) ON SIZE ERROR		END-SUBTRACT
MULTIPLY		(NOT) ON SIZE ERROR		END-MULTIPLY
DIVIDE		(NOT) ON SIZE ERROR		END-DIVIDE
COMPUTE		(NOT) ON SIZE ERROR		END-COMPUTE
WRITE	DATA-RECORD	(NOT) INVALID KEY	PERFORM ERROR-PROCEDURE	END-WRITE
REWRITE		(NOT) INVALID KEY		END-REWRITE
START		(NOT) INVALID KEY		END-START
DELETE		(NOT) INVALID KEY		END-DELETE
READ		(NOT) INVALID KEY		END-READ
STRING	A,B DELIMITED SIZE INTO C	(NOT) ON OVERFLOW	PERFORM ERROR-ROUTINE	END-STRING
UNSTRING		(NOT) ON OVERFLOW		END-UNSTRING
CALL		(NOT) ON OVERFLOW		END-CALL
READ	AN-INPUT-FILE	(NOT) AT END	PERFORM END-OF-FILE-PROC	END-READ
RETURN		(NOT) AT END		END-RETURN
IF	CONDITION-IS-TRUE		PERFORM TRUE-PROCEDURE	END-IF
EVALUATE	CONDITION	WHEN TRUE	PERFORM TRUE-PROCEDURE	END-EVALUATE
SEARCH	TABLE	WHEN MATCH	PERFORM MATCH-PROCEDURE	END-SEARCH
RECEIVE	MESSAGE-ITEM	(WITH/NO) DATA	PERFORM ERROR-PROCEDURE	END-RECEIVE
CALL	SUBROUTINE	(NOT) ON EXCEPTION	PERFORM ERROR-PROCEDURE	END-CALL
PERFORM	10 TIMES	ADD 1 TO IN-LINE-PROCEDURE-COUNTER		END-PERFORM

One of the best uses of scope terminators is in nested conditional statements. In COBOL 85, the scope of an inner conditional statement can be ended without accidentally affecting the scope of the outer conditional statement.

Consider the following *incomplete* example.

```
IF    MONDAY    READ            MONDAY-TRANS
                AT END          DISPLAY "MONDAY ENDED"
                                EXIT PROGRAM
                WRITE           MASTER-REC
                  INVALID KEY   DISPLAY FILE-STAT
                                STOP RUN
                PERFORM         MONDAY-PROCESS

IF    TUESDAY . . .
```

In earlier versions of COBOL, we are faced with the dilemma of where to place the periods to make this code execute properly. If we were to place a period after either the **EXIT PROGRAM** statement or the **STOP RUN** statement, we would be properly ending the scope of the **READ** or **WRITE** statements, respectively, but we would have inadvertently ended the scope of the **IF MONDAY** statement as well.

To end the scope of an inner conditional statement without affecting the outer conditional statement, we use scope terminators as follows:

```
IF    MONDAY    READ            MONDAY-TRANS
                AT END          DISPLAY "MONDAY-ENDED"
                                EXIT PROGRAM
                END-READ
                WRITE           MASTER-REC
                  INVALID KEY   DISPLAY FILE-STAT
                                STOP RUN
                END-WRITE
                PERFORM         MONDAY-PROCESS
      END-IF

IF    TUESDAY . . .
```

When an **IF** statement is nested inside another **IF** statement (or any other conditional statement nested inside a similar

conditional statement), each scope terminator will be paired
with the most recent occurrence of its respective verb, as
shown in the example that follows.

```
IF        FIRST-HALF-OF-YEAR
   THEN   PERFORM S1
          IF        FIRST-QTR
             THEN   PERFORM Q1
                    IF        JANUARY
                       THEN   PERFORM M1
                    END-IF
             ELSE   IF        APRIL
                       THEN   PERFORM M4
                       ELSE   CONTINUE
                    END-IF
          END-IF
   ELSE   IF        THIRD-QTR
             THEN   PERFORM Q3
                    IF        NOT JULY
                       THEN   CONTINUE
                       ELSE   PERFORM M7
                    END-IF
             ELSE   IF        OCTOBER
                       THEN   PERFORM M10
                    END-IF
          END-IF
END-IF
```

Scope terminators provide a means of writing well-structured (nested) conditional statements without causing the programmer to create "artificial" paragraphs and without causing
the program flow to jump around a lot.

```
IF        FILE-NOT-FINISHED
   THEN   READ   INPUT-FILE
             AT END   GO TO FINAL-RTN
          END-READ
          IF   COUNT-DOWN = ZERO
             THEN PERFORM FINISH-UP
          END-IF
          DISPLAY "TOTAL", WS-AMT
   ELSE   PERFORM EMPTY-RECORD-RTN
          GO TO REST-OF-PROGRAM
END-IF
```

Segmentation
(Obsolete)

The concept of independent segments is an obsolete language element. All segments are either "fixed" or "fixed-overlayable," and all segments behave as if they are resident in the computer at all times. Since independent segments are obsolete, the **SEGMENT-LIMIT** clause of the **OBJECT-COMPUTER** paragraph is obsolete. (See *COBOL 85 Conversion*, page 200.)

```
OBJECT-COMPUTER.
          SEGMENT-LIMIT IS 75.
```

SELECT
(New)

In the **SELECT** clause, some new variations are permitted in COBOL 85.

In the following example,

```
FILE-CONTROL.
          SELECT   SEQUENTIAL-FILE-A
                   ASSIGN TO DISK
                   ORGANIZATION IS SEQUENTIAL
          SELECT   SEQUENTIAL-FILE-B
                   ASSIGN TO TAPE SEQUENTIAL.
```

the words **ORGANIZATION IS** are optional, as illustrated in the second **SELECT** statement above. (These words are required in COBOL 74. They do not exist in COBOL 68.)

The **ASSIGN** clause may specify a nonnumeric literal (e.g., **"DISK A"**).

As the example on the following page illustrates,

```
SELECT OPTIONAL  RELATIVE-FILE
                 ASSIGN TO "DISK-A"
                 ORGANIZATION IS RELATIVE.

SELECT OPTIONAL  INDEXED-FILE-A
                 ASSIGN TO DISK
                 ORGANIZATION IS INDEXED
                 RECORD DELIMITER IS STANDARD-1.

SELECT           INDEXED-FILE-B
                 ASSIGN TO DISK
                 INDEXED
                 RECORD DELIMITER IS DATA-STREAMING.
```

in COBOL 85, the **OPTIONAL** phrase may be specified for **RELATIVE** and **INDEXED** files as well as for **SEQUENTIAL** files. In COBOL 74, the **OPTIONAL** phrase can be specified only for **SEQUENTIAL** files.

The **RECORD DELIMITER** clause specifies the method for determining the length of variable-length records. **STANDARD-1** refers to the American National Standard (X3-27. 1978) for Magnetic Tape Labels. **DATA-STREAMING** is an implementor-defined mechanism for determining the record length.

In the following example,

```
SELECT        SEQUENTIAL-FILE-C
              ASSIGN TO TAPE
              PADDING CHARACTER IS "*".
SELECT        SEQUENTIAL-FILE-D
              ASSIGN TO DISK
              PADDING CHARACTER IS PAD-CHAR.
```

the new **PADDING CHARACTER** clause specifies the character to be used to fill up the unused portion at the end of each block in a **SEQUENTIAL** file.

The **PADDING CHARACTER** clause may specify either a literal, *"*"*, or an identifier, **PAD-CHAR**, that contains the actual character.

SEND   (New)

In the following example,

```
. . . SEND MESSAGE-CONTROL-AREA
        FROM  SENDING-FIELD
        WITH  ESI
        REPLACING LINE
```

the **REPLACING LINE** phrase causes the characters transmitted by the **SEND** statement to replace (rather than superimpose) characters that may have previously been transmitted to the same line. Replacement is from left to right.

SET   (New)

Some new variations of **SET**ting control switches are allowed in COBOL 85. Given the following **WORKING-STORAGE** entry,

```
WORKING-STORAGE SECTION.

01   MONTH   PIC 99.
     88  JANUARY     VALUE  1.
     88  JUNE        VALUE  6.
     88  REST-OF-YR  VALUES 2 THRU 5,
                            7 THRU 12.
```

a programmer may code:

```
SET JUNE TO TRUE
```

Note the conditional constants **TRUE** and **FALSE**, two new reserved words.

The above statement has the same effect as coding:

```
MOVE 6 TO MONTH
```

and indeed, the value **6** will be **MOVE**d to **MONTH** in both examples.

Furthermore, as the following **SPECIAL-NAMES** entry illustrates,

```
SPECIAL-NAMES.
     SWITCH-22 IS SWITCH-22.
```

implementor switch-names and user-defined mnemonic switch-names may be the same. In COBOL 85, the programmer may code the following:

```
SET SWITCH-22 ON
```

NOTE: A mnemonic-name (**SWITCH-22**) may be defined for an implementor switch without specifying an **ON STATUS** or **OFF STATUS** condition-name. Also, the reserved word **IS**, as in:

```
SWITCH-23 OFF STATUS IS SW23-OFF
```

is required in COBOL 74, but is not (though still optional) in COBOL 85, as in:

```
SWITCH-23 ON STATUS SW23-ON
```

In addition, identifiers, index data items and indexes may be mixed in a single **SET** statement, as in the following example.

```
SET NUMERIC-DATA-ITEM-A, INDEX-DATA-ITEM-A, INDEX-A TO INDEX-B.
```

In the above example, **NUMERIC-DATA-ITEM-A** is an integer data item whose **USAGE IS DISPLAY** or **COMPUTATIONAL; INDEX-DATA-ITEM-A** is defined as **USAGE IS INDEXED;** and **INDEX-A** is an **INDEX** associated with an **OCCURS** clause of a table, such as:

```
TABLE-ELEMENT OCCURS 100 TIMES PIC 99 INDEXED BY INDEX-A.
```

The following chart summarizes the **SET** statements permissible when transferring values between integer literals (10), integer data items (**PIC 99**), **INDEX**es (associated with **OC-CURS**) and **INDEX** data items (**USAGE IS INDEX**), as in the statement:

```
SET RECEIVER-B TO SENDER-A.
```

		RECEIVING ITEM		
		INTEGER DATA ITEM	INDEX	INDEX DATA ITEM
SENDING ITEM	**INTEGER LITERAL**	Invalid	Valid	Invalid
	INTEGER DATA ITEM	Invalid	Valid	Invalid
	INDEX	Valid	Valid	Valid
	INDEX DATA ITEM	Invalid	Valid	Valid

Also, in referencing an element of a multidimensional table, an **INDEX** (i.e., **DIM-INDEX**) and a data-name subscript (i.e., **ROOM-SUBSCRIPT**) may both be written in a single set of subscripts of the table element (i.e., **DIMENSION**), as in the following **MOVE** statement.

```
DATA DIVISION.
01    ROOM-SUBSCRIPT    PIC 99.
01    ROOM-SIZES.
   03    ROOM            OCCURS 12 TIMES.
      05    DIMENSION     OCCURS 3 TIMES
                         PIC 99V99
                         INDEXED BY DIM-INDEX.


PROCEDURE DIVISION.
   . . . MOVE DIMENSION (ROOM-SUBSCRIPT, DIM-INDEX) TO HEIGHT
```

SIGN

(New)

A **SIGN** clause may be written at a group level. In the example on the following page,

```
01    GROUP-ITEM        SIGN IS LEADING SEPARATE.
   03    NUMBER-ONE         PIC S9(5).
   03    NUMBER-TWO         PIC S9(3).
   03    NUMBER-THREE       PIC S9(3).
```

the **SIGN** clause **LEADING SEPARATE** will apply to all subordinate numeric data items (**NUMBER-ONE, NUMBER-TWO, NUMBER-THREE**).

In a hierarchy of multiple **SIGN** clauses, as in the following example,

```
01      GROUP-ITEM                      SIGN IS LEADING SEPARATE.
   03    NUMBER-ONE    PIC S9(5).
   03    NUMBER-TWO    PIC S9(3).
   03    NUMBER-THREE  PIC S9(3)   SIGN IS TRAILING.
   03    SUB-GROUP-ITEM-1.
      05 NUMBER-FOUR   PIC S9(5).
      05 NUMBER-FIVE   PIC S9(3)   SIGN IS LEADING.
   03    SUB-GROUP-ITEM-2           SIGN IS TRAILING SEPARATE.
      05 NUMBER-SIX    PIC S9(5)   SIGN IS LEADING.
      05 NUMBER-SEVEN  PIC S9(6).
```

the **SIGN** clauses at the "higher" group level are distributed to the subordinate numeric data items, but are overridden by a **SIGN** clause on a "lower," or subordinate, data item.

Thus, in the example above, the applicable **SIGN**s for the numeric data items are specified in the following table.

DATA ITEM	SIGN
NUMBER-ONE	LEADING SEPARATE
NUMBER-TWO	LEADING SEPARATE
NUMBER-THREE	TRAILING
NUMBER-FOUR	LEADING SEPARATE
NUMBER-FIVE	LEADING
NUMBER-SIX	LEADING
NUMBER-SEVEN	TRAILING SEPARATE

One additional new feature: the **SIGN** clause is now allowed in a report group entry in the Report Writer facility. In COBOL 74, this is not permitted.

SORT and MERGE   (New)

When **SORT**ing records with possible *duplicate keys*, the
programmer can assure that the sequence of those duplicate
records on the **OUTPUT** file(s) will be identical to the sequence
of those records on the **INPUT** file using the **WITH DUPLI-
CATES IN ORDER** phrase of the **SORT** statement, as in the
following example.

```
SORT                        SORT-WORK-FILE
   ON ASCENDING KEY         WORK-ORDER-NUMBER
                            WITH DUPLICATES IN ORDER
   INPUT PROCEDURE IS       WORK-ORDER-VALIDATION-PROCESS
   GIVING                   DAILY-WORK-ORDERS-SEQ.
```

The **OUTPUT** file (**GIVING . . .**) of a **SORT** statement may
reside on the same reel as the **INPUT** file (**USING . . .**).

Multiple **OUTPUT** files may be specified in the **GIVING**
phrase of a **SORT** or a **MERGE** statement, as shown below.

```
SORT                        SORT-WORK-FILE
   ON ASCENDING KEY         WORK-ORDER-NUMBER
                            WITH DUPLICATES IN ORDER
   INPUT PROCEDURE IS       WORK-ORDER-VALIDATION-PROCESS
   GIVING                   DAILY-WORK-ORDERS-SEQ
                            DAILY-WORK-ORDERS-RELATIVE
                            DAILY-WORK-ORDERS-INDEXED.


MERGE                       MERGE-WORK-FILE
   ON ASCENDING KEY         WORK-ORDER-NUMBER
   USING                    MONDAY-WORK-ORDERS
                            TUESDAY-WORK-ORDERS
                            WEDNESDAY-WORK-ORDERS
                            THURSDAY-WORK-ORDERS
                            FRIDAY-WORK-ORDERS
   GIVING                   WEEKLY-WORK-ORDERS-SEQ
                            WEEKLY-WORK-ORDERS-RELATIVE
                            WEEKLY-WORK-ORDERS-INDEXED.
```

NOTE: COBOL 74 allows only one **GIVING** file.

As the above examples illustrate, the **OUTPUT** files of a

SORT or a **MERGE** statement need not be **SEQUENTIAL** files (as they must be in COBOL 74). Furthermore, the **INPUT** and **OUTPUT** files (**USING/GIVING**) may now contain variable-length records (again, not allowed in COBOL 74).

Additionally, both the **INPUT** and **OUTPUT PROCE-DURES**, if specified, may reference and be referenced by procedures in any (non-**SORT/MERGE**) procedural section of the program; that is, while executing code in an **INPUT PROCE-DURE** or **OUTPUT PROCEDURE**, subroutines (paragraphs) that are coded in other **SECTION**s of the program may be **PERFORM**ed.

Likewise, while executing code in any main (non-**SORT**) **SECTION** of a COBOL program, subroutines (paragraphs) that are coded in the **INPUT** or **OUTPUT PROCEDURE SECTION**s of a **SORT/MERGE** statement can be **PERFORM**ed. The programmer is responsible for making the program exit from the **SORT PROCEDURE**s properly in order to signal the **SORT** macro that a particular phase of **SORT**ing is completed.

STOP   (Change, Obsolete)

STOP "literal.

The **STOP "literal"** format of the **STOP** statement is an obsolete language element.

```
        . . . STOP "ERROR CODE 1234"
```

NOTE: This does not affect the **STOP RUN** format of the **STOP** statement. (See *COBOL 85 Conversion*, page 201.)

STOP RUN

There are some subtle changes in the behavior of COBOL

programs that contain a **STOP RUN** (and **CANCEL** and **EXIT PROGRAM**) statement(s).

In COBOL 85, a **STOP RUN** statement causes any files that are left in the **OPEN** mode to be implicitly **CLOSE**d. Furthermore, any messages that were partially received by the Message Control System (MCS) will be eliminated, and all MCS queues will be cleared.

COBOL 74 does not specify what happens to any left-**OPEN**ed files or partial messages in the queues. Many COBOL 74 compilers did, in fact, implicitly **CLOSE** any left-**OPEN**ed files and clear the queues. There could be some COBOL 74 compliers, however, that did not, and may have relied on this behavior. (See *COBOL 85 Conversion*, page 200.)

STRING   (New, Change)

The identifier in the **INTO** phrase of the **STRING** statement may be either a group or an elementary item. In COBOL 74, it must be an elementary item.

As with the **DIVIDE**, **INSPECT**, **PERFORM** and **UNSTRING** statements, the order of evaluating subscripts in the **STRING** statement is specified in COBOL 85. This order is not specified in COBOL 74, and COBOL 68 does not include **STRING**. (See *COBOL 85 Conversion*, page 202.)

Structured Conditional Phrases   (New)

Alternate-path phrases allow the programmer to specify actions to be taken for both "true" and "false" branches of any conditional statements.

In the following COBOL 74 (and COBOL 85) example, a simple conditional phrase (**ON SIZE ERROR**) is written for the **ADD** statement.

```
ADD                     A TO B
ON SIZE ERROR           PERFORM ARITH-OVERVIEW.
```

In COBOL 85, an alternative branch may also be coded, as in the following example.

```
ADD                     A  TO B
  ON SIZE ERROR         PERFORM ARITH-OVERFLOW
  NOT ON SIZE ERROR     PERFORM NORMAL-PROCESS
END-ADD
```

There is a problem with the way these phrases were introduced into the COBOL 85 language. This problem warrants special attention from the programmer. This is true because a seemingly minor "independent" change to a program could have unexpected results under certain conditions.

Given the following COBOL 85 example:

```
ADD A TO B
    ON SIZE ERROR
                ADD C TO D
                MOVE X TO Y
    NOT ON SIZE ERROR
                PERFORM ROUTINE-CC
END-ADD
```

the rules covering this statement are clear and unambiguous. The two **ADD** instructions, one outer (**ADD A TO B**), one inner (**ADD C TO D**), are vulnerable to "misbehavior" under certain circumstances. In the example above, the outer **ADD** statement has two conditional phrases attached to it (**ON SIZE ERROR . . .** and **NOT ON SIZE ERROR. . .**)

If a (maintenance) programmer were to simply remove the statement, **MOVE X TO Y**, as in:

```
ADD A TO B
    ON SIZE ERROR
                ADD C TO D
    NOT ON SIZE ERROR
                PERFORM ROUTINE-CC
END-ADD
```

the behavior of both **ADD** instructions would change. For now, the rules state, the **NOT ON SIZE ERROR . . .** phrase is no longer attached to the outer **ADD** statement (**ADD A TO B**) but rather it is part of the inner **ADD** statement (**ADD C TO D**). This, of course, changes the logic of the original "intended" code.

It is essential therefore that a maintenance programmer be particularly careful when making such a "minor" change, to restore the original logic as follows:

```
ADD A TO B
    ON SIZE ERROR
            ADD C TO D
            END-ADD
    NOT ON SIZE ERROR
            PERFORM ROUTINE-CC
END-ADD
```

Note the use of the explicit scope terminator **END-ADD**.

Structured Programming   (New, Change)

For a discussion of COBOL 85's relationship with structured progamming see the chapter in this book "Structured Trends and the COBOL Language."

For examples of the specific COBOL 85 features dealing with structured programming see the following sections in this book:

- **CALL** (See page 73.)
- **CANCEL** (See page 76.)
- Conditional Expressions (See page 79.)
- **ENTER** (See page 84.)
- **ENVIRONMENT DIVISION** (See page 106.)
- **EVALUATE** (See page 85.)
- **EXIT PROGRAM** (See page 89.)

(list continued on following page)

- **EXTERNAL** (See page 110.)
- **GLOBAL** (See page 103.)
- **GO TO** (See page 94.)
- Nested Programs (See page 101.)
- **PERFORM** (See page 114.)
- Scope Terminators (See page 127.)
- Segmentation (See page 131.)
- Structured Conditional Phrases (See page 139.)

Subscripting   (New)

Up to seven dimensions may be defined for tables. (COBOL 74 allows only three dimensions.)

```
01   A-SEVEN-LEVEL-TABLE.
   03   LEVEL-1 OCCURS 10 TIMES.
      05   LEVEL-2 OCCURS 10 TIMES.
         07   LEVEL-3 OCCURS 10 TIMES.
            09   LEVEL-4 OCCURS 10 TIMES.
               11   LEVEL-5 OCCURS 10 TIMES.
                  13   LEVEL-6 OCCURS TO TIMES.
                     15   LEVEL-7 OCCURS 10 TIMES.
                        17   TEXT-FIELD           PIC X(3).
                        17   NUMBER-FIELD         PIC 9999 COMP.
```

This allows the writing of up to seven levels of subscripts/ indexes, as in the following example.

```
INIT-TABLE.
      ADD   SUB-1,
            SUB-2,
            SUB-3,
            SUB-4,
            SUB-5,
            SUB-6,
            SUB-7
   TO     NUMBER-FIELD (SUB-1, SUB-2, SUB-3, SUB-4, SUB-5, SUB-6, SUB-7
```

Note that data items and indexes may now be mixed as subscripts.

In addition, in COBOL 85 a limited form of arithmetic

expression may be used as a subscript. Referred to as a *relative subscript*, a numeric identifier used as a subscript may be incremented or decremented by a numeric literal, as in

```
MOVE TABLE-ENTRY (SUB) TO TABLE-ENTRY (SUB + 1)
```

SYMBOLIC CHARACTER   (New)

The **SYMBOLIC CHARACTER** clause of the **SPECIAL-NAMES** paragraph allows the programmer to name a user-defined figurative constant for any character in a known character set. This is particularly useful for referencing nonprintable characters.

In the following example,

```
SPECIAL-NAMES.
     SYMBOLIC CHARACTER BELL IS 8 IN ASCII.
```

a user-defined name **BELL** represents the **8**th ordered position of the **ASCII** character set. Other character sets may be specified. If no character set is specified, the "native" character set of the specific COBOL implementation in use is assumed (default).

This user-defined figurative constant may be used anywhere that other nonnumeric figurative constants (**SPACES**, **QUOTES**, etc.) are allowed, as in the following example which will wake up a dozing console operator.

```
DISPLAY     BELL, BELL, BELL;
            "PLEASE RESPOND TO SYSTEM ERROR";
            BELL, BELL, BELL
    UPON TERMINAL
    WITH NO ADVANCING.
```

NOTE: the new optional phrase **WITH NO ADVANCING** of the **DISPLAY** statement. This assures that the vertical position of a **DISPLAY** device will be held after the execution of the **DISPLAY** statement.

UNSTRING   (Change)

As with the **DIVIDE**, **INSPECT**, **PERFORM** and **STRING** statements, the order of evaluating subscripts in the **UNSTRING** statement is specified in COBOL 85. This order is not specified in COBOL 74, and **UNSTRING** does not exist in COBOL 68. (See *COBOL 85 Conversion*, page 203.)

USAGE IS BINARY and   (New)
USAGE IS PACKED-DECIMAL

Two new **USAGE** types (**BINARY** and **PACKED-DECIMAL**) can be specified in COBOL 85.

```
01 PACKED-DATA-ITEM PICTURE 9(18) USAGE IS PACKED-DECIMAL.

01 BINARY-DATA-ITEM PICTURE 9(18) USAGE IS BINARY.
```

Of course, the other **USAGE** types (**DISPLAY**, **COMPUTATIONAL**, and **INDEXED**) are still valid.

Although specifying **USAGE IS BINARY** or **USAGE IS PACKED-DECIMAL** does not guarantee portability between two different COBOL compilers, it does provide better program documentation.

VALUE   (New)

A **VALUE** clause can be specified in the same entry of a data item that also contains an **OCCURS** clause. COBOL 74 does not permit this. This allows a programmer to specify initial values for the elements of a table without the need to redefine that table. In the following example,

```
01.
  05  YTD-AMT     OCCURS 12 TIMES
                  PIC S9(8)
                  VALUE ZERO.
```

each of the 12 occurrences of **YTD-AMT** is given an initial value of **ZERO**.

Variable-Length Records   (Change)

A subtle change has occurred in determining the size of a variable-length table. This change affects programs where the size of a table is given by an identifier that is subordinate to the same group item to which the table is subordinate.

In the following example,

```
01  PERIOD-TABLE.
    03  NUMBER-OF-PERIODS    PIC 99.
    03  PERIOD-AMOUNT        PIC S9(6)V99
                            OCCURS 12 TIMES DEPENDING ON
                            NUMBER-OF-PERIODS.
```

NUMBER-OF-PERIODS and **PERIOD-AMOUNT** are subordinate to the same group item **PERIOD-TABLE**. Since the size of **PERIOD-AMOUNT** depends on **NUMBER-OF-PERIODS**, it is important to determine when **NUMBER-OF-PERIODS** is evaluated, as in the following **MOVE** instruction.

```
MOVE FILE-TABLE-OF-VALUES TO PERIOD-TABLE
```

In COBOL 85, the maximum number of occurrences (12) of **PERIOD-AMOUNT** is assumed, and the actual value in **NUMBER-OF-PERIODS** is ignored. In COBOL 74, the actual value in **NUMBER-OF-PERIODS** at the start of the **MOVE** instruction is used for the size of the array, **PERIOD-AMOUNT**. (See *COBOL 85 Conversion*, page 205.)

ZERO   (New)

A variable-length table (one that **OCCURS** from *n1* to *n2* times) may have **ZERO** as a minimum number of occurrences, as in the following example. COBOL 74 requires at least one occurrence.

(Example appears on page 146)

```
01        PRIOR-PERIOD-TABLE.
  05      PERIOD-AMT    PIC 9(6)
                        OCCURS ZERO TO 12 TIMES
                        DEPENDING ON PRIOR-PERIODS.
```

The figurative constant **ZERO** may now be written in arithmetic expressions, as in the following example.

```
COMPUTE REVERSE-SIGN = ZERO - YTD-AMT.
```

NOTE: COBOL 74/68 do not allow **ZERO** in arithmetic expressions.

IV

COBOL 85

Conversion of COBOL 74/68 Programs

The COBOL 85 features described in this section are the known changes in the COBOL 85 language (from COBOL 74) that are capable of causing incompatibilities. If a perfectly valid program written in ANS COBOL 74 and using one of these features were to be recompiled (with no modifications) using an ANS COBOL 85 compiler, that same program may execute differently in some subtle and not so subtle ways. It should be noted that if the same "perfectly valid" ANS COBOL 74 program were to be recompiled (with no modifications) using another ANS COBOL 74 compiler, most of the same potential incompatibilities would still exist.

These potential incompatibilities are a necessary consequence in the evolution of the COBOL programming language. They are created when poorly defined features of COBOL 74 are given clear and precise definitions in COBOL 85. In the following example of a **DIVIDE** statement,

```
DIVIDE AAA INTO BBB GIVING CCC REMAINDER D(CCC)
```

the data item used as a subscript for storing the **REMAINDER, D(CCC)**, is also the receiving field for the results in the **GIVING** phrase of the **DIVIDE** statement. This value, **CCC**, is changed during the course of executing the **DIVIDE** statement. Therefore, it is important to know precisely when the value of **CCC** is determined by the compiler. In COBOL 74, the rules for the exact behavior of this special case of the **DIVIDE** statement are poorly defined, possibly causing different COBOL 74 compilers to interpret this statement differently. For instance, some may have captured (and used as the subscript value) whatever value was in **CCC** at the start of the **DIVIDE** statement and ignored any changes to **CCC** during the actual execution of the **DIVIDE** statement. Other compilers may have chosen instead to use the value in **CCC** after the **DIVIDE** statement had executed and the result had been placed in the **GIVING** field, **CCC**. Other compilers may have chosen still other methods of interpreting this **DIVIDE** statement. In each case, a different interpretation by the compiler causes a slightly different behavior in the object program.

In COBOL 85, the rules governing this situation have been clearly defined. The subscript in the **REMAINDER** phrase, **D(CCC)**, is determined after the **DIVIDE** statement has placed the results in the **GIVING** data item, **CCC**. (See **DIVIDE**).

The **DIVIDE** statement is one of 60 changed or obsolete features that were created in the new COBOL 85 language. These potential sources of incompatibility have caused much of the controversy surrounding the new COBOL 85 language. (See the *COBOL 85 Controversy* section.)

In this section, each of these changed and obsolete features is examined and explained.

Two main sources are quoted and referenced frequently in this section: the draft-proposed International COBOL 85 Programming language*; and the National Bureau of Standards COBOL 85 Cost-Benefit Study.**

ALL "literal" (Change)

> New rules have been created for the length of **ALL "literal"**.

When the figurative constant **ALL "literal"** is not associated with another data item, the length of the string is the length of the literal. In COBOL 74, the length may be one.

COBOL 74 rules for the size of the figurative constant **ALL "literal"** vary, depending on where the figurative constant

---

*The draft proposed revised International Standards Organization (ISO) Programming Language COBOL, published October 1984 with updates contained in ANSI document X314/W-392. The International draft COBOL 85 is identical to the American draft COBOL 85.

**Cost-Benefit Impact Study on the Adoption of the Draft Proposed Revised X3.23 American National Standard Programming Language COBOL, M. Fiorello and J. Cugini U.S. Dept. of Commerce, Natl. Bureau of Standards Publ. p. 152 (new) No. NBSIR 83-2639

is used in the program. For example, if **ALL "literal"** is used in the **ALPHABET** or **CURRENCY SIGN** clause of the **SPECIAL-NAMES** paragraph, only the first character of the literal is used regardless of the number of characters specified in the literal. In other instances, such as **IF ALL "ABC,"** the size of the literal is considered to be all the characters specified in the literal. This inconsistency in the rules for the size of **ALL "literal"** causes misleading documentation of the program and its behavior. The new rules in COBOL 85 eliminate this inconsistency. The use of this COBOL 74 facility is limited to esoteric programming practices. This change should not affect many programs.

A specific use of **ALL "literal"** is made obsolete.

The figurative constant **ALL "literal"** is an obsolete language element when:

    1) associated with a numeric or numeric-edited item; and

    2) the length of the literal is greater than one character.

In the following example, the figurative constant **ALL "123"** (where the size of the literal is greater than one character) is **MOVE**d to three different numeric (numeric-edited) data items. Each **MOVE** statement produces a different result as indicated.

```
                                              RESULT AFTER MOVE

01  THREE-POINT-TWO-ITEM                PIC 999.99
    . . . MOVE ALL "123" TO THREE-POINT-TWO-ITEM.
              123123                                   123.00

01  THREE-PLUS-TWO-ITEM                 PIC 999V99.
    . . . MOVE ALL "123" TO THREE-PLUS-TWO-ITEM.
              12312                                    31200

01  AMOUNT-FIELD                        PIC $999.99.
    . . . MOVE ALL "123" TO AMOUNT-FIELD.
              1231231                                 $231.00
```

The National Bureau of Standards considers these changed and obsolete features to be of *low complexity* requiring few programming-logic modifications. Most of the conversion logic can be handled by an automatic Language Conversion Program (LCP).

ALPHABET   (Change)

> The alphabet-name clause uses the key word **ALPHABET**.

In the user-defined **ALPHABET** clause in the COBOL 74 **SPECIAL-NAMES** section, the key word **ALPHABET** does not exist. Implementor-names are system-names, and mnemonic-names are user-defined words. In COBOL 85, system-names and user-defined words may be the same word. The following COBOL 85 entry is permitted:

```
SPECIAL-NAMES. word-1 IS word-1.
```

In COBOL 85, if the implementor-name **word-1** were permitted in both the implementor-name clause (i.e., **SWITCH-1**) and the alphabet-name clause, it would not be possible to determine which clause was intended in the entry above. Introducing the key word **ALPHABET** in the alphabet-name clause resolves this ambiguity. This problem does not exist in COBOL 74 because system-names and user-defined words may not be the same words; therefore the above construct is not permitted. The alphabet-name clause, although an essential feature of the language, is limited in use to applications that use character codes or collating sequences other than "native" (or one of a few other internationally recognized character sets).

Conversion is simple (inserting the word **ALPHABET**) and can be done automatically by a Language Conversion Program (LCP).

The National Bureau of Standards, in its analysis of the COBOL 85 language, considers this changed feature to be of *low complexity* requiring no programming-logic modifications. Most of the conversion logic can be handled by an automatic Language Conversion Program (LCP).

ALPHABETIC Class   (Change)

New rules have been defined for the **ALPHABETIC** class test.

A program containing a condition test for **ALPHABETIC** may behave differently if compiled in COBOL 85 than if compiled in COBOL 74/68. In COBOL 85, the **ALPHABETIC** class test is true for uppercase letters, lowercase letters and the space character. The **ALPHABETIC-UPPER** test is true for uppercase letters and the space character; the **ALPHABETIC-LOWER** test is true for lowercase letters and the space character.

In COBOL 74/68, the rules are ambiguous in this area, and there is no clear definition for **ALPHABETIC**. Some COBOL 74/68 compilers include both uppercase and lowercase letters in their definition of **ALPHABETIC**. Other COBOL 74/68 compilers include only uppercase letters in their definition of **ALPHABETIC** (i.e., lowercase letters are not considered **ALPHA-BETIC**). There are no **UPPER/LOWER** class tests in COBOL 74/68. In the ASCII world of today, this seems archaic. This change affects only COBOL 74/68 programs that:

    a) contain an **ALPHABETIC** class test statement such as

```
IF SCREEN-NAME IS NOT ALPHABETIC
    PERFORM INVALID-SCREEN-INPUT.
```

    b) were written for a COBOL 74/68 compiler that
           interpreted **ALPHABETIC** as uppercase letters only.
    c) must distinguish between uppercase and lowercase
           letters (and considers lowercase letters as
           nonalphabetic).

Conversion of COBOL 74/68 programs is relatively easy

with the new **REPLACE** statement in COBOL 85, as shown in the following example:

```
REPLACE ==ALPHABETIC== BY ==ALPHABETIC-UPPER==
```

All **REPLACE**ments that must be made should be written into one **REPLACE** statement and be part of a general conversion module stored in the user's library. This library module should then be **COPY**ed into every program that goes through this same conversion procedure.

The National Bureau of Standards, in its analysis of the COBOL 85 language, considers this changed feature to be of *low complexity* requiring no programming-logic modifications. Most of the conversion logic can be handled by an automatic Language Conversion Program (LCP).

ALTER (Obsolete)

The **ALTER** statement has been made obsolete.

The **ALTER** statement, which changes the procedure referenced in a **GO TO** statement, is an obsolete language element. The **ALTER** statement is a nemesis for maintenance programmers.

```
. . . ALTER CONTROL-POINTER
        TO PROCEED TO LAST-PROCESS.

CONTROL-POINTER. GO TO FIRST-PROCESS.
```

To remove **ALTER** statements from a source program, each **GO TO** statement that is **ALTER**ed must be replaced with a **GO TO . . . DEPENDING ON . . .** statement or an **EVALUATE** statement. Programmers must make up a table of possible

"**GO TO**" destinations and assign each an artificial number. This is why the **GO TO . . . DEPENDING ON . . .** statement is almost as awkward as **ALTER**. (As a teacher of good COBOL programming, it hurts this author to even discuss the above programming technique.) Use **EVALUATE** logic instead.

The National Bureau of Standards, in its analysis of the COBOL 85 language, considers this obsolete feature to be of *intermediate complexity* requiring minor programming-logic modifications. Much of the conversion logic can be handled by an automatic Language Conversion Program (LCP).

NOTE: Understanding the unpopularity of the **ALTER** statement is essential to understanding the essence of maintenance programming.

CANCEL

(Change)

> The **CANCEL** statement **CLOSE**s all **OPEN**ed files.

In COBOL 85, the **CANCEL** statement implicitly **CLOSE**s any files that remain in the **OPEN** mode in the program that is being **CANCEL**led. In COBOL 74, the status of files after a **CANCEL** statement is not defined. This change produces a predictable and consistent result.

The COBOL programs that are affected by this changed feature are those that depend on the files of **CALL**ed programs to remain **OPEN**ed after executing a **CANCEL** statement in the **CALL**ing program. No other programs are affected.

This changed feature may be less benign than it appears. There are indeed some programming methodologies that suggest "suspending" and "resuming" the execution of programs. One such popular methodology recommends the use of "co-routines." This concept requires that the executing status of each co-routine be identical at resumption time to that at suspension time. Co-routines can still be used according to the new rules in COBOL 85, but they must be resident segments of a main program (one that is never **CANCEL**led); this of course detracts from the flexibility of such co-routines.

If conversion is necessary, it can be detected automatically by a Language Conversion Program (LCP). Conversion entails first determining which files, if any, must remain **OPEN**ed while a program module is "suspended." Those files in an outer program (at a higher level) must then be **SELECT**ed and declared **GLOBAL** files.

The National Bureau of Standards considers this changed feature to be of *intermediate complexity* requiring minor programming-logic modifications. Much of the conversion logic can be handled by an automatic Language Conversion Program (LCP).

Character substitution   (Obsolete)

Two-for-one-character substitution has been made obsolete.

The COBOL 74 rule that permits the substitution of double characters for a single COBOL character has been made obsolete. This rule was intended for systems whose character sets have fewer than 51 characters. Two-for-one-character substitution may still be specified by an implementor, but will no longer be required in subsequent COBOL Standards. The rules for character substitution will continue to be supported in COBOL 85.

Conversion of many programs is not likely to be necessary. The specifications in COBOL 74 are a carryover from the time when some computers could not provide the complete COBOL character set. This limitation on the number of characters available in a computer no longer exists. There may still be, however, instances where a specific COBOL character is not available on a given computer. The implementor can therefore define a substitute character for the missing COBOL character so as not to lose the "functionality" of the missing character.

The National Bureau of Standards, in its analysis of the COBOL 85 language, considers this obsolete feature to be of *low complexity* requiring no programming-logic modifications. Most of the conversion logic can be handled by an automatic Language Conversion Program (LCP).

CLOSE   (Change)

> The **NO REWIND** phrase and the **REEL/UNIT** phrase cannot be specified together in the same **CLOSE** statement.

In COBOL 85, the **NO REWIND** phrase cannot be specified in a **CLOSE** statement containing the **REEL/UNIT** phrase. The rules for the **NO REWIND** and **REEL/UNIT** phrases together in the same **CLOSE** statement in COBOL 74 are in conflict, and cannot both be processed. The syntax rule in COBOL 85 prohibits that conflict, thereby closing a loophole.

The National Bureau of Standards, in its analysis of the COBOL 85 language, considers this changed feature to be of *intermediate complexity* requiring minor programming-logic modifications. Much of the conversion logic can be handled by an automatic Language Conversion Program (LCP).

It is not clear what sort of conversion may be required if compatibility with COBOL 74/68 programs is indeed necessary. No specific meaning can be deduced for the **NO REWIND** and **REEL/UNIT** phrases together in the same **CLOSE** statement. It is assumed that COBOL implementors who provide COBOL 74 compatibility will continue using its COBOL 74 interpretation of such a situation.

Communication status key   (Change)

New communication status key values have been added.

COBOL 74 leaves the results of some communications situations undefined. COBOL 85, however, defines new status key values for these situations so that the user can check for these error conditions in a standard way, and take corrective action if appropriate.

These new status key values affect only COBOL 74 programs that rely on some other implementor-defined action taking place when the newly defined exception conditions occur.

The National Bureau of Standards, in its analysis of the COBOL 85 language, considers this changed feature to be of *intermediate complexity* requiring minor programming-logic modifications. Much of the conversion logic can be handled automatically by a Language Conversion Program (LCP).

The individual status key values that have been added are listed below.

Status Key 15

Symbolic source, or one or more queues or destinations already disabled/enabled.

If, at the time a **DISABLE** or **ENABLE** is obeyed, the source or a queue or a destination referenced is already disabled or enabled respectively, COBOL 74 returns a **00** status value. COBOL 85 returns a status value of **15**.

Status Key 21

Symbolic source is unknown.

In COBOL 74, the user must compare the **SYMBOLIC**

SOURCE data item with spaces in order to determine whether the symbolic name of the source terminal is known to the message control system (MCS) on a **RECEIVE** statement. CO-BOL 74 does not specify what happens if the symbolic source in an input **CD** referenced in an **ENABLE** or **DISABLE** statement is unknown. New status key value **21** provides this information in COBOL 85 programs.

Status Key 65

Output-queue capacity is exceeded.

COBOL 74 does not specify what happens if the capacity of the output queue is exceeded on a **SEND**. This situation in COBOL 85 gives the new status key value of **65**.

Status Key 70

One or more destinations do not have message portions associated with them.

This status key value is returned only by the new verb **PURGE**. Since the **PURGE** statement is new in COBOL 85, this condition does not exist in COBOL 74.

Status Key 80

A combination of at least two status key conditions **10**, **15** and **20** has occurred.

If the (level 2) multiple-destination facility is used, and one of the destinations is disabled while a second destination is unknown, COBOL 74 does not specify whether status key value **10** or **20** should be returned by a **SEND** statement. In COBOL 85, new status key value **80** is now defined for this situation as well as for the case of an **ENABLE** or **DISABLE** where new status key condition **15** and status key condition **20** both apply.

Status Key 9x

Implementor-defined status.

This new range of status key values in COBOL 85 allows the implementor to define a variety of different error conditions. This provides the user with a facility to test for implementor-defined error conditions, similar to the COBOL 74 facility for testing I-O status values for implementor-defined I-O errors.

Conditional Expressions   (Change)

New rules have been defined for evaluating complex conditional expressions.

In COBOL 85, each condition within the same level of a nested conditional statement is evaluated in order from left to right. Evaluation of that level ends as soon as a truth value for the entire expression is determined, regardless of whether all the other conditions within that level have been evaluated.

COBOL 85 clarifies some of the COBOL 74 rules that are ambiguous. This change might affect the execution of some COBOL 74 programs. The only programs affected are those that contain debugging declaratives for which the **ALL REFERENCES** phrase is specified as in **USE FOR DEBUGGING ON ALL REFERENCES OF AMOUNT-TWO, AMOUNT-THREE**. If the truth value of the entire complex conditional expression can be determined before the individual conditions referencing **AMOUNT-TWO** and **AMOUNT-THREE** are evaluated, then the **USE FOR DEBUGGING ON ALL REFERENCES OF AMOUNT-TWO, AMOUNT-THREE** will not be invoked. In COBOL 74, depending on the particular COBOL compiler being used, that **USE** procedure might have been invoked.

Conversion is necessary if the COBOL 74 program must evaluate all components of a complex conditional expression in order to trigger the **USE FOR DEBUGGING** mechanism.

Note also that the **DEBUG** module has been made obsolete.

The National Bureau of Standards, in its analysis of the COBOL 85 language, considers this changed feature to be of *intermediate complexity* requiring only minor programming-logic modifications. Much of the conversion logic can be handled automatically by a Language Conversion Program (LCP).

COPY   (Change)

> New rules exist for a **COPY** statement imbedded in a comment-entry.

In COBOL 85, if the word **COPY** appears in a comment-entry or in the place where a comment-entry may appear, it is considered part of the comment-entry. In COBOL 74, the appearance of the word **COPY** in a comment-entry is an undefined situation. The specification of this situation within COBOL 85 will enhance program portability.

If it is necessary for a **COPY** statement to be recognized as a **COPY** statement and not as part of the comment-entry, the **COPY** statement should be taken out of the comment-entry.

> There are new rules for a **COPY** statement appearing on a **DEBUG** line.

In COBOL 85, after all **COPY** statements have been processed, a debugging line will be considered to have all the characteristics of a comment line if the **WITH DEBUGGING MODE** clause is not specified in the **SOURCE-COMPUTER** paragraph.

COBOL 74 does not address the situation of a **COPY** statement, or a portion of a **COPY** statement, appearing on a debugging line. Consider the following **COPY** statement with a **D** in column 7.

```
        COPY        COMMON-MODULE   IN MY-USER-LIBRARY
D       REPLACING   ==ALPHABETIC== BY  ==ALPHABETIC-UPPER==.
```

If the program is compiled without the **WITH DEBUGGING MODE** clause, COBOL 74 does not state whether or not the **REPLACING** phrase is executed. In COBOL 85, the **REPLACING** phrase is executed. (In the example above, I have used the **DEBUG** facility of COBOL as a conversion facility.)

A potential incompatibility exists if a particular COBOL 74 compiler treated the **DEBUG**ging line as a comment line. If conversion is necessary, it can be detected by a Language Conversion Program (LCP).

The National Bureau of Standards considers these changed features to be of *low complexity* requiring few programming-logic modifications. Most of the conversion logic can be handled by an automatic Language Conversion Program (LCP).

CURRENCY SIGN (Change)

> No figurative constant is allowed in the
> **CURRENCY SIGN** clause.

The literal specified within the **CURRENCY SIGN** clause cannot be a figurative constant.

It is unclear in COBOL 74 whether or not the figurative constants **HIGH-VALUE** or **LOW-VALUE** are allowed in the **CURRENCY SIGN** clause, regardless of the little usefulness such a statement would provide.

It becomes very tedious to write rules to cover all uses of figurative constants in the **CURRENCY SIGN** clause. The benefits of allowing the use of figurative constants in these cases is marginal at best. It appears more likely to have been an omission of a clarifying rule in COBOL 74 rather than the inclusion of a desirable feature. This change is unlikely to affect many programs, since very few existing programs have used figurative constants in the **CURRENCY SIGN** clause.

The National Bureau of Standards considers this changed feature to be of *low complexity* requiring no programming-logic modifications. Most of the conversion logic can be handled by an automatic Language Conversion Program (LCP).

Debug (Obsolete)

> Debug has been made obsolete.

The Debug facility is an obsolete language element. Therefore, the "compile-time" **DEBUGGING** switch—**WITH DEBUGGING MODE**—in the **SOURCE-COMPUTER** paragraph of the **ENVIRONMENT DIVISION** is obsolete.

```
SOURCE-COMPUTER.   SYT-VX WITH DEBUGGING MODE.
```

The **USE FOR DEBUGGING** procedure in the **DECLARATIVES** is also obsolete.

```
DECLARATIVES.
DEBUG-PROCESS SECTION.
    USE FOR DEBUGGING ON FILE-A.
       . . .
```

Any program that uses the ANS COBOL 74 **DEBUG** facility will be affected by this obsolete feature. It is likely that there are very few of these programs, however.

There will be no equivalent in the revision that follows COBOL 85 (COBOL 95 perhaps?) of the COBOL 74 **DEBUG** facility to which to convert this feature. The programmer will have to:

1) rely on non-COBOL tools to duplicate interactive debugging or
2) write "debugging trace" statements manually to test the program or
3) use one of the many compilers expected to continue supporting the COBOL Debug facility as an implementor-extension.

In my analysis of the COBOL 85 language, I consider this changed feature to be of *high complexity* requiring major programming logic modifications. Little of the required conversion logic can be handled by an automatic Language Conversion Program (LCP).

NOTE: Debug lines, indicated by a **D** in column 7 of a COBOL source line, is technically not considered part of the Debug facility and is *not* an obsolete language element.

DISABLE ... KEY   (Obsolete)

The **KEY** phrase of the **DISABLE** statement has been made obsolete.

The rules for determining when the **KEY** value "matches" the system password are not specified in COBOL 74, and are therefore implementor-defined. The removal of this implementor-defined feature should increase program portability.

If conversion is required, the COBOL implementor must provide an alternative method of matching a system password to gain access to a terminal device. This will probably be done through Job Control Language (JCL) (as it is in most cases presently). Implementors may choose to retain this feature as an extension when the ANS COBOL 85 language is fully revised (in 1995 perhaps). *This feature will continue to be supported in COBOL 85.* Compatibility of this feature between a standard-conforming COBOL 74 compiler and a standard-conforming COBOL 85 compiler is assured by no one (nor between two different COBOL 74 compilers).

The National Bureau of Standards, in its analysis of the COBOL 85 language, considers this obsolete feature to be of *high complexity* requiring major programming-logic modifications. It is possible that some of the code is sensitive to the source hardware or operating system, and equivalent features may be lacking in the COBOL 85 environment. Little of the conversion logic can be handled by an automatic Language Conversion Program (LCP).

DISPLAY

(Change)

> The hardware positioning after a **DISPLAY** statement is now specified.

In a COBOL 85 **DISPLAY** statement that does not specify **WITH NO ADVANCING**, the positioning of the hardware device will be reset to the leftmost position of the next line of the device after the last operand has been transferred.

In COBOL 74, the positioning of the hardware device is undefined after the last operand is transferred. The new rule in COBOL 85 is necessary for a complete specification of the new **WITH NO ADVANCING** clause. Conversion is expected to be unlikely. Most compilers already function according to the new rule.

The National Bureau of Standards considers this changed feature to be of *low complexity* requiring few programming-logic modifications. Most of the conversion logic can be handled by an automatic Language Conversion Program (LCP).

DIVIDE

(Change)

> The order of evaluating subscripts in a **DIVIDE** statement is defined.

In COBOL 85, any subscripts used in the **REMAINDER** data item of a **DIVIDE** statement are evaluated after the result of the **DIVIDE** operation is stored in the **GIVING** data item.

In COBOL 74, it is undefined at which point in the processing of the **DIVIDE** statement any subscripts in the **REMAINDER** phrase are determined. This change should improve portability of COBOL 85 programs.

```
DIVIDE A INTO B GIVING C REMAINDER D(C)
```

Conversion from COBOL 74/68 is required if the value of **C** to be used in the **REMAINDER D(C)** is its current value before the **DIVIDE** operation.

This situation can be detected automatically by a Language Conversion Program. If the program must use the value of the data item in the **GIVING** clause prior to execution of the **DIVIDE** statement, simply **MOVE** that value to a new "holding" data item (**HOLD-SUBSCRIPT**), and use this new "holding" data item as the subscript in the **DIVIDE** statement. The following example illustrates this suggested conversion.

```
MOVE        C
   TO       HOLD-SUBSCRIPT


DIVIDE      A
   INTO     B
   GIVING   C
   REMAINDER D (HOLD-SUBSCRIPT)
```

The National Bureau of Standards, in its analysis of the COBOL 85 language, considers this changed feature to be of *low complexity* requiring few programming-logic modifications. Most of the conversion logic can be handled by an automatic Language Conversion Program (LCP).

ENABLE ... KEY   (Obsolete)

> The **KEY** phrase of the **ENABLE** statement has been made obsolete.

The rules for determining when the **KEY** value "matches" the system password are not specified in COBOL 74, and are therefore defined by the implementor. As in the similar case of **DISABLE**, the eventual removal of this implementor-defined feature should increase program portability. This feature will continue to be supported in COBOL 85 although no portability is assured.

If conversion is required, the COBOL implementor must provide an alternative method of matching a system password to gain access to a terminal device. This will probably be provided through JCL (as it is in most cases presently). *This feature will continue to be supported in COBOL 85.* As with a few other poorly defined features, program portability and compatibility are assured by no one. When the ANS COBOL 85 language is revised (in 1995 perhaps), implementors may choose to retain this feature as an extension to the standard COBOL language.

The National Bureau of Standards, in its analysis of the COBOL 85 language, considers this changed feature to be of *high complexity* requiring major programming-logic modifications. It is possible that some of the code is sensitive to the source hardware or operating system, and equivalent features may be lacking in the COBOL 85 environment. Little of the conversion logic can be handled by an automatic Language Conversion Program (LCP).

ENTER (Obsolete)

The **ENTER** statement has been made obsolete.

The **ENTER** statement has traditionally been used to write non-COBOL subprograms within COBOL programs.

In COBOL 74, the **ENTER** statement is optional, and not every COBOL 74 compiler includes it. Furthermore, when it is included in a particular COBOL 74 compiler, there are few rules governing how the mechanism should work. The eventual deletion of this feature from COBOL detracts little from the standard COBOL language. *The **ENTER** statement is still included in COBOL 85.* Its portability is assured by no one. Removing **ENTER** statements from COBOL 74/68 programs will require, in most cases, substituting a **CALL** statement to a separately compiled subprogram (subroutine, procedure). Each "alien" subroutine (coded in a non-COBOL language) that is currently imbedded in a COBOL 74/68 program must be separately compiled and accessible as an "executable" module to the run unit. Care should be taken when passing parameters to and from this newly created **CALL**ing subprogram.

The National Bureau of Standards, in its analysis of the COBOL 85 language, considers this obsolete feature to be of *high complexity* requiring major programming-logic modifications. Little of the conversion logic can be handled automatically by a Language Conversion Program (LCP).

EXIT PROGRAM (Change)

EXIT PROGRAM rules have been added for **PERFORM** loops.

The following COBOL 85 rule appears for the **EXIT PRO-**

GRAM statement: ". . . the ends of the ranges of all **PERFORM** statements executed by the called program are considered to have been reached." This situation is undefined in COBOL 74.

An ambiguity is resolved in COBOL 85 by the addition of a new general rule. The COBOL 85 rules provide a safeguard against inaccurately executing programs. Note, however, that it provides no safeguard against inaccurately coded programs. Programmer beware! COBOL is becomming more forgiving, and thus more tolerant of sloppy programming.

This potential incompatibility between COBOL 74/68 programs and COBOL 85 programs is perhaps more serious than most of the others. This language change will indeed help more programs written in the future than it will hurt programs written in the past. There is, however, a popular programming methodology that recommends the use of "co-routines." This concept requires that the executing status of the co-routine be identical at resumption time to that at suspension time. Co-routines can still be used according to the new rules in COBOL 85, but they must be resident segments of a main program (one that contains no **EXIT PROGRAM** statement); this of course detracts from the flexibility of such "co-routines."

The National Bureau of Standards considers this changed feature to be of *intermediate complexity* requiring minor programming-logic modifications. Much of the conversion logic can be handled by an automatic Language Conversion Program (LCP).

New **EXIT PROGRAM** default rules have been defined.

In COBOL 85, when there is no next executable statement in a **CALL**ed program, an implicit **EXIT PROGRAM** statement is executed. This situation is undefined in COBOL 74. This change increases COBOL 85's portability.

This affects only programs whose compilers behave differently from described above. If conversion is necessary, it is expected that implementors will provide a method in their COBOL 85 compilers to produce "COBOL 74" behavior (perhaps ABEND).

The National Bureau of Standards considers this changed feature to be of *intermediate complexity* requiring minor programming-logic modifications. Much of the conversion logic can be handled by an automatic Language Conversion Program (LCP).

Exponentiation   (Change)

> New rules have been defined for exponentiation.

The following special cases of exponentiation are defined in COBOL 85:

1) If a value less than or equal to 0 is raised to a power of 0, the size error condition exists.
2) If the evaluation of the exponentiation yields both a positive and a negative real number, the positive number is returned.
3) If no real number exists as the result of the evaluation, the size error condition exists.

Since COBOL 74 does not state what happens in these special cases of exponentiation, implementors are free to choose how to handle them. This change is the resolution of an undefined situation and will help promote program portability.

This change may produce "slightly different arithmetic results" in cases where a specific method of exponentiation has changed. If a compiler has indeed changed its algorithm for exponentiation, implementors must inform users how to duplicate the previous method of calculating arithmetic expressions involving exponents. It is assumed that implementors will offer programmers to use the same algorithms in their COBOL 85 compilers as in their COBOL 74 compilers.

FD (Obsolete)

Three clauses in the **FD** paragraph of the **DATA DIVISION—LABEL RECORDS, VALUE OF, DATA RECORDS**—are obsolete language elements.

```
FD  COBOL-74-FILE
    LABEL RECORD IS STANDARD
    VALUE OF IDENTIFICATION IS "COBOL-74"
    DATA RECORD IS COBOL-74-RECORD.
01  COBOL-74-RECORD.
```

It is felt that this information is more appropriately supplied outside the COBOL language (in the JCL, for instance). Many COBOL 74 compilers already treat these clauses as documentation or override their values when in conflict with JCL parameters. For these compilers, there will be no incompatibility when these clauses are actually deleted from the COBOL language (in 1995 perhaps). However, many compilers still give some "functionality" to these clauses. To convert these programs, some alternative mechanism (probably through JCL) must be provided by implementors to relay the file information to the operating system.

These clauses are supported (however implementor-defined they may be) in COBOL 85. They will, however, be deleted from the Standard when COBOL is fully revised.

The National Bureau of Standards considers this obsolete feature to be of *low complexity* requiring few programming-logic modifications. Most of the required logic can be handled by an automatic Language Conversion Program (LCP).

File Position Indicator (Change)

> New File Position Indicator replaces Current Record Pointer.

The concept of a *current record pointer* (CRP) in COBOL 74

along with some semantics have been changed to the concept of a *file position indicator* (FPI) in COBOL 85.

In certain combinations of **READ/WRITE/DELETE**, the generalized concept of current record pointer (CRP) in COBOL 74 gives rise to undefined and surprising results. Also, it is sometimes confusing that an entity termed "current record pointer" can point to a nonexistent record. This concept has been replaced by the file position indicator, which more clearly defines file position.

> The behavior of the File Position Indicator is redefined after an **OPEN** statement.

Following an **OPEN I-O** statement in COBOL 85, the file position indicator is set to the first record in the file. Execution of a **WRITE** statement of a record with a new low key (lower than the original lowest key) followed by a **READ NEXT** statement retrieves the record just written. In COBOL 74, this same situation of an **OPEN I-O**, **WRITE** (new low key) and **READ NEXT** execution sequence causes the access of the original first record in the file (now the second record).

In COBOL 85, a successful execution of the **OPEN** statement results in the file position indicator being set to **1** in the case of a **SEQUENTIAL** or a **RELATIVE** file, or for an **INDEXED** file to the characters that have the lowest ordinal position in the collating sequence associated with that **INDEXED** file. In COBOL 74, the result is to set the current record pointer to the first record currently existing in the file when the **OPEN** is executed.

Since the **WRITE** statement does not affect the file position indicator (or current record pointer), it is more logical that on execution of the first **READ NEXT** statement following an **OPEN** statement, the record accessed should be the very first record of the file, regardless of whether or not execution of a **WRITE** statement of a record with a lower key has occurred.

The National Bureau of Standards, in its analysis of the COBOL 85 language, considers these changed features to be of *high complexity* possibly requiring major programming-logic modifications. Little of the required logic can be handled by an automatic Language Conversion Program (LCP).

FOOTING

(Change)

> New rules exist for the **FOOTING** phrase of a print-file File Description (**FD**).

In COBOL 85, if the **FOOTING** phrase is not specified in the **FD** of a print-file, no **END-OF-PAGE** condition, independent of the page overflow condition, exists.

In COBOL 74, the specifications for the existence of the **FOOTING** are contradictory between the **LINAGE** clause and the **WRITE** statement. Some existing compilers provide an implicit one-line **FOOTING** area, while others provide no **FOOTING** area when the **FOOTING** phrase is not specified. There is no way to resolve the ambiguity without affecting some existing compilers. The solution in COBOL 85 reflects the intuition that if no **FOOTING** area is specified, then none is wanted. Thus, if no **FOOTING** phrase is specified in the **LINAGE** clause of a print-file **FD**, no **FOOTING** area exists, and no end-of-page condition occurs. This change will affect only those programs that:

1) specify no **FOOTING** phrase in the **LINAGE** clause for a file;
2) use a **WRITE** statement with the **END-OF-PAGE** phrase for that file; and
3) use an existing compiler that provides a **FOOTING** area.

The National Bureau of Standards, in its analysis of the

COBOL 85 language, considers this changed feature to be of *low complexity* requiring few programming-logic modifications. Most of the conversion logic can be handled by an automatic Language Conversion Program (LCP).

IDENTIFICATION   (Obsolete)
DIVISION—Comment-entries

Five paragraphs in the **IDENTIFICATION DIVISION** are obsolete.

The following paragraphs in the **IDENTIFICATION DIVISION** are obsolete language elements:

AUTHOR
INSTALLATION
DATA-WRITTEN
DATA-COMPILED
SECURITY

```
IDENTIFICATION DIVISION.
PROGRAM-ID.     TEST-EDIT.
AUTHOR.         R. KNIGHTS.
INSTALLATION.   PIGGOTT ET AL.
DATE-WRITTEN.   JANUARY 1, 1985.
DATE-COMPILED.  JULY 24, 1985.
SECURITY.       FOR YOUR EYES ONLY.
```

There is no reason for comment-entries to be as structured as they have been in COBOL. A simple asterisk (*) in column 7 identifies a comment-entry throughout the COBOL program. Conversion is trivial: It is simply a matter of placing an asterisk in column 7.

These five comment-entries in the **IDENTIFICATION DIVISION** are supported in ANS COBOL 85. They will be deleted from the COBOL language when COBOL is fully revised (in 1995 perhaps). If they appear in any compilers after that, it will be as extensions to the Standard.

INDEXED File　　　　　　　　　(Change)

> The collating sequence of an **INDEXED** file is "native."

The collating sequence used to access an **INDEXED** file is the collating sequence associated with the "native" character set that was in effect for the file at the time the file was created.

COBOL 74 lacks rules that state which collating sequence is used for the retrieving and storing of records when accessing an **INDEXED** file. Two different interpretations are possible:

1) the native collating sequence or
2) the collating sequence specified by the **PROGRAM COLLATING SEQUENCE** clause.

The new rule in COBOL 85 specifies that the "native" collating sequence will be used. This is logical since files are generally shared by different programs. Thus, they should contain attributes of a systems-operating environment rather than of a specific program.

Most existing COBOL 74 compilers use the "native" collating sequence. Therefore, even though the change represents a potential incompatibility between COBOL 74 and COBOL 85, this change is not likely to affect many existing programs.

The National Bureau of Standards, in its analysis of the COBOL 85 language, considers this changed feature to be of *high complexity* requiring major programming-logic modifications, possibly because some of the code is sensitive to the source hardware or operating system, and equivalent features are lacking in the COBOL 85 environment. Little of the conver-

sion can be handled by an automatic Language Conversion
Program (LCP).

INSPECT   (Change)

The order of evaluating subscripts in an **INSPECT** statement
is defined.

COBOL 74 does not state when subscripts in an **INSPECT**
statement are evaluated. In COBOL 85, a general rule of the
INSPECT statement states: "Subscripting associated with any
identifier is evaluated only once as the first operation in the
execution of the **INSPECT** statement." This change resolves an
ambiguity in COBOL 74, and increases COBOL's portability.

Conversion from COBOL 74 (and its counterpart in
COBOL 68, **EXAMINE**) is unlikely to be necessary as this
change presumably deals with a very esoteric programming
technique. If conversion is necessary, it can be detected automatically by a Language Conversion Program (LCP). Conversion is necessary only if a COBOL 74 program contains an
INSPECT statement in which:

1) subscripts are used that may be changed during the
   course of executing the **INSPECT** statement and
2) the COBOL 74 compiler for which the program was
   written did not evaluate subscripts prior to executing
   the **INSPECT** statement.

The National Bureau of Standards, in its analysis of the
COBOL 85 language, considers this changed feature to be of
intermediate complexity requiring minor programming-logic
modifications. Much of the conversion logic can be handled
by an automatic Language Conversion Program (LCP).

I-O Status codes   (Change)

Seventeen standard I-O Status codes have been added.

The new I-O status codes that have been added include **04**, **05**, **07**, **14**, **15**, **24**, **25**, **34**, **35**, **37**, **38**, **39**, **41**, **42**, **43**, **46**, **49**.

COBOL 74 specifies only a few I-O status code conditions. As a result, users cannot always distinguish between many different I-O exception conditions that they might wish to treat in a variety of ways. In addition, each implementor specified a different set of implementor-defined status codes that covered similar situations in a variety of ways. COBOL 74 leaves the results of many I-O situations undefined or says that certain criteria are to be met, but does not specify what happens when they are not; hence, execution of the object program becomes undefined.

Potential incompatibilities with COBOL 74 programs may occur if these programs have equated a successful I-O operation to a **00** status code. Such programs will have to be modified in COBOL 85 to include **04**, **05**, **07** as additional successful status codes.

It is also possible that some COBOL 74 compilers assigned some other (implementor-defined) meaning to one of the new I-O status codes. This should not occur because these numbers are reserved for the CODASYL COBOL Committee's use. If such a conflict does occur, however, new implementor-defined I-O status codes will have to be assigned for those implementor-defined I-O exceptions.

The National Bureau of Standards, in its analysis of the COBOL 85 language, considers this changed feature to be of *intermediate complexity* requiring minor programming-logic modifications. Much of the conversion logic can be handled by an automatic Language Conversion Program (LCP).

COBOL 85 defines several more common I-O exceptions and the resultant status codes, so that each of these situations can be programmed in a standard way. They include:

I-O status 04

A **READ** statement is successfully executed, but the length of the record being processed does not conform to the fixed file attributes for the file. COBOL 74 does not define the consequences if a **READ** statement accesses a record containing more or fewer characters than the maximum and minimum, respectively, specified for that file. The new I-O status value of "**04**" defines the result in these circumstances.

I-O status 05

An **OPEN** statement is successfully executed, but the referenced optional file is not present at the time the **OPEN** statement is executed. According to COBOL 74, the absence of an optional file is not notified to the program until the first **READ** statement is attempted for this file. The new I-O status value **05** makes this status information available at the time the file is referenced by an **OPEN** statement, allowing the program to take action immediately when this condition occurs.

I-O status 07

The input-output statement is successfully executed. However, for a **CLOSE** statement with the **NO REWIND**, **REEL/UNIT**, or **FOR REMOVAL** phrase, or for an **OPEN** statement with the **NO REWIND** phrase, the referenced file is on a non-**REEL/UNIT** medium. According to COBOL 74, **OPEN . . . NO REWIND** can be used only with sequential single **REEL/UNIT** files, and **CLOSE . . . REEL/UNIT** must be used only for sequential files. However, with mass-storage files, these instances of **OPEN** and **CLOSE** can be considered successful in essence, if the anomaly of the **NO REWIND** or **REEL/UNIT** phrase is overlooked. The new I-O status value of **07** makes successful completion possible, while preserving the information for the user in case specific action is desired.

I-O status 14

A sequential **READ** statement is attempted for a relative file, and the number of significant digits in the relative record number is larger than the size of the relative key data item described for the file. COBOL 74 states that successful execution of a format 1 **READ** statement referencing a relative file updates the contents of the relative key data item (if specified) to contain the relative record number of the record available. COBOL 74 does not define the result if the number of significant digits of the relative record number is larger than the relative key data item. The new I-O status value of **14** defines the result.

I-O status 15

A sequential **READ** statement is attempted for the first time on an optional file that is not present. The new I-O status value of **15** distinguishes the absence of an optional file from other **AT END** conditions.

I-O status 24

An attempt is made to **WRITE** beyond the externally defined boundaries of a relative or indexed file; or a sequential **WRITE** statement is attempted for a relative file, and the number of significant digits in the relative record number is larger than the relative key data item. COBOL 74 does not define the result if the number of significant digits of the relative record number is larger than the relative key data item. The new I-O status value of **24** has been enhanced beyond its definition in COBOL 74 to include this additional case.

I-O status 25

A I-O status **25** indicates that a **START** statement or a random **READ** statement has been attempted on an **OPTIONAL** file that is not present.

I-O status 34

An attempt is made to **WRITE** beyond the externally defined boundaries of a sequential file. The only difference between COBOL 74 and COBOL 85 is the absence from COBOL 74 of the sentence: "The implementor specifies the manner in which these boundaries are defined."

I-O status 35

An **OPEN** statement with the **INPUT** phrase is attempted on a nonoptional file that is not present. COBOL 74 requires that the **OPTIONAL** phrase be specified for input files that are not necessarily present each time the object program is executed. However, COBOL 74 does not specify what happens when this requirement is not met. The new I-O status value of **35** allows the user to test for this condition and take specific corrective action if desired.

I-O status 37

An **OPEN** statement with an **I-O** phrase is attempted on a file that is not a mass-storage file (a terminal, for instance). COBOL 74 specifies that the file must be a mass-storage file, but does not specify what happens if it is not. The new I-O status value of **37** permits the user to test for this condition and take specific action if desired. This would prohibit the use of a terminal as an I-O file in a COBOL 85 program (unless the terminal can be considered as a mass-storage device). Using a terminal for I-O can still be accomplished easily with the Communication Section.

I-O status 38

An **OPEN** statement is attempted on a file previously **CLOSE**d **WITH LOCK**. COBOL 74 specifies that the **OPEN** statement may not follow a **CLOSE WITH LOCK** statement, but does not specify what happens if this rule is violated. The new I-O status value of **38** permits the user to test for this condition and take corrective action if desired.

I-O status 39

An **OPEN** statement is unsuccessful because a conflict has been detected between the fixed file attributes and the attributes specified for the file in the program. COBOL 74 specifies that the attributes must agree, but does not specify what happens if they do not. The new I-O status value of **39** allows the user to test for this condition and take corrective action if desired.

I-O status 41

An **OPEN** statement is attempted for a file already in the **OPEN** mode. COBOL 74 does not allow an **OPEN** statement to refer to a file that is already in the **OPEN** mode, but does not define the consequences. The new I-O status value of **41** permits the user to test for the condition and take corrective action if desired.

I-O status 42

A **CLOSE** statement is attempted for a file that is not in the **OPEN** mode. COBOL 74 does not allow a **CLOSE** statement to refer to a file that is not in the **OPEN** mode, but it does not define what happens if the file is *not* in the **OPEN** mode at the time of a **CLOSE** statement. The new I-O status code **42** permits the programmer to test for this situation.

I-O status 43

For a mass storage file in the sequential access mode, the last input-output statement executed for the associated file prior to the execution of a **DELETE** or **REWRITE** statement was not a successfully executed **READ** statement. COBOL 74 specifies that this must be the case, but does not specify what happens if the requirement is not satisfied. The new I-O status value of **43** allows the user to test for this condition and take corrective action if desired.

I-O status 46

A sequential **READ** statement is attempted on a file opened in the **INPUT** or **INPUT-OUTPUT** mode, and no valid next record has been established. COBOL 74 specifies that in these circumstances the execution of the **READ** statement is unsuccessful, but does not specify any status code value to indicate this situation. The new I-O status value of **46** allows the user to test for this condition and take action if desired.

I-O status 49

The execution of a **DELETE** or **REWRITE** statement is attempted on a file not opened in the **INPUT-OUTPUT** mode. COBOL 74 requires that the file be opened in the **INPUT-OUTPUT** mode, but does not specify what happens if the requirement is not met. The new I-O status value of **49** allows the user to test for this condition and take corrective action if desired.

LINAGE and EXTEND   (Change)

New restrictions have been placed on the use of **LINAGE** and **EXTEND** clauses together.

Files whose **FD**s contain a **LINAGE** clause that has been specified must not be **OPEN**ed in the **EXTEND** mode.

In COBOL 74, the size of the first logical page for a file **OPEN**ed in the **EXTEND** mode is undefined, and the page number is reset to one. There seems to be little utility for such a feature. This change should affect few, if any, COBOL 74 programs.

The National Bureau of Standards, in its analysis of the COBOL 85 language, considers this changed feature to be of *intermediate complexity* requiring minor programming-logic modifications. Much of the required logic can be handled by an automatic Language Conversion Program (LCP).

MEMORY SIZE   (Obsolete)

The **MEMORY SIZE** clause of the **OBJECT-COMPUTER** paragraph has been made obsolete.

In COBOL 74, the facility provided by the **MEMORY SIZE** clause is a function more appropriately controlled by the operating system. Because this feature is implementor defined, no true portability exists between many different COBOL compilers. Therefore, deletion of this feature will enhance standardization of future programs. Some compilers have assigned "functionality" to this clause, and some conversion may be necessary in those cases. This conversion is likely to include substituting JCL paramters for the information provided by the **MEMORY SIZE** clause. These changes may have been necessary regardless of whether or not the feature was deleted. The **MEMORY SIZE** clause will continue to be supported in COBOL 85.

The National Bureau of Standards considers this obsolete feature to be of *intermediate complexity* requiring minor programming-logic modifications. Much of the conversion logic can be handled by an automatic Language Conversion Program (LCP).

MERGE   (Change)

MERGE files cannot use **SAME AREA**.

In COBOL 85, no two files in a **MERGE** statement may be specified in the **SAME AREA** clause or **SAME SORT-MERGE AREA** clause. The only files in a **MERGE** statement that can be specified in the **SAME RECORD AREA** clause are those associated with the **GIVING** phrase of the **MERGE** statement. This rule is not present in COBOL 74.

This rule clarifies the COBOL 74 rule for the **SAME AREA** clause and the **MERGE** statement. Although not stated explicitly in COBOL 74, the **MERGE** statement will probably not perform properly if this rule is violated. It is unlikely that this affects many (if any) programs.

The National Bureau of Standards, in its analysis of the COBOL 85 language, considers this changed feature to be of *intermediate complexity* requiring minor programming-logic modifications. Much of the conversion logic can be handled by an automatic Language Conversion Program (LCP).

MULTIPLE FILE TAPE   (Change)

Limits have been placed on the **MULTIPLE FILE TAPE** clause.

New rules in COBOL 85 state:

1) each file in a series of files sharing the same physical reel of tape must be created with a uniform labeling convention; and

2) a **SORT** or **MERGE** file may not be specified in the **MULTIPLE FILE TAPE** clause.

Not all files in a **MULTIPLE FILE** set need be described in the COBOL 74 program. If the undescribed files had different label conventions, it would not be possible for the compiler to know how to properly position to the start of any given file. Most COBOL 74 compilers already have such a restriction.

SORT and **MERGE** files are essentially "scratch" files and are not **OPENed** or **CLOSEd** by the user. If one file of a multiple file set were to be used as a **SORT** file, it would be impossible for the user to **CLOSE** the file, which would be necessary before other files in the set could be accessed. There is no reasonable application for the use of such a file, and few existing COBOL 74 programs are likely to be affected by this change.

The National Bureau of Standards, in its analysis of the COBOL 85 language, considers this changed feature to be of *intermediate complexity* requiring minor programming-logic modifications. Much of the required logic can be handled by an automatic Language Conversion Program (LCP).

OPEN REVERSED   (Obsolete)

> The **REVERSED** option of the **OPEN** statement has been made obsolete.

The **REVERSED** phrase of the **OPEN** statement has been made obsolete. COBOL 74 allows a sequential file, **OPEN**ed for input, to be read in a **REVERSED** order.

The necessary hardware to perform this function is not very widely available; hence, this was an infrequently implemented feature and not a good candidate for standardization. An implementor is free to continue to support this feature as a non-standard extension. This feature will continue to be supported (as poorly defined as in the past) in COBOL 85. Few, if any, programs are expected to be affected by making this feature obsolete.

The National Bureau of Standards considers this obsolete feature to be of *high complexity* possibly requiring major programming-logic modifications. Some of the code is sensitive to the source hardware, and equivalent hardware may be lacking in the COBOL 85 environment. Little of the conversion logic can be handled by an automatic Language Conversion Program (LCP).

PERFORM

(Change)

> New rules have been added for initializing nested
> **PERFORM** statements.

COBOL 85 states that when a **PERFORM** statement contains multiple **VARYING** identifiers (i.e., a **PERFORM** within a **PERFORM**), the initial value of the outer identifier is set first. COBOL 74/68 do not state the order of initialization of multiple **VARYING** identifiers; the **PERFORM** statements of two different COBOL 74/68 compilers may have behaved differently. In the following example, the initial value of the **INNER-COUNTER** is set to the "current" value of the **OUTER-COUNTER**. (This is a "cute and clever" programming technique that I suggest not using; instead, both **COUNTERS** should be equated to an intermediate, local data item.)

```
MOVE 2 TO OUTER-COUNTER
PERFORM SUB-ROUTINE
    VARYING OUTER-COUNTER
            FROM 1  BY  1
            UNTIL OUTER-COUNTER = 3
    AFTER INNER-COUNTER
            FROM OUTER-COUNTER  BY  1
            UNTIL INNER-COUNTER = 3
```

In COBOL 85, the initial value of **OUTER-COUNTER** is **1**, and the initial value of **INNER-COUNTER** is **1**. In COBOL 74/68, depending on the particular COBOL compiler in use, **INNER-COUNTER** may have been set first. If it was, the initial value of **OUTER-COUNTER** would still be **1**, but the initial value of **INNER-COUNTER** would be **2**. This change affects programs that:

1) contain a "nested" **PERFORM** statement that sets the initial value of the **INNER-COUNTER** to the current value of the **OUTER-COUNTER** and

2) were compiled using a COBOL 74/68 compiler that initialized the **INNER-COUNTER** first.

In this case, conversion may be accomplished by creating a new "holding" data item, **INITIAL-INNER-COUNTER**, and by coding the following:

```
MOVE OUTER-COUNTER TO INITIAL-INNER-COUNTER
PERFORM SUB-ROUTINE
   VARYING OUTER-COUNTER
           FROM 1
           BY   1
           UNTIL OUTER-COUNTER = 3
   AFTER INNER-COUNTER
           FROM  INITIAL-INNER-COUNTER
           BY    1
           UNTIL INNER-COUNTER = 3
```

In addition, the following statement should be inserted at the end of **SUB-ROUTINE**.

```
MOVE OUTER-COUNTER TO INITIAL-INNER-COUNTER.
```

> There are new rules for augmenting identifiers in a nested **PERFORM** statement.

The order of augmenting the inner and outer identifiers in each "cycle" of a nested **PERFORM** statement has been changed. In COBOL 85, the **OUTER-COUNTER** is augmented first. Consider the following example (similar but not identical to the previous example).

```
PERFORM SUB-ROUTINE
   VARYING OUTER-COUNTER
           FROM 1  BY  1
           UNTIL OUTER-COUNTER > 3
   AFTER INNER-COUNTER
           FROM OUTER-COUNTER  BY  1
           UNTIL INNER-COUNTER > 3
```

The following chart states the respective values of **OUTER-COUNTER** and **INNER-COUNTER** in each cycle of the COBOl 85 **PERFORM** statement above.

COBOL 85 PERFORM

	C	Y	C	L	E	
1	2	3	4	5	6	
OUTER-COUNTER	1	1	1	2	2	3
INNER-COUNTER	1	2	3	2	3	3

In COBOL 74 (where the **INNER-COUNTER** is reset first), the same **PERFORM** example above produces the following table of values.

COBOL 74 PERFORM

	C	Y	C	L	E		
1	2	3	4	5	6	7	8
OUTER-COUNTER	1	1	1	2	2	2	3	3
INNER-COUNTER	1	2	3	1	2	3	2	3

NOTE: COBOL 85 results in two fewer iterations of the **PERFORM**ed **SUB-ROUTINE**.

The effect of the new **PERFORM** rules in COBOL 85 is to make this **PERFORM** statement:

```
PERFORM SUB-ROUTINE
   VARYING OUTER-COUNTER
           FROM   1
           BY     1
           UNTIL OUTER-COUNTER > 3
   AFTER INNER-COUNTER
           FROM   OUTER-COUNTER
           BY     1
           UNTIL INNER-COUNTER > 3
```

logically equivalent to the following code.

```
PERFORM           OUTER-ROUTINE
     VARYING      OUTER-COUNTER
     FROM         1
     BY           1
     UNTIL        OUTER-COUNTER > 3.


OUTER-ROUTINE.
     PERFORM      SUB-ROUTINE
       VARYING    INNER-COUNTER
       FROM       OUTER-COUNTER
       BY         1
       UNTIL      INNER-COUNTER > 3.
```

In COBOL 74, the two previous examples are not logically equivalent. In COBOL 85, these two examples are logically equivalent.

A new order is defined for evaluating subscripts in a **PERFORM** statement.

An additional change in the **PERFORM** statement in COBOL 85 that may affect COBOL 74/68 programs is the evaluation of subscripts in the **VARYING** phrase. As with **DIVIDE**, **INSPECT**, **STRING** and **UNSTRING**, the order of evaluating subscripts in the **PERFORM VARYING** statement is specified in COBOL 85. This order is not specified in COBOL 74/68. In the following example,

```
PERFORM           SUB-ROUTINE
     VARYING      X-SUB
     FROM         Y
     BY           Z
     UNTIL        COUNTER (X-SUB) > 3.
```

the subscript in the identifier of this **VARYING** phrase, **COUNTER (X-SUB)**, is evaluated for each iteration (loop) of the **PERFORM**ed **SUB-ROUTINE**. It is evaluated at the time the identifier is used, either in a setting, or augmenting or condition testing operation. This change affects COBOL 74/68 programs that:

1) use subscripted identifiers in the **VARYING** phrase as in the example above;
2) change the values of those subscripts while the **PERFORM** statement is still active (in **SUB-ROUTINE**); and
3) were previously compiled using a COBOL 74/68 compiler that specified a different order of subscript evaluation. In other words, subscripts in the **VARYING** phrase remain static during all iterations of the **PERFORM** statement.

If conversion is required, it can be detected automatically by a Language Conversion Program. If the program must use different values for the data items in a **PERFORM** statement (that is, different from their values just prior to the execution of each phase of the **PERFORM** statement), those values must be captured and stored and used in place of the data items now being used. Although it is expected that this incompatibility will occur infrequently, if conversion is necessary, it may require considerable manual reprogramming. This change in COBOL 85 is the resolution of an ambiguity and will help promote program portability.

The National Bureau of Standards considers these changed features described above to be of *low complexity*.

PICTURE P   (Change)

New restrictions have been placed on **PIC P**.

When a data item described by a **PICTURE** clause containing the character **P** is referenced, the digit positions specified by **P** will be considered to contain zeros when:

1) the reference requires a numeric item or
2) the data item is moved to a numeric or numeric-edited item or
3) the data item is compared to a numeric item.

In COBOL 74, such digit positions are considered to contain zeros when used in an operation involving conversion of data from one form of internal representation to another. However, it is not specified in COBOL 74 when such conversion is required. COBOL 85 specifies that these digit positions will contain zeros when the referenced item is required to be numeric or when it is used in association with a numeric item. This clarification agrees with current compilers for the most common cases. For the more obscure cases (such as moving an item with **PICTURE 9P** to one with **PICTURE XX**), the clarification takes the most intuitive approach.

The National Bureau of Standards considers this changed feature to be of *low complexity*, requiring few programming-logic modifications. Most of the conversion logic can be handled by an automatic Language Conversion Program (LCP).

PROCEDURE DIVISION   (Change)

New variations for **PROCEDURE DIVISION** are allowed.

In COBOL 85, a data item appearing in the **USING** phrase of the **PROCEDURE DIVISION** header must not have a **REDEFINES** clause in its data description entry.

In COBOL 74, such a restriction is not stated. As a result, strange, undefined code can be written. In COBOL 74, the following example is legal.

```
LINKAGE SECTION
01  A   PIC X(10)
01  B   REDEFINES A PIC 9(10)

PROCEDURE DIVISION USING A,B.
```

If the calling program specifies two different parameters, the results are undefined. Allowing an item with a **REDEFINES** clause to be specified in the **USING** phrase of the **PROCEDURE DIVISION** header could allow programming errors to remain undetected. Furthermore, it provides no additional "functionality". A program that specifies a redefining item in the **USING** phrase of the **PROCEDURE DIVISION** header can be converted automatically by substituting the redefined item.

The National Bureau of Standards considers this changed feature to be of *low complexity* requiring few programming-logic modifications. Most of the conversion logic can be handled by an automatic Language Conversion Program (LCP).

READ   (Change)

New restrictions have been placed on a **READ INTO** statement.

In COBOL 85, the **INTO** phrase cannot be specified unless:

1) all records associated with the file and the data item specified in the **INTO** phrase are group items or elementary alphanumeric items, or
2) only one record description is subordinate to the file description entry.

In COBOL 74, there are few rules describing the movement of the record to the **INTO** field. For a file with multiple elementary records, it is not stated whether any conversion of data takes place or whether a group move is performed. Thus, different COBOL 74 compilers may produce different results for such **READ INTO** statements. The new rule in COBOL 85 increases COBOL program portability.

If conversion is required, it will require knowing what precedence was used by a former compiler when dealing with multiple, or conflicting, receiving field data descriptions. The program must then singularly define the **INTO** field with this same data description.

The National Bureau of Standards considers this changed feature to be of *intermediate complexity* requiring minor programming-logic modifications. Much of the conversion logic can be handled by an automatic Language Conversion Program (LCP).

> There are new rules for using the **READ NEXT RECORD** option with an **ALTERNATE KEY**.

In COBOL 85, if an **ALTERNATE KEY** is the **KEY** of reference and it is changed by a **REWRITE** statement to a value between the current value and the next value in the file, a subsequent **READ NEXT** statement will obtain the same record just rewritten. In COBOL 74, the subsequent **READ** statement obtains the record with the next value for that **ALTERNATE KEY** prior to the **REWRITE** being executed.

It is logically consistent that if the **ALTERNATE KEY** value (and possibly other values) had changed, the subsequent **READ** statement should obtain the record just written, since that record at that moment is the next existing record in the file whose key value is greater than that of the record made available by the last **READ** statement. This is consistent with the file position indicator mechanism after **OPEN**ing files.

The National Bureau of Standards, considers this changed feature to be of *high complexity* requiring major programming-logic modifications, since some of the code is sensitive to the source hardware or operating system, and equivalent features are lacking in the COBOL 85 environment. Little of the required logic can be handled automatically by a Language Conversion Program (LCP).

RELATIVE KEY   (Change)

> New restrictions have been placed on the **RELATIVE KEY** phrase.

The data item specified in the **RELATIVE KEY** phrase of a **SELECT** clause must not contain the **PICTURE** symbol **P** in the data decription entry.

In COBOL 74, a **RELATIVE KEY** is allowed to have a **P** in the **PICTURE** character-string. If a **RELATIVE KEY** were so described, some of the records in the file would be inaccessible to the program. For example, a **RELATIVE KEY** with a **PICTURE** **9P** can have only the values **0**, **10**, **20**, **30**, **40**, **50**, **60**, **70**, **80** and **90**. This means that only records with these relative numbers could be accessed.

Use of such a key description is probably an error, and can be diagnosed easily in COBOL 85. If such coding were not in error, the programmer would have to substitute an algorithm to generate **RELATIVE KEY** values in multiples of ten. It is unlikely that many existing programs use such a key.

The National Bureau of Standards, in its analysis of the COBOL 85 language, considers this changed feature to be of *intermediate complexity* requiring minor programming-logic modifications. Much of the required logic can be handled by an automatic Language Conversion Program (LCP).

RERUN

(Obsolete)

> The **RERUN** clause of the **I-O-CONTROL** paragraph has been made obsolete.

In COBOL 74, there are seven forms of the **RERUN** clause of which the implementor is required to support at least one. Therefore, there is no guarantee that a program using the **RERUN** clause will run the same on another system. Most implementors provide a restart capability external to the COBOL language. **RERUN** should be external to COBOL as well.

Conversion is not likely to be necessary. Implementors are expected to continue defining the **RERUN** statement as they did in their COBOL 74 compilers. The **RERUN** statement will continue to be supported in COBOL 85 in the same poorly-defined manner it has in the past. It will be dropped from the Standard COBOL language when the ANS COBOL 85 language is fully revised (1995 perhaps?).

The National Bureau of Standards considers this obsolete feature to be of *high complexity* requiring major programming-logic modifications. Little of the conversion logic can be handled by an automatic Language Conversion Program (LCP).

Reserved words

(Change)

> Forty-nine new reserved words have been added.

The following 49 reserved words have been added to COBOL 85.

ALPHABET	END-RETURN
ALPHABETIC-LOWER	END-REWRITE
ALPHABETIC-UPPFR	END SEARCII
ALPHANUMERIC	END-START
ALPHANUMERIC-EDITED	END-SUBTRACT
ANY	END-UNSTRING
BINARY	END-WRITE
CLASS	EVALUATE
COMMON	EXTERNAL
CONTENT	FALSE
CONTINUE	GLOBAL
CONVERTING	INITIALIZE
DAY-OF-WEEK	NUMERIC-EDITED
END-STRING	ORDER
END-ADD	OTHER
END-CALL	PACKED-DECIMAL
END-COMPUTE	PADDING
END-DELETE	PURGE
END-DIVIDE	REFERENCE
END-EVALUATE	REPLACE
END-IF	STANDARD-2
END-MULTIPLY	TEST
END-PERFORM	THEN
END-READ	TRUE
END-RECEIVE	

Conversion of COBOL 74/68 programs that used these reserved words as user names is simple with the **REPLACE** statement. **REPLACE** should be used to change the spelling of all the invalid user-defined words, as in the following example.

```
REPLACE   ==WITH DEBUGGING MODE==   BY   ====
          ==END-READ==              BY   ==END-OF-READ==
          ==END-WRITE==             BY   ==END-OF-WRITE==
          ==TRUE==                  BY   ==TRUE-STATUS==
          ==FALSE==                 BY   ==FALSE-STATUS==
          ==CONTINUE==              BY   ==CONTINUE-ON==
          ==OTHER==                 BY   ==ALL-OTHER==
          ==ALPHABETIC==            BY   ==ALPHABETIC-UPPER==
          ==INITIALIZE==            BY   ==INITIALIZE-PROCESS==.
```

The programmer need not verify the presence (or absence) of any of these words in the program to be converted.

The CODASYL COBOL Committee, responsible for COBOL's development, has agreed to some rules regarding the formation of future reserved words in the COBOL language. These rules in effect establish a small category of data names that are "safe" for a programmer to use for user-defined data items. "Safe" is meant to imply a minimum chance of conflict with a future COBOL reserved word. I say a "minimum" chance, because the CODASYL COBOL Committee can of course change the rules later, but probably will not do so.

The rules adopted by the committee state:

1. Reserved words do not begin with the digits **0** through **9**, nor with the letters **X**, **Y** or **Z** (except the word **ZERO/ZEROS/ZEROES**).
2. Reserved words do not consist of a single letter.
3. Reserved words do not start with one or two characters, followed by a hyphen, except:
    *   the word **I-O-CONTROL**,
    *   words that begin with **B —** , such as **B-AND**, **B-OR**, **B-LESS**, **B-EXOR** (used for Boolean operators in the CODASYL COBOL *Journal of Development*) and
    *   words that begin with **DB**- (used in the COBOL Data Base Supplement).
4. Reserved words do not have two hyphens (--) together.

The National Bureau of Standards, in its analysis of the COBOL 85 language, considers this changed feature to be of *low complexity* requiring no programming-logic modifications. Most of the conversion logic can be handled by an automatic Language Conversion Program (LCP).

RETURN INTO (Change)

> New restrictions have been placed on the **RETURN INTO** statement.

In COBOL 85, the **INTO** phrase cannot be specified unless:

1) all records associated with the file and the data item specified in the **INTO** phrase are group items or elementary alphanumeric items, or
2) only one record description is subordinate to the file description entry.

The rationale for this change is identical to the rationale regarding **READ INTO**. In COBOL 74, the semantics for the **MOVE** of the record to the **INTO** identifier are not supplied. For a file with multiple elementary records, it is not stated whether any conversion of data takes place or whether a group move is performed. Different COBOL 74 compilers may produce different results for such **RETURN INTO** statements. In COBOL 85, the rules clarify the type of implicit **MOVE** expected.

If conversion is required, it will require knowing what precedence was used by a former compiler when dealing with multiple (conflicting) receiving field data descriptions. The program must then singularly define the **INTO** field with this same data description.

The National Bureau of Standards, in its analysis of the COBOL 85 language, considers this changed feature to be of *intermediate complexity* requiring minor programming-logic modifications. Much of the conversion logic can be handled by an automatic Language Conversion Program (LCP).

Segmentation   (Obsolete)

Independent segments are obsolete.

The concept of *independent segments* is an obsolete language element. All segments are either "fixed" or "fixed-overlayable." All segments behave as if they were resident in the computer at all times. It should be transparent to programmers whether or not a segment is permanently or temporarily resident in the computer. Since independent segments are obsolete, the **SEGMENT-LIMIT** clause of the **OBJECT-COMPUTER** paragraph is obsolete as well.

```
OBJECT-COMPUTER.
       SEGMENT-LIMIT IS 75.
```

The concept of *independent segments* as well as the **SEGMENT-LIMIT** clause are supported in COBOL 85. They will be deleted from the standard when ANS COBOL 85 is fully revised (in 1995 perhaps).

If conversion is required, it can be detected automatically by a Language Conversion Program (LCP). If it is necessary for some segments to be "refreshed" each time they are loaded into the computer, these segments should be created in "stand-alone" executable programs and **CALL**ed into execution when appropriate. **IS INITIAL** should be specified in the **PROGRAM-ID** entry to assure that a "fresh" (initialized) version of the program is loaded each time.

STOP   (Change)

The **STOP RUN** statement implicity **CLOSE**s all files.

In COBOL 74, the status of files, which remain **OPEN**ed

at the time of run completion, is not specified; this situation could lead to errors in some cases.

In COBOL 85, however, the **STOP RUN** statement implicitly **CLOSE**s all **OPEN**ed files. This change eliminates an undefined situation and increases program portability.

It is not clear under what circumstances a program would ever want files to remain **OPEN**ed after the execution of a **STOP RUN** statement. No conversion is suggested.

STOP RUN statement clears queues.

In COBOL 85, if the run unit has been accessing messages, the **STOP RUN** statement causes the Message Control System (MCS) to eliminate from the queue any message partially received by that run unit.

In COBOL 74, what happens to partially received messages when a run unit executes a **STOP RUN** statement is undefined.

Conversion is likely never to be necessary since so few programs in existence today use the Message Control System specified in American National Standard COBOL 74.

The **STOP "literal"** statement is obsolete.

The **STOP "literal"** format of the **STOP** statement which causes the program execution to pause while waiting for some "operations" response has been made obsolete. In this age of multitasking computers, such a feature could be disruptive.

The National Bureau of Standards, considers these changed features to be of *intermediate complexity* requiring minor programming-logic modifications. Much of the conversion logic can be handled by an automatic Language Conversion Program (LCP).

STRING   (Change)

> The order of evaluating subscripts in a **STRING** statement
> is defined.

In COBOL 85, the evaluation of subscripts in the **STRING**
statement is done once, before the first operation in the execution of the **STRING** statement. This order is undefined in
COBOL 74, and this change will increase COBOL program
portability.

Given the following **WORKING-STORAGE** items,

```
01   A               PIC  X(100).
01   B.
     03   FILLER      PIC  X(20).
     03   PNTR        PIC  99.
     03   FILLER      PIC  X(78).
01   C-TABLE.
     03   C           PIC  999     OCCURS 10 TIMES.
```

the subscript, **PNTR**, is contained in the receiving item **B** and
may be "overwritten" by the operation of the following **STRING**
statement.

```
    . . . STRING        A   DELIMITED BY SPACE
           INTO         B
           WITH POINTER C(PNTR)
```

In COBOL 85, the subscript in **C (PNTR)** is evaluated once,
prior to the **STRING** operation. Conversion from COBOL 74
is unlikely to be necessary.

If conversion is required, it can be detected automatically
by a Language Conversion Program. If the program must use
different values of the data items in a **STRING** statement (different from their values just prior to the execution of the **STRING**
statement), those values must be captured and stored and used
in place of the data items now being used.

The National Bureau of Standards, in its analysis of the

COBOL 85 language, considers this changed feature to be of *low complexity* requiring few programming-logic modifications. Most of the conversion logic can be handled by an automatic Language Conversion Program (LCP).

UNSTRING   (Change)

> The order of evaluating subscripts in an **UNSTRING** statement is defined.

In the COBOL 85 **UNSTRING** statement, any subscripting associated with the delimiter identifiers is evaluated once, immediately before the examination of the sending fields for the delimiters.

In COBOL 74, the order of evaluation of subscripts is not specified; this change eliminates an implementor-defined feature and improves portability.

If conversion is required, it can be detected automatically by a Language Conversion Program. If the program must use different values of the data items in a **UNSTRING** statement (different from their values just prior to the execution of the **UNSTRING** statement), those values must be captured and stored and used in place of the data items now being used.

Given the following **WORKING-STORAGE** items,

```
01  A              PICTURE X(100).
01  B.
   03   FILLER     PICTURE X(20).
   03   PNTR       PICTURE 99.
   03   FILLER     PICTURE X(78).
01  C-TABLE.
   03   C          PICTURE 999
                   OCCURS 10 TIMES.
01  D              PICTURE X(10).
01  DEL            OCCURS 14 TIMES
                   PICTURE X.
```

the subscript, **PNTR**, is contained in the receiving item **B**, and may be overwritten by the operation of the **UNSTRING** statement that follows.

```
UNSTRING        A    DELIMITED BY DEL (PNTR)
   INTO         B, D
   WITH POINTER PNTR.
```

In COBOL 85, the subscript in the **DELIMITER**, **DEL (PNTR)** is evaluated once, prior to the **UNSTRING** operation. This **DELIMITER** remains static during the entire **UNSTRING** operation.

In COBOL 74, the subscript in **DEL (PNTR)** is reevaluated prior to sending the second string of characters to **C**.

Conversion from COBOL 74 can be accomplished by using a new **DELIMITER** subscript, **NEW-PNTR**, which is not contained in the receiving item **B**.

```
UNSTRING A DELIMITED  BY   DEL(NEW-PNTR)
           INTO B, C
           WITH  POINTER  NEW-PNTR
```

The National Bureau of Standards, in its analysis of the COBOL 85 language, considers this changed feature to be of *low complexity* requiring no programming-logic modifications. Most of the conversion logic can be handled by an automatic Language Conversion Program (LCP).

Variable-length Tables (Change)

> There are new rules for determining the size of variable-length tables.

In COBOL 85, when a receiving item is a variable-length data item and contains the object of the **DEPENDING ON** phrase (of an **OCCURS** clause), the maximum length of the item will be used. In COBOL 74, the actual rather than the maximum length is used.

In COBOL 74, the length of such a receiving item is computed based on the value of the data item in the **DEPENDING ON** phrase prior to the execution of the procedural statement. The COBOL 74 rules for a **READ INTO** statement can result in the loss of data. Data is lost if the value of the **DEPENDING ON** data item is not set to indicate the length of the record to be read before the **READ** takes place. Many current COBOL 74 compilers actually use the rules as specified in COBOL 85 (as an implementor extension to the COBOL 74 compiler).

If the conversion is required, that is, if a COBOL 74 program requires the actual value of **NUMBER-OF-PERIODS** to be used to determine the size of the table, the following conversion strategy is suggested.

A new data item, containing the value of **TABLE-SIZE**, should be created. The remainder of the input-record is immaterial and can be truncated or defined as **FILLER**. The **OCCURS DEPENDING ON** clause of **PERIOD-AMOUNT** should be changed to reference this new data item: **TABLE-SIZE**.

```
01    TABLE-SIZE            PIC 99.
01    PERIOD-TABLE.
   03    NUMBER-OF-PERIODS  PIC 99.
   03    PERIOD-AMOUNT      PIC S9(6)V99
                            OCCURS 12 TIMES DEPENDING ON TABLE-SIZE.


      MOVE NUMBER-OF-PERIODS TO TABLE-SIZE
      MOVE FILE-TABLE-OF-VALUES TO PERIOD-TABLE.
```

This is one of the serious incompatibilities remaining in COBOL 85. The National Bureau of Standards in its analysis of the new COBOL 85 language concurs that this is one of four principal incompatibilities. In that same analysis, NBS considers this changed feature to be of *intermediate complexity* requiring minor programming-logic modifications. Much of the conversion logic can be handled by an automatic Language Conversion Program (LCP).

If conversion is required, that is, if it is important that the size of a table be determined by the value of the **DEPENDING ON** variable prior to executing the **READ INTO** statement, that value must be captured and stored just prior to the **READ** statement. The object of the **DEPENDING ON** phrase should then refer to this stored data item.

WRITE ADVANCING   (Change)

New restrictions on the **WRITE** statement have been added.

The phrases **ADVANCING PAGE** and **END-OF-PAGE** must not both be specified in a single **WRITE** statement.

In COBOL 74, it is syntactically possible to specify both of these phrases within one **WRITE** statement; no rules are provided to explain the behavior, or semantics, of such a statement; its behavior therefore is implementor-defined.

In COBOL 85, attempting the actions of these two phrases in one statement is considered illogical. This change to COBOL removes an implementor-defined feature and thereby increases COBOL program portability.

As it is not clear what behavior is intended by the inclusion of both phrases in the same **WRITE** statement, no conversion is suggested.

The National Bureau of Standards considers this changed feature to be of *low complexity* requiring few programming-logic modifications. Most of the required logic can be handled by an automatic Language Conversion Program (LCP).

V

COBOL 85

Appendices

APPENDIX A
Summary of COBOL 85 Features

Differences: COBOL 85 - COBOL 74

The following list of differences between COBOL 85 and COBOL 74 is divided into three sections. The first section contains *new* features in COBOL 85: additions to the language or a relaxation of previous restrictions. None of these items will cause incompatibilities with existing ANS COBOL 74 (or earlier) programs (except perhaps the new reserved words associated with new verbs or phrases).

The second section contains a list of *changes* in COBOL 85 that can impact existing programs. These changes are for the most part clarifications of previously ambiguous rules or implementor-defined features of COBOL 74.

The third section contains a list of *obsolete* language elements. These are features that will remain in the COBOL 85 language although marked for deletion in the subsequent revision. (1994 perhaps?) This section will serve as an early warning system to the COBOL user community.

COBOL 85: New Features

- Lowercase letters equivalent to uppercase letters (except in nonnumeric literals)
- Colon(:) character added to COBOL character set (for use in Reference Modification)
- Interchangeable separators (comma, semicolon, space)
- User-defined words and system-names may be the same

- New **SYMBOLIC-CHARACTER** clause for nonprintable characters
- Nonnumeric literal size limit is 160
- Figurative constant **ZERO** allowed in arithmetic expressions
- Uniqueness of reference not required
- Fifty levels of qualification
- Seven levels of subscripting
- Relative subscripting
- Mixing data-names and indexes in a subscript allowed
- Reference modification (substring facility)
- Sequence number may contain nonnumeric characters
- **END PROGRAM** header
- Nested source programs
- **INITIAL** clause in **PROGRAM-ID** paragraph
- **COMMON** clause in **PROGRAM-ID** paragraph
- **ENVIRONMENT DIVISION** is optional
- **CONFIGURATION SECTION** is optional
- **SOURCE-COMPUTER** paragraph is optional
- **OBJECT-COMPUTER** paragraph is optional
- **FILE-CONTROL** entries are optional
- **I-O-CONTROL** entries are optional
- **I-O-CONTROL** entries may be in any order
- A switch in **SPECIAL-NAMES** paragraph need not specify **ON/OFF STATUS** name
- Optional word **IS** in **SPECIAL-NAMES** paragraph
- **STANDARD-2** (ISO ASCII) option in **ALPHABET** clause
- **OPTIONAL** phrase in **FILE-CONTROL** can apply to **RELATIVE** or **INDEXED** files opened in **INPUT**, **I-O** and **EXTEND** modes

- The words **ORGANIZATION IS** in the **FILE-CONTROL** entry are optional
- **CODF-SET** clause may be specified for any **SEQUEN-TIAL** file
- New **RECORD DELIMITER** clause specifies a method to determine variable-length record size
- New **PADDING CHARACTER** clause
- **DATA DIVISION** is optional
- **LABEL RECORDS** clause is optional
- In the **LINAGE** clause, data-names may be qualified
- New **EXTERNAL** clause
- New **GLOBAL** clause
- **FILLER** may be an **01** Level item
- The word **FILLER** is optional
- In the **OCCURS** clause, the minimum number of occurrences is zero

- **PICTURE** character-string continuation
- **PICTURE** clause may conclude with a period or a comma
- **RECORD VARYING** clause for variable-length records
- **REDEFINES** clause with unequal data items
- Multiple **SIGN** clauses
- **SIGN** clause **REPORT SECTION**
- **SYNCHRONIZED** clause for **INDEX**
- Communication Description (**CD**) entries may be in any order
- New **FOR I-O** phrase in Communication Description entry
- **PROCEDURE DIVISION** is optional
- **PROCEDURE DIVISION** header need not contain only **LINKAGE SECTION** data items

- Segment-number **O**
- New Scope Terminators (19) for nested conditional statements (**END-IF**, **END-ADD**, etc.)
- New **DAY-OF-WEEK** phrase of **ACCEPT** statement
- In **ADD** statement, **TO** and **GIVING** allowed together
- New **CALL BY CONTENT** for data protection
- In **CALL** statement, data-names need not be Level **01** or Level **77** items
- **CLOSE REEL/UNIT** may be specified for single **REEL/UNIT** files
- **CLOSE FOR REMOVAL** may be specified for **SEQUENTIAL** single **REEL/UNIT** files
- New **CONTINUE** statement
- New **DISPLAY WITH NO ADVANCING**
- New **EVALUATE** statement
- **EXIT PROGRAM** statement need not be in a separate paragraph
- **GO TO . . . DEPENDING ON . ..** statement may specify only one operand
- **IF . . . THEN . . . ELSE . . . END-IF** format
- New **INITIALIZE** statement
- In **INSPECT**, **ALL/LEADING** may be distributed over identifier series
- In **INSPECT**, multiple **REPLACING** allowed
- In **INSPECT**, **BEFORE/AFTER** allowed together
- New **INSPECT CONVERTING** statement
- In **MERGE**, multiple **GIVING** files allowed
- In **MERGE**, files may contain variable-length records
- In **MERGE**, **USING/GIVING** files may be **RELATIVE** or **INDEXED**

- In **MERGE**, **INPUT/OUTPUT** procedures may access (and be accessed by) main section paragraphs
- De-edited **MOVE**
- **EXTEND** phrase of the **OPEN** statement allowed for **RELATIVE** and **INDEXED** files

- New **PURGE** statement
- In-line **PERFORM**
- **PERFORM WITH TEST AFTER/BEFORE**
- **PERFORM** with multiple (up to six) **AFTER** phrases
- Variable-length records allowed with **READ INTO**
- **READ NEXT** allowed for **SEQUENTIAL** files
- New **REPLACE** statement
- Variable-length records allowed with **RETURN INTO**
- **REWRITE** records of different lengths
- **SEND REPLACING**
- **SET** statement with mixed receiving identifiers (subscripts, index items, indexes)

- **SET** condition to **TRUE**
- In **SORT**, multiple **GIVING** files allowed
- In **SORT**, files may contain variable-length records
- In **SORT**, **USING/GIVING** files may be **RELATIVE** or **INDEXED**
- In **SORT**, **INPUT/OUTPUT** procedures may access (and be accessed by) main section paragraphs

- **USE** declaratives with file-names takes precedence over **USE** with **OPEN** mode

- **USE GLOBAL BEFORE REPORTING** statement
- New user-defined **CLASS**
- New **USAGE IS BINARY/PACKAGED-DECIMAL**

- Alternative conditional branches (**NOT AT END, NOT ON SIZE ERROR**, etc.)
- **ASSIGN** clause may specify a nonnumeric literal
- **BLOCK CONTAINS** clause is optional
- **VALUE** clause may be specified with an item containing an **OCCURS** clause
- New relational operators **> =** and **< =**
- **DISPLAY ALL "literal"** allowed

COBOL 85: Changes

- Length of **ALL "literal"** is length of string
- Alphabet-name clause uses keyword **ALPHABET**
- Collating sequence of **INDEXED** file is **NATIVE**
- **CURRENCY SIGN** literal cannot be figurative constant
- **RELATIVE KEY** cannot contain **P** in **PICTURE** description
- Files in **MULTIPLE FILE TAPE** clause must have similar labels
- Files with a **LINAGE** clause must not be opened in **EXTEND** mode
- **FOOTING** phrase must be specified for **END-OF-PAGE** condition
- Variable-length item uses maximum length in some circumstances
- **PIC P** with incompatible data interpreted differently
- **PROCEDURE DIVISION USING** item must not have **REDEFINES** clause
- Exponentiation specified

- Incomplete evaluation within complex conditional expressions
- **ALPHABETIC** class test includes lowercase
- **CANCEL** closes all opened files
- **CLOSE WITH NO REWIND** not allowed with **REEL/UNIT** phrase
- **COPY** in comment-entry will be ignored
- **COPY** with **DEBUG** may be ignored in some circumstances
- **DISPLAY** statement positioning specified
- Order of evaluation of subscripts in **DIVIDE** specified
- Implicit **EXIT PROGRAM** if no next statement
- **EXIT PROGRAM** terminates range of left-open **PERFORM** paragraphs
- Order of evaluation of subscripts in **INSPECT** specified
- **MERGE** files cannot use **SAME AREA**
- Order of initialization of **PERFORM** identifiers specified
- Order of augmenting and setting nested **PERFORM** identifiers changed
- Order of evaluation of subscripts in **PERFORM VARYING** specified
- **READ INTO** not allowed for two different record descriptions
- Qualified queue name required in **RECEIVE** statement
- **RETURN INTO** not allowed for two different record descriptions
- **STOP RUN** closes all files
- **STOP RUN** clears queues
- Order of evaluation of subscripts in **STRING** specified
- Order of evaluation of subscripts in **UNSTRING** specified

- Cannot specify both **ADVANCING** and **END-OF-PAGE**
- Concept of file position indicator replaced current record pointer
- Change file pointer initialization after **OPEN** statement
- Change semantics of **READ NEXT** after **REWRITE** statement
- Forty-nine new reserved words
- New I-O status codes
- New communication status-key values
- New communication error keys

COBOL 85: Obsolete Elements

Features that have been identified as "obsolete" have the following characteristics:

1. Implementors must include them in ANS COBOL 85 (i.e., they are not necessarily optional).
2. These features will definitely be deleted in the subsequent COBOL revision (unless of course ANSI X3J4 changes this rule).
3. Compilers must provide an optional "warning flag" for programmers to highlight the occurrence of any obsolete language element in a program.
4. Obsolete language elements will not be modified, enhanced or maintained by the ANSI COBOL committee.
5. The interaction between obsolete elements and other language elements is undefined.
6. Any feature to be deleted from COBOL in the future must first be placed in the "Obsolete" category in order to give the COBOL community some time to deal with potential conversion problems.

- In the **IDENTIFICATION DIVISION**, the following comment entries:

     AUTHOR
     INSTALLATION
     DATE-WRITTEN
     DATE-COMPILED
     SECURITY

- In the **FD**, (File Description), the following entries:

     LABEL RECORDS clause
     VALUE OF clause
     DATA RECORD clause

- The literal variation of the **STOP** statement

- The Debug facility containing **DEBUG-ITEM** and the **USE FOR DEBUGGING** statement

- **ENTER** statement

- **RERUN** statement

- **ALTER** statement

- Independent segments and the **SEGMENT-LIMIT** clause in the **OBJECT-COMPUTER** paragraph

- **ALL** "literal" greater than one character with numeric items

- The **REVERSED** option in the **OPEN** statement

- The **MEMORY SIZE** clause in the **OBJECT-COMPUTER** paragraph

- The **WITH KEY** phrase in the **ENABLE** and **DISABLE** statements

- Two-for-one-character substitution

APPENDIX B
COBOL 85 Reserved Words

ACCEPT
ACCESS
ADD
ADVANCING
AFTER
ALL
ALPHABET
ALPHABETIC
ALPHABETIC-LOWER
ALPHABETIC-UPPER
ALPHANUMERIC
ALPHANUMERIC-EDITED
ALSO
ALTER
ALTERNATE
AND
ANY
ARE
AREA
AREAS
ASCENDING
ASSIGN
AT
AUTHOR

BEFORE
BINARY
BLANK
BLOCK
BOTTOM
BY

CALL
CANCEL
CD
CF
CH
CHARACTER
CHARACTERS
CLASS
CLOCK-UNITS
CLOSE
COBOL
CODE
CODE-SET
COLLATING
COLUMN
COMMA
COMMON
COMMUNICATION
COMP
COMPUTATIONAL
COMPUTE
CONFIGURATION
CONTAINS
CONTENT
CONTINUE
CONTROL
CONTROLS
CONVERTING
COPY
CORR
CORRESPONDING

COUNT
CURRENCY

DATA
DATE
DATE-COMPILED
DATE-WRITTEN
DAY
DAY-OF-WEEK
DE
DEBUG-CONTENTS
DEBUT-ITEM
DEBUG-LINE
DEBUG-NAME
DEBUG-SUB-1
DEBUG-SUB-2
DEBUG-SUB-3
DEBUGGING
DECIMAL-POINT
DECLARATIVES
DELETE
DELIMITED
DELIMITER
DEPENDING
DESCENDING
DESTINATION
DETAIL
DISABLE
DISPLAY
DIVIDE
DIVISION
DOWN
DUPLICATES
DYNAMIC

EGI

ELSE
EMI
ENABLE
END
END-ADD
END-CALL
END-COMPUTE
END-DELETE
END-DIVIDE
END-EVALUATE
END-IF
END-MULTIPLY
END-OF-PAGE
END-PERFORM
END-READ
END-RECEIVE
END-RETURN
END-REWRITE
END-SEARCH
END-START
END-STRING
END-SUBTRACT
END-UNSTRING
END-WRITE
ENTER
ENVIRONMENT
EOP
EQUAL
ERROR
ESI
EVALUATE
EVERY
EXCEPTION
EXIT
EXTEND
EXTERNAL

FALSE
FD
FILE
FILE-CONTROL
FILLER
FINAL
FIRST
FOOTING
FOR
FROM

GENERATE
GIVING
GLOBAL
GO
GREATER
GROUP

HEADING
HIGH-VALUE
HIGH-VALUES

I-O
I-O-CONTROL
IDENTIFICATION
IF
IN
INDEX
INDEXED
INDICATE
INITIAL
INITIALIZE
INITIATE
INPUT
INPUT-OUTPUT
INSPECT

INSTALLATION
INTO
INVALID
IS

JUST
JUSTIFIED

KEY

LABEL
LAST
LEADING
LEFT
LENGTH
LESS
LIMIT
LIMITS
LINAGE
LINAGE-COUNTER
LINE
LINE-COUNTER
LINES
LINKAGE
LOCK
LOW-VALUE
LOW-VALUES

MEMORY
MERGE
MESSAGE
MODE
MODULES
MOVE
MULTIPLE
MULTIPLY

NATIVE
NEGATIVE
NEXT
NO
NOT
NUMBER
NUMERIC
NUMERIC-EDITED

OBJECT-COMPUTER
OCCURS
OF
OFF
OMITTED
ON
OPEN
OPTIONAL
OR
ORDER
ORGANIZATION
OTHER
OUTPUT
OVERFLOW

PACKED-DECIMAL
PADDING
PAGE
PAGE-COUNTER
PERFORM
PF
PH
PIC
PICTURE
PLUS
POINTER
POSITION

POSITIVE
PRINTING
PROCEDURE
PROCEDURES
PROCEED
PROGRAM
PROGRAM-ID
PURGE

QUEUE
QUOTE
QUOTES

RANDOM
RD
READ
RECEIVE
RECORD
RECORDS
REDEFINES
REEL
REFERENCE
REFERENCES
RELATIVE
RELEASE
REMAINDER
REMOVAL
RENAMES
REPLACE
REPLACING
REPORT
REPORTING
REPORTS
RERUN
RESERVE
RESET

RETURN
REVERSED
REWIND
REWRITE
RF
RH
RIGHT
ROUNDED
RUN

SAME
SD
SEARCH
SECTION
SECURITY
SEGMENT
SEGMENT-LIMIT
SELECT
SEND
SENTENCE
SEPARATE
SEQUENCE
SEQUENTIAL
SET
SIGN
SIZE
SORT
SORT-MERGE
SOURCE
SOURCE-COMPUTER
SPACE
SPACES
SPECIAL-NAMES
STANDARD
STANDARD-1
STANDARD-2

START
STATUS
STOP
STRING
SUB-QUEUE-1
SUB-QUEUE-2
SUB-QUEUE-3
SUBTRACT
SUM
SUPPRESS
SYMBOLIC
SYNC
SYNCHRONIZED

TABLE
TALLYING
TAPE
TERMINAL
TERMINATE
TEST
TEXT
THAN
THEN
THROUGH
THRU
TIME
TIMES
TO
TOP
TRAILING
TRUE
TYPE

UNIT
UNSTRING
UNTIL

UP	ZERO
UPON	ZEROES
USAGE	ZEROS
USE	
USING	+
	−
VALUE	*
VALUES	/
VARYING	**
	>
WHEN	<
WITH	=
WORDS	>=
WORKING-STORAGE	<=
WRITE	

APPENDIX C
COBOL 68 Syntax Skeleton

Identification division

       IDENTIFICATION   DIVISION.
       PROGRAM-ID. program-name.
       [AUTHOR. [comment-entry] . . .]
       [INSTALLATION. [comment-entry] . . .]
       [DATE-WRITTEN. [comment-entry] . . .]
       [DATE-COMPILED. [comment-entry] . . .]
       [SECURITY. [comment-entry] . . .]
       [REMARKS. [comment-entry] . . .]

Environment division

       ENVIRONMENT   DIVISION.

Configuration section

       CONFIGURATION   SECTION.

Source-computer Format 1:

       SOURCE-COMPUTER.   COPY library-name

$$\left[\text{REPLACING word-1 } \underline{BY} \left\{ \begin{array}{l} \text{word-2} \\ \text{identifier-1} \\ \text{literal-1} \end{array} \right\} \right.$$

$$\left. \left[\text{, word-3 } \underline{BY} \left\{ \begin{array}{l} \text{word-4} \\ \text{identifier-2} \\ \text{literal-2} \end{array} \right\} \right] \cdots \right].$$

Format 2:

       SOURCE-COMPUTER.   computer-name.

Object-computer Format 1:

       OBJECT-COMPUTER.   COPY library-name

$$\left[\text{REPLACING word-1 } \underline{BY} \left\{ \begin{array}{l} \text{word-2} \\ \text{identifier-1} \\ \text{literal-1} \end{array} \right\} \right.$$

$$\left. \left[\text{, word-3 } \underline{BY} \left\{ \begin{array}{l} \text{word-4} \\ \text{identifier-2} \\ \text{literal-2} \end{array} \right\} \right] \cdots \right].$$

Format 2:

       OBJECT-COMPUTER.   computer-name

$$\left[\text{, } \underline{MEMORY} \text{ SIZE integer} \left\{ \begin{array}{l} \underline{WORDS} \\ \underline{CHARACTERS} \\ \underline{MODULES} \end{array} \right\} \right]$$

       [, SEGMENT-LIMIT IS priority-number]

Special-names
Format 1:

SPECIAL-NAMES. <u>COPY</u> library-name

$$\left[\underline{\text{REPLACING}} \text{ word-1 } \underline{\text{BY}} \left\{ \begin{array}{l} \text{word-2} \\ \text{identifier-1} \\ \text{literal-1} \end{array} \right\} \right.$$

$$\left. \left[, \text{word-3 } \underline{\text{BY}} \left\{ \begin{array}{l} \text{word-4} \\ \text{identifier-2} \\ \text{literal-2} \end{array} \right\} \right] \dots \right] .$$

Format 2:

SPECIAL-NAMES.   [implementor-name

$$\left\{ \begin{array}{l} \underline{\text{IS}} \text{ mnemonic-name } \quad [, \underline{\text{ON}} \text{ STATUS } \underline{\text{IS}} \text{ condition-name-1} \\ \underline{\text{IS}} \text{ mnemonic-name } \quad [, \underline{\text{OFF}} \text{ STATUS } \underline{\text{IS}} \text{ condition-name-2} \\ \underline{\text{ON}} \text{ STATUS } \underline{\text{IS}} \text{ condition-name-1} \\ \underline{\text{OFF}} \text{ STATUS } \underline{\text{IS}} \text{ condition-name-2} \end{array} \right.$$

$$\left. \begin{array}{l} [, \underline{\text{OFF}} \text{ STATUS } \underline{\text{IS}} \text{ condition-name-2}]] \\ [, \underline{\text{ON}} \text{ STATUS } \underline{\text{IS}} \text{ condition-name-1}]] \\ [, \underline{\text{OFF}} \text{ STATUS } \underline{\text{IS}} \text{ condition-name-2}] \\ [, \underline{\text{ON}} \text{ STATUS } \underline{\text{IS}} \text{ condition-name-1}] \end{array} \right\} \dots \right]$$

[, <u>CURRENCY</u> SIGN <u>IS</u> literal]   [, <u>DECIMAL-POINT</u> <u>IS</u> <u>COMMA</u>] .

Input-output section

INPUT-OUTPUT <u>SECTION</u>.

File-control
Format 1:

FILE-CONTROL. <u>COPY</u> library-name

$$\left[\underline{\text{REPLACING}} \text{ word-1 } \underline{\text{BY}} \left\{ \begin{array}{l} \text{word-2} \\ \text{identifier-1} \\ \text{literal-1} \end{array} \right\} \right.$$

$$\left. \left[, \text{word-3 } \underline{\text{BY}} \left\{ \begin{array}{l} \text{word-4} \\ \text{identifier-2} \\ \text{literal-2} \end{array} \right\} \right] \dots \right] .$$

Format 2:

FILE-CONTROL. {SELECT [OPTIONAL] file-name
ASSIGN TO [integer-1] implementor-name-1 [, implementor-name-2] ...

$$\left[\text{FOR } \underline{\text{MULTIPLE}} \left\{ \begin{array}{l} \underline{\text{REEL}} \\ \underline{\text{UNIT}} \end{array} \right\} \right] \left[, \underline{\text{RESERVE}} \left\{ \begin{array}{l} \text{integer-2} \\ \underline{\text{NO}} \end{array} \right\} \text{ALTERNATE} \left[\begin{array}{l} \text{AREA} \\ \text{AREAS} \end{array} \right] \right]$$

$$\left[, \left\{ \begin{array}{l} \underline{\text{FILE-LIMIT}} \underline{\text{IS}} \\ \underline{\text{FILE-LIMITS}} \underline{\text{ARE}} \end{array} \right\} \left\{ \begin{array}{l} \text{data-name-1} \\ \text{literal-1} \end{array} \right\} \underline{\text{THRU}} \left\{ \begin{array}{l} \text{data-name-2} \\ \text{literal-2} \end{array} \right\} \right.$$

$$\left. \left[, \left\{ \begin{array}{l} \text{data-name-3} \\ \text{literal-3} \end{array} \right\} \underline{\text{THRU}} \left\{ \begin{array}{l} \text{data-name-4} \\ \text{literal-4} \end{array} \right\} \right] \dots \right]$$

$$\left[, \underline{\text{ACCESS}} \text{ MODE } \underline{\text{IS}} \left\{ \begin{array}{l} \underline{\text{SEQUENTIAL}} \\ \underline{\text{RANDOM}} \end{array} \right\} \right]$$

[, PROCESSING MODE IS SEQUENTIAL]
[, ACTUAL KEY IS data-name-5] . } ...

Format 3:

FILE-CONTROL. { SELECT file-name ASSIGN TO implementor-name-1
[, implementor-name-2] ... OR implementor-name-3

$$\left[, \text{implementor-name-4} \right] \dots \left[\text{FOR } \underline{\text{MULTIPLE}} \left\{ \begin{array}{l} \underline{\text{REEL}} \\ \underline{\text{UNIT}} \end{array} \right\} \right] . \} \dots$$

I-O-Control
Format 1:

I-O-CONTROL. COPY library-name

$$\left[\underline{\text{REPLACING}} \text{ word-1 } \underline{\text{BY}} \left\{ \begin{array}{l} \text{word-2} \\ \text{identifier-1} \\ \text{literal-1} \end{array} \right\} \right.$$

$$\left. \left[, \text{word-3 } \underline{\text{BY}} \left\{ \begin{array}{l} \text{word-4} \\ \text{identifier-2} \\ \text{literal-2} \end{array} \right\} \right] \dots \right] .$$

Format 2:

$$\text{I-O-CONTROL.} \left[; \underline{\text{RERUN}} \left[\underline{\text{ON}} \left\{ \begin{array}{l} \text{file-name-1} \\ \text{implementor-name} \end{array} \right\} \right] \right.$$

$$\underline{\text{EVERY}} \left\{ \begin{array}{l} \left\{ [\underline{\text{END OF}}] \left\{ \begin{array}{l} \underline{\text{REEL}} \\ \underline{\text{UNIT}} \end{array} \right\} \right\} \text{ OF file-name-2} \\ \text{integer-1 } \underline{\text{RECORDS}} \\ \text{integer-2 } \underline{\text{CLOCK-UNITS}} \\ \text{condition-name} \end{array} \right\} \dots \right]$$

$$\left[; \underline{\text{SAME}} \left[\left\{ \begin{array}{l} \underline{\text{RECORD}} \\ \underline{\text{SORT}} \end{array} \right\} \right] \text{ AREA FOR file-name-3 } \{ , \text{file-name-4} \} \dots \right] \dots$$

[; MULTIPLE FILE TAPE CONTAINS file-name-5 [POSITION integer-3]
[, file-name-6 [POSITION integer-4]] ...] ... .

data division

    <u>DATA</u> <u>DIVISION</u>.

file section

    <u>FILE</u> <u>SECTION</u>.

file description
Format 1:

    <u>FD</u> file-name; <u>COPY</u> library-name

$$\left[\ \underline{\text{REPLACING}}\ \text{word-1}\ \underline{\text{BY}}\ \left\{ \begin{array}{l} \text{word-2} \\ \text{identifier-1} \\ \text{literal-1} \end{array} \right\} \right.$$

$$\left. \left[\ ,\ \text{word-3}\ \underline{\text{BY}}\ \left\{ \begin{array}{l} \text{word-4} \\ \text{identifier-2} \\ \text{literal-2} \end{array} \right\} \right] \ \ldots \right] \ .$$

Format 2:

    <u>FD</u> file-name

$$\left[\ ;\ \underline{\text{BLOCK}}\ \text{CONTAINS}\ [\text{integer-1}\ \underline{\text{TO}}]\ \text{integer-2}\ \left\{ \begin{array}{l} \underline{\text{RECORDS}} \\ \underline{\text{CHARACTERS}} \end{array} \right\} \right]$$

$$\left[\ ;\ \underline{\text{DATA}}\ \left\{ \begin{array}{l} \underline{\text{RECORD}}\ \text{IS} \\ \underline{\text{RECORDS}}\ \text{ARE} \end{array} \right\}\ \text{data-name-1}\ [\ ,\ \text{data-name-2}]\ \ldots \right]$$

$$;\ \underline{\text{LABEL}}\ \left\{ \begin{array}{l} \underline{\text{RECORD}}\ \text{IS} \\ \underline{\text{RECORDS}}\ \text{ARE} \end{array} \right\}\ \left\{ \begin{array}{l} \underline{\text{STANDARD}} \\ \underline{\text{OMITTED}} \\ \text{data-name-3}\ [\ ,\ \text{data-name-4}]\ \ldots \end{array} \right\}$$

$$[\ ;\ \underline{\text{RECORD}}\ \text{CONTAINS}\ [\text{integer-3}\ \underline{\text{TO}}]\ \text{integer-4}\ \text{CHARACTERS}]$$

$$\left[\ ;\ \underline{\text{VALUE}}\ \underline{\text{OF}}\ \text{data-name-5}\ \text{IS} \left\{ \begin{array}{l} \text{data-name-6} \\ \text{literal-1} \end{array} \right\} \right.$$

$$\left. \left[\ ,\ \text{data-name-7}\ \text{IS} \left\{ \begin{array}{l} \text{data-name-8} \\ \text{literal-2} \end{array} \right\} \right] \ \ldots \right] \ .$$

Format 3:

FD file-name

$$\left[\text{.; } \underline{\text{BLOCK}} \text{ CONTAINS [integer-1 } \underline{\text{TO}} \text{] integer-2} \left\{ \begin{array}{l} \underline{\text{RECORDS}} \\ \underline{\text{CHARACTERS}} \end{array} \right\} \right]$$

$$\text{; } \underline{\text{LABEL}} \left\{ \begin{array}{l} \underline{\text{RECORD}} \text{ IS} \\ \underline{\text{RECORDS}} \text{ ARE} \end{array} \right\} \left\{ \begin{array}{l} \underline{\text{STANDARD}} \\ \underline{\text{OMITTED}} \\ \text{data-name-1 [, data-name-2] ...} \end{array} \right\}$$

[; RECORD CONTAINS [integer-3 TO] integer-4 CHARACTERS]

$$\text{; } \left\{ \begin{array}{l} \underline{\text{REPORT}} \text{ IS} \\ \underline{\text{REPORTS}} \text{ ARE} \end{array} \right\} \text{report-name-1 [, report-name-2] ...}$$

$$\left[\text{; } \underline{\text{VALUE}} \underline{\text{OF}} \text{ data-name-3 IS} \left\{ \begin{array}{l} \text{data-name-4} \\ \text{literal-1} \end{array} \right\} \right.$$

$$\left. , \text{data-name-5 IS} \left\{ \begin{array}{l} \text{data-name-6} \\ \text{literal-2} \end{array} \right\} \right] ... \right] .$$

Sort description
Format 1:

SD file-name; COPY library-name

$$\left[\underline{\text{REPLACING}} \text{ word-1 } \underline{\text{BY}} \left\{ \begin{array}{l} \text{word-4} \\ \text{identifier-1} \\ \text{literal-1} \end{array} \right\} \right.$$

$$\left[, \text{word-3 } \underline{\text{BY}} \left\{ \begin{array}{l} \text{word-4} \\ \text{identifier-2} \\ \text{literal-2} \end{array} \right\} \right] ... \right] .$$

Format 2:

SD file-name

$$\left[\text{; } \underline{\text{DATA}} \left\{ \begin{array}{l} \underline{\text{RECORD}} \text{ IS} \\ \underline{\text{RECORDS}} \text{ ARE} \end{array} \right\} \text{data-name-1 [, data-name-2] ...} \right]$$

[; RECORD CONTAINS [integer-1 TO] integer-2 CHARACTERS] .

Record description
Format 1:

01 data-name-1; COPY library-name

$$\left[\underline{\text{REPLACING}} \text{ word-1 } \underline{\text{BY}} \left\{ \begin{array}{l} \text{word-2} \\ \text{identifier-1} \\ \text{literal-1} \end{array} \right\} \right.$$

$$\left[, \text{word-3 } \underline{\text{BY}} \left\{ \begin{array}{l} \text{word-4} \\ \text{identifier-2} \\ \text{literal-2} \end{array} \right\} \right] ... \right] .$$

Format 2:

level-number $\left\{ \begin{array}{l} \text{data-name-1} \\ \underline{\text{FILLER}} \end{array} \right\}$ [; <u>REDEFINES</u> data-name-2]

[; <u>BLANK</u> WHEN <u>ZERO</u>]

$\left[\; \left\{ \begin{array}{l} \underline{\text{JUSTIFIED}} \\ \underline{\text{JUST}} \end{array} \right\} \text{RIGHT} \right]$

$\left[\; \underline{\text{OCCURS}} \left\{ \begin{array}{l} \text{integer-1 } \underline{\text{TO}} \text{ integer-2 TIMES [}\underline{\text{DEPENDING}} \text{ ON data-name-3]} \\ \text{integer-2 } \underline{\text{TIMES}} \end{array} \right\} \right.$

$\left. \left[\left\{ \begin{array}{l} \underline{\text{ASCENDING}} \\ \underline{\text{DESCENDING}} \end{array} \right\} \text{KEY IS data-name-4 [, data-name-5] } \ldots \right] \ldots \right.$

[<u>INDEXED</u> BY index-name-1 [, index-name-2] ...]]

$\left[\; \left\{ \begin{array}{l} \underline{\text{PICTURE}} \\ \underline{\text{PIC}} \end{array} \right\} \text{IS character-string} \right]$

$\left[\; \left\{ \begin{array}{l} \underline{\text{SYNCHRONIZED}} \\ \underline{\text{SYNC}} \end{array} \right\} \left[\begin{array}{l} \underline{\text{LEFT}} \\ \underline{\text{RIGHT}} \end{array} \right] \right]$

$\left[\; [\underline{\text{USAGE}} \text{ IS}] \left\{ \begin{array}{l} \underline{\text{COMPUTATIONAL}} \\ \underline{\text{COMP}} \\ \underline{\text{DISPLAY}} \\ \underline{\text{INDEX}} \end{array} \right\} \right]$

[; <u>VALUE</u> IS literal-3].

Format 3:

66 data-name-1; <u>RENAMES</u> data-name-2 [<u>THRU</u> data-name-3] .

Format 4:

88 condition-name

$\quad \; \left\{ \begin{array}{l} \underline{\text{VALUE}} \text{ IS} \\ \underline{\text{VALUES}} \text{ ARE} \end{array} \right\}$ literal-1 [<u>THRU</u> literal-2]

[, literal-3 [<u>THRU</u> literal-4]] ... .

Working storage section

<u>WORKING-STORAGE</u> <u>SECTION</u>.

Report section

<u>REPORT</u> <u>SECTION</u>.

Report description
Format 1:

<u>RD</u> report-name; <u>COPY</u> library-name

$\left[\underline{\text{REPLACING}} \text{ word-1 } \underline{\text{BY}} \left\{ \begin{array}{l} \text{word-2} \\ \text{identifier-1} \\ \text{literal-1} \end{array} \right\} \right.$

$\left. \left[\text{ , word-3 } \underline{\text{BY}} \left\{ \begin{array}{l} \text{word-4} \\ \text{identifier-2} \\ \text{literal-2} \end{array} \right\} \right] \ldots \right] .$

Format 2:

    <u>RD</u> report-name
      [; <u>CODE</u> mnemonic-name-1]

$$\left[\; ; \; \left\{ \begin{array}{l} \underline{\text{CONTROL}} \text{ IS} \\ \underline{\text{CONTROLS}} \text{ ARE} \end{array} \right\} \left\{ \begin{array}{l} \underline{\text{FINAL}} \\ \text{identifier-1} \; [\; , \; \text{identifier-2}] \; \ldots \\ \underline{\text{FINAL}}, \text{identifier-1} \; [\; , \; \text{identifier-2}] \; \ldots \end{array} \right\} \right]$$

$$\left[\; ; \; \underline{\text{PAGE}} \left[\begin{array}{l} \text{LIMIT IS} \\ \text{LIMITS ARE} \end{array} \right] \text{integer-1} \left\{ \begin{array}{l} \underline{\text{LINE}} \\ \underline{\text{LINES}} \end{array} \right\} [\; , \; \underline{\text{HEADING}} \text{ integer-2} \right.$$

      [, <u>FIRST</u> <u>DETAIL</u> integer-3] [, <u>LAST</u> <u>DETAIL</u> integer-4]
      [, <u>FOOTING</u> integer-5]] .

Report group description
Format 1:

    01 data-name-1; <u>COPY</u> library-name

$$\left[\underline{\text{REPLACING}} \text{ word-1 } \underline{\text{BY}} \left\{ \begin{array}{l} \text{word-2} \\ \text{identifier-1} \\ \text{literal-1} \end{array} \right\} \right.$$

$$\left[\; , \text{word-3 } \underline{\text{BY}} \left\{ \begin{array}{l} \text{word-4} \\ \text{identifier-2} \\ \text{literal-2} \end{array} \right\} \right] \; \ldots \; \right] .$$

Format 2:

01 [data-name-1]

$$
\left[\; ;\; \underline{\text{LINE}}\;\text{NUMBER}\;\text{IS}\;
\left\{
\begin{array}{l}
\text{integer-1} \\
\underline{\text{PLUS}}\;\text{integer-2} \\
\underline{\text{NEXT}}\;\underline{\text{PAGE}}
\end{array}
\right\}
\right]
$$

$$
\left[\; ;\; \underline{\text{NEXT}}\;\text{GROUP}\;\text{IS}\;
\left\{
\begin{array}{l}
\text{integer-3} \\
\underline{\text{PLUS}}\;\text{integer-4} \\
\underline{\text{NEXT}}\;\underline{\text{PAGE}}
\end{array}
\right\}
\right]
$$

$$
;\; \underline{\text{TYPE}}\;\text{IS}\;
\left\{
\begin{array}{l}
\underline{\text{REPORT}}\;\underline{\text{HEADING}} \\
\underline{\text{RH}} \\
\underline{\text{PAGE}}\;\underline{\text{HEADING}} \\
\underline{\text{PH}} \\
\left\{\begin{array}{l}\underline{\text{CONTROL}}\;\underline{\text{HEADING}}\\ \underline{\text{CH}}\end{array}\right\}\;\left\{\begin{array}{l}\text{identifier-1}\\ \underline{\text{FINAL}}\end{array}\right\} \\
\underline{\text{DETAIL}} \\
\underline{\text{DE}} \\
\left\{\begin{array}{l}\underline{\text{CONTROL}}\;\underline{\text{FOOTING}}\\ \underline{\text{CF}}\end{array}\right\}\;\left\{\begin{array}{l}\text{identifier-2}\\ \underline{\text{FINAL}}\end{array}\right\} \\
\underline{\text{PAGE}}\;\underline{\text{FOOTING}} \\
\underline{\text{PF}} \\
\underline{\text{REPORT}}\;\underline{\text{FOOTING}} \\
\underline{\text{RF}}
\end{array}
\right\}
$$

[; [<u>USAGE</u> IS] <u>DISPLAY</u>] .

Format 3:

    level-number [data-name-1]
        [; **BLANK** WHEN **ZERO**]
        [; **COLUMN** NUMBER IS integer-1]
        [; **GROUP** INDICATE]

$$\left[\; \left\{ \begin{array}{l} \textbf{JUSTIFIED} \\ \textbf{JUST} \end{array} \right\} \text{RIGHT} \right]$$

$$\left[\; \text{\underline{LINE}} \text{ NUMBER IS} \left\{ \begin{array}{l} \text{integer-2} \\ \textbf{PLUS} \text{ integer-3} \\ \textbf{NEXT} \; \textbf{PAGE} \end{array} \right\} \right]$$

$$\left[\; \left\{ \begin{array}{l} \textbf{PICTURE} \\ \textbf{PIC} \end{array} \right\} \text{IS character-string} \right]$$

$$\left[\; \text{\underline{RESET}} \text{ ON} \left\{ \begin{array}{l} \text{identifer-1} \\ \textbf{FINAL} \end{array} \right\} \right]$$

$$\left\{ \begin{array}{l} ; \; \textbf{SOURCE IS} \text{ identifier-2} \\ ; \; \textbf{\underline{SUM}} \text{ identifier-3 [, identifier-4] ...} [\textbf{UPON} \text{ data-name-2}] \\ ; \; \textbf{VALUE IS} \text{ literal-1} \end{array} \right\}$$

        [; [**USAGE** IS] **DISPLAY**].

Procedure division

   PROCEDURE DIVISION.

Accept

   ACCEPT identifier [**FROM** mnemonic-name]

Add
Format 1:

$$\underline{\textbf{ADD}} \left\{ \begin{array}{l} \text{identifier-1} \\ \text{literal-1} \end{array} \right\} \left[\begin{array}{l} , \text{ identifier-2} \\ , \text{ literal-2} \end{array} \right] ... \; \textbf{\underline{TO}} \text{ identifier-m} [\textbf{ROUNDED}]$$

        [, identifier-n [**ROUNDED**]] ...
        [; **ON** **SIZE** **ERROR** imperative-statement]

Format 2:

$$\underline{\textbf{ADD}} \left\{ \begin{array}{l} \text{identifier-1} \\ \text{literal-1} \end{array} \right\} , \left\{ \begin{array}{l} \text{identifier-2} \\ \text{literal-2} \end{array} \right\} \left[\begin{array}{l} , \text{ identifier-3} \\ , \text{ literal-3} \end{array} \right] ...$$

        GIVING identifier-m [**ROUNDED**]
        [; **ON** **SIZE** **ERROR** imperative-statement]

Format 3:

$$\text{\underline{ADD}} \left\{ \begin{array}{l} \text{\underline{CORRESPONDING}} \\ \text{\underline{CORR}} \end{array} \right\} \text{identifier-1} \ \text{\underline{TO}} \ \text{identifier-2} \ [\text{\underline{ROUNDED}}]$$

[; **ON** **SIZE** **ERROR** imperative-statement]

Alter

ALTER procedure-name-1 **TO** [**PROCEED** **TO**] procedure-name-2
   [, procedure-name-3 **TO** [**PROCEED** **TO**] procedure-name-4] . . .

Close

$$\text{\underline{CLOSE}} \ \text{file-name-1} \left[\begin{array}{l} \text{\underline{REEL}} \\ \text{\underline{UNIT}} \end{array} \right] \left[\text{WITH} \left\{ \begin{array}{l} \text{\underline{NO} REWIND} \\ \text{\underline{LOCK}} \end{array} \right\} \right]$$

$$\left[, \ \text{file-name-2} \left[\begin{array}{l} \text{\underline{REEL}} \\ \text{\underline{UNIT}} \end{array} \right] \left[\text{WITH} \left\{ \begin{array}{l} \text{\underline{NO} REWIND} \\ \text{\underline{LOCK}} \end{array} \right\} \right] \right] \ . . .$$

Compute

$$\text{\underline{COMPUTE}} \ \text{identifier-1} \ [\text{\underline{ROUNDED}}] = \left\{ \begin{array}{l} \text{identifier-2} \\ \text{literal-1} \\ \text{arithmetic-expression} \end{array} \right\}$$

[; **ON** **SIZE** **ERROR** imperative-statement]

Copy

COPY library-name

$$\left[\text{\underline{REPLACING}} \ \text{word-1} \ \text{\underline{BY}} \left\{ \begin{array}{l} \text{word-2} \\ \text{identifier-1} \\ \text{literal-1} \end{array} \right\} \right.$$

$$\left[, \ \text{word-3} \ \text{\underline{BY}} \left\{ \begin{array}{l} \text{word-4} \\ \text{identifier-2} \\ \text{literal-2} \end{array} \right\} \right] \ . . . \right] .$$

Declaratives

DECLARATIVES.
   {section-name **SECTION**. declarative-sentence
   {paragraph-name. {sentence} . . . } . . . } . . .
   END **DECLARATIVES**.

Display

$$\text{\underline{DISPLAY}} \left\{ \begin{array}{l} \text{literal-1} \\ \text{identifier-1} \end{array} \right\} \left[\begin{array}{l} , \ \text{literal-2} \\ , \ \text{identifier-2} \end{array} \right] \ . . . \ [\text{\underline{UPON}} \ \text{mnemonic-name}]$$

Divide
Format 1:

$$\underline{\text{DIVIDE}} \left\{ \begin{array}{l} \text{identifier-1} \\ \text{literal-1} \end{array} \right\} \underline{\text{INTO}} \text{ identifier-2 } [\underline{\text{ROUNDED}}]$$

[; ON **SIZE ERROR** imperative-statement]

Format 2:

$$\underline{\text{DIVIDE}} \left\{ \begin{array}{l} \text{identifier-1} \\ \text{literal-1} \end{array} \right\} \underline{\text{INTO}} \left\{ \begin{array}{l} \text{identifier-2} \\ \text{literal-2} \end{array} \right\}$$

GIVING identifier-3 [**ROUNDED**}
[; ON **SIZE ERROR** imperative-statement]

Format 3:

$$\underline{\text{DIVIDE}} \left\{ \begin{array}{l} \text{identifier-1} \\ \text{literal-1} \end{array} \right\} \underline{\text{BY}} \left\{ \begin{array}{l} \text{identifier-2} \\ \text{literal-2} \end{array} \right\}$$

GIVING identifier-3 [**ROUNDED**]
[; ON **SIZE ERROR** imperative-statement]

Format 4:

$$\underline{\text{DIVIDE}} \left\{ \begin{array}{l} \text{identifier-1} \\ \text{literal-1} \end{array} \right\} \underline{\text{INTO}} \left\{ \begin{array}{l} \text{identifier-2} \\ \text{literal-2} \end{array} \right\}$$

GIVING identifier-3 [**ROUNDED**] **REMAINDER** identifier-4
[; ON **SIZE ERROR** imperative-statement]

Format 5:

$$\underline{\text{DIVIDE}} \left\{ \begin{array}{l} \text{identifier-1} \\ \text{literal-1} \end{array} \right\} \underline{\text{BY}} \left\{ \begin{array}{l} \text{identifier-2} \\ \text{literal-2} \end{array} \right\}$$

GIVING identifier-3 [**ROUNDED**] **REMAINDER** identifier-4
[; ON **SIZE ERROR** imperative-statement]

Enter

ENTER language-name [routine-name].

Examine

EXAMINE identifier

$$\left\{ \begin{array}{l} \underline{\text{TALLYING}} \left\{ \begin{array}{l} \underline{\text{UNTIL}} \ \underline{\text{FIRST}} \\ \underline{\text{ALL}} \\ \underline{\text{LEADING}} \end{array} \right\} \text{literal-1} [\underline{\text{REPLACING}} \ \text{BY literal-2}] \\ \\ \underline{\text{REPLACING}} \left\{ \begin{array}{l} \underline{\text{ALL}} \\ \underline{\text{LEADING}} \\ [\underline{\text{UNTIL}}] \ \underline{\text{FIRST}} \end{array} \right\} \text{literal-3} \ \underline{\text{BY}} \ \text{literal-4} \end{array} \right\}$$

Exit

EXIT.

Generate

> GENERATE identifier

Go

Format 1:

> GO TO [procedure-name-1]

Format 2:

> GO TO procedure-name-1 [, procedure-name-2] . . .
> , procedure-name-n DEPENDING ON identifier

If

$$\text{IF condition;} \left\{ \begin{array}{l} \text{statement-1} \\ \underline{\text{NEXT}} \;\; \underline{\text{SENTENCE}} \end{array} \right\} ; \; \underline{\text{ELSE}} \left\{ \begin{array}{l} \text{statement-2} \\ \underline{\text{NEXT}} \;\; \underline{\text{SENTENCE}} \end{array} \right\}$$

Initiate

> INITIATE report-name-1 [, report-name-2] . . .

Move

Format 1:

$$\underline{\text{MOVE}} \left\{ \begin{array}{l} \text{identifier-1} \\ \text{literal-1} \end{array} \right\} \underline{\text{TO}} \text{ identifier-2 [, identifier-3] . . .}$$

Format 2:

$$\underline{\text{MOVE}} \left\{ \begin{array}{l} \underline{\text{CORRESPONDING}} \\ \underline{\text{CORR}} \end{array} \right\} \text{ identifier-1 } \underline{\text{TO}} \text{ identifier-2}$$

Multiply

Format 1:

$$\underline{\text{MULTIPLY}} \left\{ \begin{array}{l} \text{identifier-1} \\ \text{literal-1} \end{array} \right\} \underline{\text{BY}} \text{ identifier-2 [}\underline{\text{ROUNDED}}\text{]}$$

[; ON SIZE ERROR imperative-statement]

Format 2:

$$\underline{\text{MULTIPLY}} \left\{ \begin{array}{l} \text{identifier-1} \\ \text{literal-1} \end{array} \right\} \underline{\text{BY}} \left\{ \begin{array}{l} \text{identifier-2} \\ \text{literal-2} \end{array} \right\}$$

GIVING identifier-3 [ROUNDED]
[; ON SIZE ERROR imperative-statement]

Note

> NOTE character-string.

Open

$$\text{OPEN} \left\{ \begin{array}{l} \underline{\text{INPUT}} \text{ file-name-1} \left\{ \begin{array}{l} \underline{\text{REVERSED}} \\ \text{WITH } \underline{\text{NO}} \text{ REWIND} \end{array} \right\} \\ \underline{\text{OUTPUT}} \text{ file-name-3} \text{ [WITH } \underline{\text{NO}} \text{ REWIND]} \\ \underline{\text{I-O}} \text{ file-name-5} \end{array} \right.$$

$$\left. \left[\text{ , file-name-2} \left[\left\{ \begin{array}{l} \underline{\text{REVERSED}} \\ \text{WITH } \underline{\text{NO}} \text{ REWIND} \end{array} \right\} \right] \right] \cdots \right\} \cdots$$

[, file-name-4 [WITH <u>NO</u> REWIND]] ...
[, file-name-6] ...

Paragraph names

{paragraph-name. {sentence} ... } ...

Perform

Format 1:

<u>PERFORM</u> procedure-name-1 [<u>THRU</u> procedure-name-2]

Format 2:

$$\underline{\text{PERFORM}} \text{ procedure-name-1 } [\underline{\text{THRU}} \text{ procedure-name-2}] \left\{ \begin{array}{l} \text{identifier-1} \\ \text{integer-1} \end{array} \right\} \underline{\text{TIMES}}$$

Format 3:

<u>PERFORM</u> procedure-name-1 [<u>THRU</u> procedure-name-2] <u>UNTIL</u> condition-1

Format 4:

<u>PERFORM</u> procedure-name-1 [<u>THRU</u> procedure-name-2]

$$\underline{\text{VARYING}} \left\{ \begin{array}{l} \text{index-name-1} \\ \text{identifier-1} \end{array} \right\} \underline{\text{FROM}} \left\{ \begin{array}{l} \text{index-name-2} \\ \text{literal-2} \\ \text{identifier-2} \end{array} \right\}$$

$$\underline{\text{BY}} \left\{ \begin{array}{l} \text{literal-3} \\ \text{identifier-3} \end{array} \right\} \underline{\text{UNTIL}} \text{ condition-1}$$

$$\left[\underline{\text{AFTER}} \left\{ \begin{array}{l} \text{index-name-4} \\ \text{identifier-4} \end{array} \right\} \underline{\text{FROM}} \left\{ \begin{array}{l} \text{index-name-5} \\ \text{literal-5} \\ \text{identifier-5} \end{array} \right\} \right.$$

$$\underline{\text{BY}} \left\{ \begin{array}{l} \text{literal-6} \\ \text{identifier-6} \end{array} \right\} \underline{\text{UNTIL}} \text{ condition-2}$$

$$\left[\underline{\text{AFTER}} \left\{ \begin{array}{l} \text{index-name-7} \\ \text{identifier-7} \end{array} \right\} \underline{\text{FROM}} \left\{ \begin{array}{l} \text{index-name-8} \\ \text{literal-8} \\ \text{identifier-8} \end{array} \right\} \right.$$

$$\left. \left. \underline{\text{BY}} \left\{ \begin{array}{l} \text{literal-9} \\ \text{identifier-9} \end{array} \right\} \underline{\text{UNTIL}} \text{ condition-3} \right] \right]$$

Read

  READ file-name RECORD [INTO identifier]

  $\left\{ \begin{array}{l} \text{; AT END imperative-statement} \\ \text{; INVALID KEY imperative-statement} \end{array} \right\}$

Release

  RELEASE record-name [FROM identifier]

Return

  RETURN file-name RECORD [INTO identifier]
    ; AT END imperative-statement

Search
Format 1:

  SEARCH identifier-1 $\left[\text{VARYING} \left\{ \begin{array}{l} \text{index-name-1} \\ \text{identifier-1} \end{array} \right\} \right]$

    [; AT END imperative-statement-1]

      ; WHEN condition-1 $\left\{ \begin{array}{l} \text{imperative-statement-2} \\ \text{NEXT SENTENCE} \end{array} \right\}$

      $\left[\text{; WHEN condition-2} \left\{ \begin{array}{l} \text{imperative-statement-3} \\ \text{NEXT SENTENCE} \end{array} \right\} \right]$ . . .

Format 2:

  SEARCH ALL identifier-1 [; AT END imperative-statement-1]

    ; WHEN condition-1 $\left\{ \begin{array}{l} \text{imperative-statement-2} \\ \text{NEXT SENTENCE} \end{array} \right\}$

Section names

  {section-name SECTION [priority-number].
  {paragraph-name. {sentence} . . . } . . . } . . .

Seek

  SEEK file-name RECORD

Set

Format 1:

$$\underline{SET} \begin{Bmatrix} \text{identifier-1 [, identifier-2] \dots} \\ \text{index-name-1 [, index-name-2] \dots} \end{Bmatrix} \underline{TO} \begin{Bmatrix} \text{identifier-3} \\ \text{index-name-3} \\ \text{literal-1} \end{Bmatrix}$$

Format 2:

$$\underline{SET} \text{ index-name-1 [, index-name-2] \dots} \begin{Bmatrix} \underline{UP\ BY} \\ \underline{DOWN\ BY} \end{Bmatrix} \begin{Bmatrix} \text{identifier-1} \\ \text{literal-1} \end{Bmatrix}$$

Sort

$$\underline{SORT} \text{ file-name-1 } \underline{ON} \begin{Bmatrix} \underline{ASCENDING} \\ \underline{DESCENDING} \end{Bmatrix} \text{KEY data-name-1 [, data-name-2] \dots}$$

$$\left[\text{; } \underline{ON} \begin{Bmatrix} \underline{ASCENDING} \\ \underline{DESCENDING} \end{Bmatrix} \text{KEY data-name-3 [, data-name-4] \dots} \right] \dots$$

$$\begin{Bmatrix} \underline{INPUT}\ \underline{PROCEDURE}\ IS\ \text{section-name-1 [}\underline{THRU}\ \text{section-name-2]} \\ \underline{USING}\ \text{file-name-2} \end{Bmatrix}$$

$$\begin{Bmatrix} \underline{OUTPUT}\ \underline{PROCEDURE}\ IS\ \text{section-name-3 [}\underline{THRU}\ \text{section-name-4]} \\ \underline{GIVING}\ \text{file-name-3} \end{Bmatrix}$$

Stop'

$$\underline{STOP} \begin{Bmatrix} \text{literal} \\ \underline{RUN} \end{Bmatrix}$$

Subtract

Format 1:

$$\underline{SUBTRACT} \begin{Bmatrix} \text{literal-1} \\ \text{identifier-1} \end{Bmatrix} \begin{bmatrix} \text{, literal-2 .} \\ \text{, identifier-2} \end{bmatrix} \dots$$

$$\underline{FROM} \text{ identifier-m [}\underline{ROUNDED}\text{] [, identifier-n [}\underline{ROUNDED}\text{] } \} \dots$$
$$\text{[; } \underline{ON}\ \underline{SIZE}\ \underline{ERROR}\ \text{imperative-statement]}$$

Format 2:

$$\underline{SUBTRACT} \begin{Bmatrix} \text{literal-1} \\ \text{identifier-1} \end{Bmatrix} \begin{bmatrix} \text{, literal-2} \\ \text{, identifier-2} \end{bmatrix} \dots$$

$$\underline{FROM} \begin{Bmatrix} \text{literal-m} \\ \text{identifier-m} \end{Bmatrix} \underline{GIVING} \text{ identifier-n [}\underline{ROUNDED}\text{]}$$

$$\text{[; } \underline{ON}\ \underline{SIZE}\ \underline{ERROR}\ \text{imperative-statement]}$$

Format 3:

$$\underline{SUBTRACT} \begin{Bmatrix} \underline{CORRESPONDING} \\ \underline{CORR} \end{Bmatrix} \text{identifier-1 } \underline{FROM} \text{ identifier-2 [}\underline{ROUNDED}\text{]}$$

$$\text{[; } \underline{ON}\ \underline{SIZE}\ \underline{ERROR}\ \text{imperative-statement]}$$

Terminate

    TERMINATE report-name-1 [, report-name-2] . . .

Use
Format 1:

    USE AFTER STANDARD ERROR PROCEDURE ON

$$\left\{ \begin{array}{l} \text{file-name-1 [, file-name-2] . . .} \\ \underline{\text{INPUT}} \\ \underline{\text{OUTPUT}} \\ \underline{\text{I-O}} \end{array} \right\}$$

Format 2:

    USE $\left\{ \begin{array}{l} \underline{\text{BEFORE}} \\ \underline{\text{AFTER}} \end{array} \right\}$ STANDARD $\left[\begin{array}{l} \underline{\text{BEGINNING}} \\ \underline{\text{ENDING}} \end{array} \right]$ $\left[\begin{array}{l} \underline{\text{REEL}} \\ \underline{\text{FILE}} \\ \underline{\text{UNIT}} \end{array} \right]$ LABEL PROCEDURE ON

$$\left\{ \begin{array}{l} \text{file-name-1 [, file-name-2] . . .} \\ \underline{\text{INPUT}} \\ \underline{\text{OUTPUT}} \\ \underline{\text{I-O}} \end{array} \right\}$$

Format 3:

    USE BEFORE REPORTING identifier-1

Write
Format 1:

    WRITE record-name [FROM identifier-1]

$$\left[\left\{ \begin{array}{l} \underline{\text{BEFORE}} \\ \underline{\text{AFTER}} \end{array} \right\} \text{ ADVANCING} \left\{ \begin{array}{l} \text{identifier LINES} \\ \text{integer LINES} \\ \text{mnemonic-name} \end{array} \right\} \right]$$

Format 2:

    WRITE record-name [FROM identifier-1]]
    ; INVALID KEY imperative-statement

APPENDIX D
COBOL 74 Syntax Skeleton

General Format For Identification Division

IDENTIFICATION DIVISION.

PROGRAM-ID. program-name.

[AUTHOR. [comment-entry] . . .]

[INSTALLATION. [comment-entry] . . .]

[DATE-WRITTEN. [comment-entry] . . .]

[DATE-COMPILED. [comment-entry] . . .]

[SECURITY. [comment-entry] . . .]

General Format For Environment Division

ENVIRONMENT DIVISION.

CONFIGURATION SECTION.

SOURCE-COMPUTER. computer-name [WITH DEBUGGING MODE] .

OBJECT-COMPUTER. computer-name

$$\left[\;,\; \underline{\text{MEMORY}}\; \text{SIZE integer} \left\{ \begin{array}{l} \text{WORDS} \\ \underline{\text{CHARACTERS}} \\ \underline{\text{MODULES}} \end{array} \right\} \right]$$

    [, SEGMENT-LIMIT IS segment-number] .

[SPECIAL-NAMES. [implementor-name

$$\left\{ \begin{array}{l} \underline{\text{IS}}\text{ mnemonic-name }\; [\;,\; \underline{\text{ON}}\text{ STATUS }\underline{\text{IS}}\text{ condition-name-1 }\; [\;,\; \underline{\text{OFF}}\text{ STATUS }\underline{\text{IS}}\text{ condition-name-2}]\;] \\ \underline{\text{IS}}\text{ mnemonic-name }\; [\;,\; \underline{\text{OFF}}\text{ STATUS }\underline{\text{IS}}\text{ condition-name-2 }\; [\;,\; \underline{\text{ON}}\text{ STATUS }\underline{\text{IS}}\text{ condition-name-1}]\;] \\ \underline{\text{ON}}\text{ STATUS }\underline{\text{IS}}\text{ condition-name-1 }\; [\;,\; \underline{\text{OFF}}\text{ STATUS }\underline{\text{IS}}\text{ condition-name-2}] \\ \underline{\text{OFF}}\text{ STATUS }\underline{\text{IS}}\text{ condition-name-2 }\; [\;,\; \underline{\text{ON}}\text{ STATUS }\underline{\text{IS}}\text{ condition-name-1}] \end{array} \right\} \; \cdots \;$$

[, CURRENCY SIGN IS literal]

[, DECIMAL-POINT IS COMMA] .]

[INPUT-OUTPUT SECTION.

FILE-CONTROL.

    {file-control-entry} . . .

[I-O-CONTROL.

$$\left[\underline{\text{RERUN}} \left[\underline{\text{ON}} \left\{ \begin{array}{l} \text{file-name-1} \\ \text{implementor-name} \end{array} \right\} \right] \right.$$

$$\left. \text{EVERY} \left\{ \begin{array}{l} \left\{ \begin{array}{l} [\underline{\text{END}}\text{ OF]} \left\{ \begin{array}{l} \underline{\text{REEL}} \\ \underline{\text{UNIT}} \end{array} \right\} \\ \text{integer-1 }\underline{\text{RECORDS}} \end{array} \right\} \text{ OF file-name-2} \\ \text{integer-2 }\underline{\text{CLOCK-UNITS}} \\ \text{condition-name} \end{array} \right\} \cdots \right]$$

$$\left[\;;\; \underline{\text{SAME}} \left[\begin{array}{l} \underline{\text{RECORD}} \\ \underline{\text{SORT}} \\ \underline{\text{SORT-MERGE}} \end{array} \right] \text{AREA FOR file-name-3} \; \{ \;,\; \text{file-name-4} \} \; \cdots \right] \cdots$$

    [; MULTIPLE FILE TAPE CONTAINS file-name-5 [POSITION integer-3]

       [, file-name-6 [POSITION integer-4]] . . .] . . . .]]

General Format For File Control Entry

FORMAT 1

<u>SELECT</u> [<u>OPTIONAL</u>] file-name

    <u>ASSIGN</u> **TO** implementor-name-1 [, implementor-name-2] . . .

    $\left[\text{ , } \underline{\text{RESERVE}} \text{ integer-1} \left[\begin{array}{l} \textbf{AREA} \\ \textbf{AREAS} \end{array} \right] \right]$

    [, <u>ORGANIZATION</u> **IS** <u>SEQUENTIAL</u>]

    [, <u>ACCESS</u> **MODE IS** <u>SEQUENTIAL</u>]

    [, **FILE** <u>STATUS</u> **IS** data-name-1] .

FORMAT 2

<u>SELECT</u> file-name

    <u>ASSIGN</u> **TO** implementor-name-1 [, implementor-name-2] . . .

    $\left[\text{ , } \underline{\text{RESERVE}} \text{ integer-1} \left[\begin{array}{l} \textbf{AREA} \\ \textbf{AREAS} \end{array} \right] \right]$

    , <u>ORGANIZATION</u> **IS** <u>RELATIVE</u>

    $\left[\text{, } \underline{\text{ACCESS}} \text{ MODE IS } \left\{ \begin{array}{l} \underline{\text{SEQUENTIAL}} \quad [\text{, } \underline{\text{RELATIVE}} \text{ KEY IS data-name-1}] \\ \left\{ \begin{array}{l} \text{RANDOM} \\ \text{DYNAMIC} \end{array} \right\} \text{, } \underline{\text{RELATIVE}} \text{ KEY IS data-name-1} \end{array} \right\} \right]$

    [, **FILE** <u>STATUS</u> **IS** data-name-2] .

FORMAT 3

<u>SELECT</u> file-name

    <u>ASSIGN</u> **TO** implementor-name-1 [, implementor-name-2] . . .

    $\left[\text{ , } \underline{\text{RESERVE}} \text{ integer-1} \left[\begin{array}{l} \textbf{AREA} \\ \textbf{AREAS} \end{array} \right] \right]$

    , <u>ORGANIZATION</u> **IS** <u>INDEXED</u>

    $\left[\text{, } \underline{\text{ACCESS}} \text{ MODE IS } \left\{ \begin{array}{l} \underline{\text{SEQUENTIAL}} \\ \underline{\text{RANDOM}} \\ \underline{\text{DYNAMIC}} \end{array} \right\} \right]$

    , <u>RECORD</u> **KEY IS** data-name-1

    [, <u>ALTERNATE</u> <u>RECORD</u> **KEY IS** data-name-2 [**WITH** <u>DUPLICATES</u>]] . . .

    [, **FILE** <u>STATUS</u> **IS** data-name-3] .

General Format For Data Division

<u>DATA</u> <u>DIVISION</u>.

[<u>FILE</u> <u>SECTION</u>.

[<u>FD</u> file-name

$\left[\text{ ; } \underline{\text{BLOCK}} \text{ CONTAINS } [\text{integer-1 } \underline{\text{TO}}] \text{ integer-2 } \left\{ \begin{array}{l} \text{RECORDS} \\ \text{CHARACTERS} \end{array} \right\} \right]$

[; <u>RECORD</u> CONTAINS [integer-3 <u>TO</u>] integer-4 CHARACTERS]

; <u>LABEL</u> $\left\{ \begin{array}{l} \text{RECORD IS} \\ \text{RECORDS ARE} \end{array} \right\}$ $\left\{ \begin{array}{l} \underline{\text{STANDARD}} \\ \underline{\text{OMITTED}} \end{array} \right\}$

$\left[\text{ ; } \underline{\text{VALUE OF}} \text{ implementor-name-1 IS} \left\{ \begin{array}{l} \text{data-name-1} \\ \text{literal-1} \end{array} \right\} \right.$

$\left. \left[\text{ , implementor-name-2 IS} \left\{ \begin{array}{l} \text{data-name-2} \\ \text{literal-2} \end{array} \right\} \right] \ldots \right]$

$\left[\text{ ; } \underline{\text{DATA}} \left\{ \begin{array}{l} \underline{\text{RECORD}} \text{ IS} \\ \underline{\text{RECORDS}} \text{ ARE} \end{array} \right\} \text{ data-name-3 } [\text{ , data-name-4}] \ldots \right]$

$\left[\text{ ; } \underline{\text{LINAGE}} \text{ IS } \left\{ \begin{array}{l} \text{data-name-5} \\ \text{integer-5} \end{array} \right\} \text{ LINES } \left[\text{ , WITH } \underline{\text{FOOTING}} \text{ AT } \left\{ \begin{array}{l} \text{data-name-6} \\ \text{integer-6} \end{array} \right\} \right] \right.$

$\left. \left[\text{ , LINES AT } \underline{\text{TOP}} \left\{ \begin{array}{l} \text{data-name-7} \\ \text{integer-7} \end{array} \right\} \right] \left[\text{ , LINES AT } \underline{\text{BOTTOM}} \left\{ \begin{array}{l} \text{data-name-8} \\ \text{integer-8} \end{array} \right\} \right] \right]$

$\left[\text{ ; } \left\{ \begin{array}{l} \underline{\text{REPORT}} \text{ IS} \\ \underline{\text{REPORTS}} \text{ ARE} \end{array} \right\} \text{ report-name-1 } [\text{ , report-name-2}] \ldots \right]$.

[record-description-entry] . . .] . . .

[<u>SD</u> file-name

[; <u>RECORD</u> CONTAINS [integer-1 <u>TO</u>] integer-2 CHARACTERS]

$\left[\text{ ; } \underline{\text{DATA}} \left\{ \begin{array}{l} \underline{\text{RECORD}} \text{ IS} \\ \underline{\text{RECORDS}} \text{ ARE} \end{array} \right\} \text{ data-name-1 } [\text{ , data-name-2}] \ldots \right]$.

{record-description-entry} . . .] . . .]

[<u>WORKING-STORAGE</u> <u>SECTION</u>.

$\left[\begin{array}{l} \text{77-level-description-entry} \\ \text{record-description-entry} \end{array} \right] \ldots$

General Format For Data Division

[<u>LINKAGE</u> <u>SECTION</u>.

$\begin{bmatrix} \text{77-level-description-entry} \\ \text{record-description-entry} \end{bmatrix} \dots]$

[<u>COMMUNICATION</u> <u>SECTION</u>.

[communication-description-entry

[record-description-entry] . . .] . . .]

[<u>REPORT</u> <u>SECTION</u>.

[<u>RD</u> report-name

    [; <u>CODE</u> literal-1]

    $\left[; \left\{ \begin{matrix} \underline{\text{CONTROL}} \text{ IS} \\ \underline{\text{CONTROLS}} \text{ ARE} \end{matrix} \right\} \left\{ \begin{matrix} \text{data-name-1 } [\text{ , data-name-2}] \dots \\ \underline{\text{FINAL}} \ [\text{ , data-name-1 } [\text{ , data-name-2}] \dots] \end{matrix} \right\} \right]$

    $\left[; \underline{\text{PAGE}} \left[\begin{matrix} \text{LIMIT IS} \\ \text{LIMITS ARE} \end{matrix} \right] \text{integer-1} \left[\begin{matrix} \text{LINE} \\ \text{LINES} \end{matrix} \right] [, \underline{\text{HEADING}} \text{ integer-2}] \right.$

       [, <u>FIRST</u> <u>DETAIL</u> integer-3] [, <u>LAST</u> <u>DETAIL</u> integer-4]

       [, <u>FOOTING</u> integer-5]] .

   {report-group-description-entry} . . .] . . .]

General Format For Data Description Entry

FORMAT 1:

level-number $\left\{ \begin{array}{l} \text{data-name-1} \\ \underline{\text{FILLER}} \end{array} \right\}$

$\left[\text{; } \underline{\text{REDEFINES}} \text{ data-name-2} \right]$

$\left[\text{; } \left\{ \begin{array}{l} \underline{\text{PICTURE}} \\ \underline{\text{PIC}} \end{array} \right\} \text{ IS character-string} \right]$

$\left[\text{; [USAGE IS]} \left\{ \begin{array}{l} \underline{\text{COMPUTATIONAL}} \\ \underline{\text{COMP}} \\ \underline{\text{DISPLAY}} \\ \underline{\text{INDEX}} \end{array} \right\} \right]$

$\left[\text{; [SIGN IS]} \left\{ \begin{array}{l} \underline{\text{LEADING}} \\ \underline{\text{TRAILING}} \end{array} \right\} \text{ [SEPARATE CHARACTER]} \right]$

$\left[\text{; } \underline{\text{OCCURS}} \left\{ \begin{array}{l} \text{integer-1 } \underline{\text{TO}} \text{ integer-2 TIMES } \underline{\text{DEPENDING}} \text{ ON data-name-1} \\ \text{integer-2 } \text{TIMES} \end{array} \right\} \right.$

$\left[\left\{ \begin{array}{l} \underline{\text{ASCENDING}} \\ \underline{\text{DESCENDING}} \end{array} \right\} \text{ KEY IS data-name-2 [, data-name-3] } \dots \right] \dots$

$\left. \text{[INDEXED BY index-name-1 [, index-name-2] } \dots \text{]]} \right.$

$\left[\text{; } \left\{ \begin{array}{l} \underline{\text{SYNCHRONIZED}} \\ \underline{\text{SYNC}} \end{array} \right\} \left[\begin{array}{l} \underline{\text{LEFT}} \\ \underline{\text{RIGHT}} \end{array} \right] \right]$

$\left[\text{; } \left\{ \begin{array}{l} \underline{\text{JUSTIFIED}} \\ \underline{\text{JUST}} \end{array} \right\} \text{ RIGHT} \right]$

$\left[\text{; } \underline{\text{BLANK}} \text{ WHEN } \underline{\text{ZERO}} \right]$

$\left[\text{; } \underline{\text{VALUE}} \text{ IS literal} \right]$.

FORMAT 2:

66 data-name-1; $\underline{\text{RENAMES}}$ data-name-2 $\left[\left\{ \begin{array}{l} \underline{\text{THROUGH}} \\ \underline{\text{THRU}} \end{array} \right\} \text{ data-name-3} \right]$.

FORMAT 3:

88 condition-name; $\left\{ \begin{array}{l} \underline{\text{VALUE}} \text{ IS} \\ \underline{\text{VALUES}} \text{ ARE} \end{array} \right\}$ literal-1 $\left[\left\{ \begin{array}{l} \underline{\text{THROUGH}} \\ \underline{\text{THRU}} \end{array} \right\} \text{ literal-2} \right]$

$\left[\text{, literal-3 } \left[\left\{ \begin{array}{l} \underline{\text{THROUGH}} \\ \underline{\text{THRU}} \end{array} \right\} \text{ literal-4} \right] \right] \dots$.

General Format For Communication Description Entry

FORMAT 1:

<u>CD</u> cd-name;

FOR [<u>INITIAL</u>] <u>INPUT</u>

[[; SYMBOLIC <u>QUEUE</u> IS data-name-1]

[; SYMBOLIC <u>SUB-QUEUE-1</u> IS data-name-2]

[; SYMBOLIC <u>SUB-QUEUE-2</u> IS data-name-3]

[; SYMBOLIC <u>SUB-QUEUE-3</u> IS data-name-4]

[; <u>MESSAGE</u> <u>DATE</u> IS data-name-5]

[; <u>MESSAGE</u> <u>TIME</u> IS data-name-6]

[; SYMBOLIC <u>SOURCE</u> IS data-name-7]

[; <u>TEXT</u> <u>LENGTH</u> IS data-name-8]

[; <u>END</u> <u>KEY</u> IS data-name-9]

[; <u>STATUS</u> <u>KEY</u> IS data-name-10]

[; <u>QUEUE</u> <u>DEPTH</u> IS data-name-11]]

[data-name-1, data-name-2, . . . , data-name 11]

FORMAT 2:

<u>CD</u> cd-name; FOR <u>OUTPUT</u>

[; <u>DESTINATION</u> <u>COUNT</u> IS data-name-1]

[; <u>TEXT</u> <u>LENGTH</u> IS data-name-2]

[; <u>STATUS</u> <u>KEY</u> IS data-name-3]

[; <u>DESTINATION</u> <u>TABLE</u> <u>OCCURS</u> integer-2 <u>TIMES</u>

[; <u>INDEXED</u> BY index-name-1 [, index-name-2]] . . .]

[; <u>ERROR</u> KEY IS data-name-4]

[; SYMBOLIC <u>DESTINATION</u> IS data-name-5] .

General Format For Report Group Description Entry

FORMAT 1:

01 [data-name-1]

$$\left[\text{; } \underline{\text{LINE}} \text{ NUMBER IS } \left\{ \begin{array}{l} \text{integer-1 } [\text{ON } \underline{\text{NEXT}} \underline{\text{PAGE}}] \\ \underline{\text{PLUS}} \text{ integer-2} \end{array} \right\} \right]$$

$$\left[\text{; } \underline{\text{NEXT}} \underline{\text{GROUP}} \text{ IS } \left\{ \begin{array}{l} \text{integer-3} \\ \underline{\text{PLUS}} \text{ integer-4} \\ \underline{\text{NEXT}} \underline{\text{PAGE}} \end{array} \right\} \right]$$

$$\text{; } \underline{\text{TYPE}} \text{ IS } \left\{ \begin{array}{l} \left\{ \begin{array}{l} \underline{\text{REPORT}} \text{ HEADING} \\ \underline{\text{RH}} \end{array} \right\} \\ \left\{ \begin{array}{l} \underline{\text{PAGE}} \text{ HEADING} \\ \underline{\text{PH}} \end{array} \right\} \\ \left\{ \begin{array}{l} \underline{\text{CONTROL}} \ \underline{\text{HEADING}} \\ \underline{\text{CH}} \end{array} \right\} \left\{ \begin{array}{l} \text{data-name-2} \\ \underline{\text{FINAL}} \end{array} \right\} \\ \left\{ \begin{array}{l} \underline{\text{DETAIL}} \\ \underline{\text{DE}} \end{array} \right\} \\ \left\{ \begin{array}{l} \underline{\text{CONTROL}} \ \underline{\text{FOOTING}} \\ \underline{\text{CF}} \end{array} \right\} \left\{ \begin{array}{l} \text{data-name-3} \\ \underline{\text{FINAL}} \end{array} \right\} \\ \left\{ \begin{array}{l} \underline{\text{PAGE}} \ \underline{\text{FOOTING}} \\ \underline{\text{PF}} \end{array} \right\} \\ \left\{ \begin{array}{l} \underline{\text{REPORT}} \ \underline{\text{FOOTING}} \\ \underline{\text{RF}} \end{array} \right\} \end{array} \right\}$$

[; [USAGE IS] DISPLAY] .

FORMAT 2:

level-number [data-name-1]

$$\left[\text{; } \underline{\text{LINE}} \text{ NUMBER IS } \left\{ \begin{array}{l} \text{integer-1 } [\text{ON } \underline{\text{NEXT}} \underline{\text{PAGE}}] \\ \underline{\text{PLUS}} \text{ integer-2} \end{array} \right\} \right]$$

[; [USAGE IS] DISPLAY] .

General Format For Report Group Description Entry

FORMAT 3:

level-number [data-name-1]

   [; **BLANK** WHEN **ZERO**]

   [; **GROUP** INDICATE]

$$\left[; \left\{ \begin{matrix} \underline{JUSTIFIED} \\ \underline{JUST} \end{matrix} \right\} \text{RIGHT} \right]$$

$$\left[; \underline{LINE} \text{ NUMBER IS } \left\{ \begin{matrix} \text{integer-1} \quad [\text{ON } \underline{NEXT} \ \underline{PAGE}] \\ \underline{PLUS} \text{ integer-2} \end{matrix} \right\} \right]$$

[; **COLUMN** NUMBERS IS integer-3]

$$; \left\{ \begin{matrix} \underline{PICTURE} \\ \underline{PIC} \end{matrix} \right\} \text{ IS character-string}$$

$$\left\{ \begin{matrix} ; \ \underline{SOURCE} \text{ IS identifier-1} \\ ; \ \underline{VALUE} \text{ IS literal} \\ \{ ; \ \underline{SUM} \ \text{ identifier-2 } [, \text{ identifier-3}] \ldots \\ \quad [\underline{UPON} \text{ data-name-2 } [, \text{ data-name-3} \ldots]] \} \ldots \\ \left[\underline{RESET} \text{ ON } \left\{ \begin{matrix} \text{data-name-4} \\ \underline{FINAL} \end{matrix} \right\} \right] \end{matrix} \right\}$$

[;[**USAGE** IS] **DISPLAY**] .

General Format For Procedure Division

FORMAT 1:

<u>PROCEDURE</u> <u>DIVISION</u>   [<u>USING</u> identifier-1 [, identifier-2] . . .] .

[<u>DECLARATIVES</u>.

{section-name <u>SECTION</u>. declarative-sentence

[paragraph-name. [sentence] . . .] . . . } . . .

[<u>END</u> <u>DECLARATIVES</u>.]

{section-name <u>SECTION</u> [segment-number] .

[paragraph-name. [sentence] . . .] . . . } . . .

FORMAT 2:

<u>PROCEDURE</u> <u>DIVISION</u>   [<u>USING</u> identifier-1 [, identifier-2] . . .] .

{paragraph-name. [sentence] . . . } . . .

General Format For Verbs

<u>ACCEPT</u> identifier [<u>FROM</u> mnemonic-name]

<u>ACCEPT</u> identifier <u>FROM</u> $\left\{ \begin{array}{l} \underline{\text{DATE}} \\ \underline{\text{DAY}} \\ \underline{\text{TIME}} \end{array} \right\}$

<u>ADD</u> $\left\{ \begin{array}{l} \text{identifier-1} \\ \text{literal-1} \end{array} \right\}$ $\left[\begin{array}{l} \text{, identifier-2} \\ \text{, literal-2} \end{array} \right]$ ... <u>TO</u> identifier-m [<u>ROUNDED</u>]

    [, identifier-n [<u>ROUNDED</u>]] ... [; <u>ON</u> <u>SIZE</u> <u>ERROR</u> imperative-statement]

<u>ADD</u> $\left\{ \begin{array}{l} \text{identifier-1} \\ \text{literal-1} \end{array} \right\}$, $\left\{ \begin{array}{l} \text{identifier-2} \\ \text{literal-2} \end{array} \right\}$ $\left[\begin{array}{l} \text{, identifier-3} \\ \text{, literal-3} \end{array} \right]$ ...

    <u>GIVING</u> identifier-m [<u>ROUNDED</u>] [, identifier-n [<u>ROUNDED</u>]] ...

    [; <u>ON</u> <u>SIZE</u> <u>ERROR</u> imperative-statement]

<u>ADD</u> $\left\{ \begin{array}{l} \underline{\text{CORRESPONDING}} \\ \underline{\text{CORR}} \end{array} \right\}$ identifier-1 <u>TO</u> identifier-2 [<u>ROUNDED</u>]

    [; <u>ON</u> <u>SIZE</u> <u>ERROR</u> imperative-statement]

<u>ALTER</u> procedure-name-1 <u>TO</u> [<u>PROCEED</u> <u>TO</u>] procedure-name-2

    [, procedure-name-3 <u>TO</u> [<u>PROCEED</u> <u>TO</u>] procedure-name-4] ...

<u>CALL</u> $\left\{ \begin{array}{l} \text{identifier-1} \\ \text{literal-1} \end{array} \right\}$ [<u>USING</u> identifier-2 [, identifier-3] ...]

    [; <u>ON</u> <u>OVERFLOW</u> imperative-statement]

<u>CANCEL</u> $\left\{ \begin{array}{l} \text{identifier-1} \\ \text{literal-1} \end{array} \right\}$ $\left[\begin{array}{l} \text{, identifier-2} \\ \text{, literal-2} \end{array} \right]$ ...

<u>CLOSE</u> file-name-1 $\left[\begin{array}{l} \left\{ \begin{array}{l} \underline{\text{REEL}} \\ \underline{\text{UNIT}} \end{array} \right\} \left[\begin{array}{l} \text{WITH} \ \underline{\text{NO}} \ \underline{\text{REWIND}} \\ \text{FOR} \ \underline{\text{REMOVAL}} \end{array} \right] \\ \\ \text{WITH} \left\{ \begin{array}{l} \underline{\text{NO}} \ \underline{\text{REWIND}} \\ \underline{\text{LOCK}} \end{array} \right\} \end{array} \right]$

    $\left[\begin{array}{l} \text{, file-name-2} \ \left\{ \begin{array}{l} \underline{\text{REEL}} \\ \underline{\text{UNIT}} \end{array} \right\} \left[\begin{array}{l} \text{WITH} \ \underline{\text{NO}} \ \underline{\text{REWIND}} \\ \text{FOR} \ \underline{\text{REMOVAL}} \end{array} \right] \\ \\ \text{WITH} \left\{ \begin{array}{l} \underline{\text{NO}} \ \underline{\text{REWIND}} \\ \underline{\text{LOCK}} \end{array} \right\} \end{array} \right]$ ...

<u>CLOSE</u> file-name-1 [<u>WITH</u> <u>LOCK</u>] [, file-name-2 [<u>WITH</u> <u>LOCK</u>]] ...

<u>COMPUTE</u> identifier-1 [<u>ROUNDED</u>] [, identifier-2 [<u>ROUNDED</u>]] ...

    = arithmetic-expression [; <u>ON</u> <u>SIZE</u> <u>ERROR</u> imperative-statement]

General Format For Verbs

<u>DELETE</u> file-name RECORD [; <u>INVALID</u> KEY imperative-statement]

<u>DISABLE</u> $\left\{ \begin{matrix} \underline{INPUT} \ [\underline{TERMINAL}] \\ \underline{OUTPUT} \end{matrix} \right\}$ cd--name WITH <u>KEY</u> $\left\{ \begin{matrix} identifier-1 \\ literal-1 \end{matrix} \right\}$

<u>DISPLAY</u> $\left\{ \begin{matrix} identifier-1 \\ literal-1 \end{matrix} \right\}$ $\left[\begin{matrix} , identifier-2 \\ , literal-2 \end{matrix} \right]$ ... [<u>UPON</u> mnemonic-name]

<u>DIVIDE</u> $\left\{ \begin{matrix} identifier-1 \\ literal-1 \end{matrix} \right\}$ <u>INTO</u> identifier-2 [<u>ROUNDED</u>]

    [, identifier-3 [<u>ROUNDED</u>]] ... [; ON <u>SIZE</u> <u>ERROR</u> imperative-statement]

<u>DIVIDE</u> $\left\{ \begin{matrix} identifier-1 \\ literal-1 \end{matrix} \right\}$ <u>INTO</u> $\left\{ \begin{matrix} identifier-2 \\ literal-2 \end{matrix} \right\}$ <u>GIVING</u> identifier-3 [<u>ROUNDED</u>]

    [, identifier-4 [<u>ROUNDED</u>]] ... [; ON <u>SIZE</u> <u>ERROR</u> imperative-statement]

<u>DIVIDE</u> $\left\{ \begin{matrix} identifier-1 \\ literal-1 \end{matrix} \right\}$ <u>BY</u> $\left\{ \begin{matrix} identifier-2 \\ literal-2 \end{matrix} \right\}$ <u>GIVING</u> identifier-3 [<u>ROUNDED</u>]

    [, identifier-4 [<u>ROUNDED</u>]] ... [; ON <u>SIZE</u> <u>ERROR</u> imperative-statement]

<u>DIVIDE</u> $\left\{ \begin{matrix} identifier-1 \\ literal-1 \end{matrix} \right\}$ <u>INTO</u> $\left\{ \begin{matrix} identifier-2 \\ literal-2 \end{matrix} \right\}$ <u>GIVING</u> identifier-3 [<u>ROUNDED</u>]

    <u>REMAINDER</u> identifier-4 [; ON <u>SIZE</u> <u>ERROR</u> imperative-statement]

<u>DIVIDE</u> $\left\{ \begin{matrix} identifier-1 \\ literal-1 \end{matrix} \right\}$ <u>BY</u> $\left\{ \begin{matrix} identifier-2 \\ literal-2 \end{matrix} \right\}$ <u>GIVING</u> identifier-3 [<u>ROUNDED</u>]

    <u>REMAINDER</u> identifier-4 [; ON <u>SIZE</u> <u>ERROR</u> imperative-statement]

<u>ENABLE</u> $\left\{ \begin{matrix} \underline{INPUT} \ [\underline{TERMINAL}] \\ \underline{OUTPUT} \end{matrix} \right\}$ cd-name WITH <u>KEY</u> $\left\{ \begin{matrix} identifier-1 \\ literal-1 \end{matrix} \right\}$

<u>ENTER</u> language-name [routine-name] .

<u>EXIT</u> [<u>PROGRAM</u>] .

<u>GENERATE</u> $\left\{ \begin{matrix} data-name \\ report-name \end{matrix} \right\}$

<u>GO</u> TO [procedure-name-1]

General Format For Verbs

<u>GO</u> TO procedure-name-1 [, procedure-name-2] . . . , procedure-name-n

<u>DEPENDING</u> ON identifier

<u>IF</u> condition; $\left\{ \begin{array}{l} \text{statement-1} \\ \underline{\text{NEXT}}\ \underline{\text{SENTENCE}} \end{array} \right\}$ $\left\{ \begin{array}{l} ; \underline{\text{ELSE}}\ \text{statement-2} \\ . \underline{\text{ELSE}}\ \underline{\text{NEXT}}\ \underline{\text{SENTENCE}} \end{array} \right\}$

<u>INITIATE</u> report-name-1 [, report-name-2] . . .

<u>INSPECT</u> identifier-1 <u>TALLYING</u>

$$\left\{ , \text{identifier-2} \underline{\text{FOR}} \left\{ , \left\{ \begin{array}{l} \left\{ \begin{array}{l} \underline{\text{ALL}} \\ \underline{\text{LEADING}} \end{array} \right\} \left\{ \begin{array}{l} \text{identifier-3} \\ \text{literal-1} \end{array} \right\} \\ \text{CHARACTERS} \end{array} \right\} \left[\left\{ \begin{array}{l} \underline{\text{BEFORE}} \\ \underline{\text{AFTER}} \end{array} \right\} \text{INITIAL} \left\{ \begin{array}{l} \text{identifier-4} \\ \text{literal-2} \end{array} \right\} \right] \right\} \cdots \right\} \cdots$$

<u>INSPECT</u> identifier-1 <u>REPLACING</u>

$$\left\{ \begin{array}{l} \text{CHARACTERS} \underline{\text{BY}} \left\{ \begin{array}{l} \text{identifier-6} \\ \text{literal-4} \end{array} \right\} \left[\left\{ \begin{array}{l} \underline{\text{BEFORE}} \\ \underline{\text{AFTER}} \end{array} \right\} \text{INITIAL} \left\{ \begin{array}{l} \text{identifier-7} \\ \text{literal-5} \end{array} \right\} \right] \\ \left\{ \left\{ \begin{array}{l} \underline{\text{ALL}} \\ \underline{\text{LEADING}} \\ \underline{\text{FIRST}} \end{array} \right\} \left\{ , \left\{ \begin{array}{l} \text{identifier-5} \\ \text{literal-3} \end{array} \right\} \underline{\text{BY}} \left\{ \begin{array}{l} \text{identifier-6} \\ \text{literal-4} \end{array} \right\} \left[\left\{ \begin{array}{l} \underline{\text{BEFORE}} \\ \underline{\text{AFTER}} \end{array} \right\} \text{INITIAL} \left\{ \begin{array}{l} \text{identifier-7} \\ \text{literal-5} \end{array} \right\} \right] \right\} \cdots \right\} \end{array} \right\}$$

<u>INSPECT</u> identifier-1 <u>TALLYING</u>

$$\left\{ , \text{identifier-2} \underline{\text{FOR}} \left\{ , \left\{ \begin{array}{l} \left\{ \begin{array}{l} \underline{\text{ALL}} \\ \underline{\text{LEADING}} \end{array} \right\} \left\{ \begin{array}{l} \text{identifier-3} \\ \text{literal-1} \end{array} \right\} \\ \text{CHARACTERS} \end{array} \right\} \left[\left\{ \begin{array}{l} \underline{\text{BEFORE}} \\ \underline{\text{AFTER}} \end{array} \right\} \text{INITIAL} \left\{ \begin{array}{l} \text{identifier-4} \\ \text{literal-2} \end{array} \right\} \right] \right\} \cdots \right\} \cdots$$

<u>REPLACING</u>

$$\left\{ \begin{array}{l} \text{CHARACTERS} \underline{\text{BY}} \left\{ \begin{array}{l} \text{identifier-6} \\ \text{literal-4} \end{array} \right\} \left[\left\{ \begin{array}{l} \underline{\text{BEFORE}} \\ \underline{\text{AFTER}} \end{array} \right\} \text{INITIAL} \left\{ \begin{array}{l} \text{identifier-4} \\ \text{literal-2} \end{array} \right\} \right] \\ \left\{ \left\{ \begin{array}{l} \underline{\text{ALL}} \\ \underline{\text{LEADING}} \\ \underline{\text{FIRST}} \end{array} \right\} \left\{ , \left\{ \begin{array}{l} \text{identifier-5} \\ \text{literal-3} \end{array} \right\} \underline{\text{BY}} \left\{ \begin{array}{l} \text{identifier-6} \\ \text{literal-4} \end{array} \right\} \left[\left\{ \begin{array}{l} \underline{\text{BEFORE}} \\ \underline{\text{AFTER}} \end{array} \right\} \text{INITIAL} \left\{ \begin{array}{l} \text{identifier-7} \\ \text{literal-5} \end{array} \right\} \right] \right\} \cdots \right\} \end{array} \right\}$$

General Format For Verbs

<u>MERGE</u> file-name-1 ON $\left\{ \begin{array}{l} \underline{ASCENDING} \\ \underline{DESCENDING} \end{array} \right\}$ <u>KEY</u> data-name-1 [, data-name-2] . . .

$\left[ON \left\{ \begin{array}{l} \underline{ASCENDING} \\ \underline{DESCENDING} \end{array} \right\} \underline{KEY} \text{ data-name-3 } [, \text{ data-name-4}] . . . \right]$ . . .

    <u>USING</u> file-name-2, file-name-3 [, file-name-4] . . .

$\left\{ \begin{array}{l} \underline{OUTPUT} \ \underline{PROCEDURE} \text{ IS section-name-1} \left[\left\{ \begin{array}{l} \underline{THROUGH} \\ \underline{THRU} \end{array} \right\} \text{ section-name-2} \right] \\ \underline{GIVING} \text{ file-name-5} \end{array} \right\}$

<u>MOVE</u> $\left\{ \begin{array}{l} \text{identifier-1} \\ \text{literal} \end{array} \right\}$ <u>TO</u> identifier-2 [, identifier-3] . . .

<u>MOVE</u> $\left\{ \begin{array}{l} \underline{CORRESPONDING} \\ \underline{CORR} \end{array} \right\}$ identifier-1 <u>TO</u> identifier-2

<u>MULTIPLY</u> $\left\{ \begin{array}{l} \text{identifier-1} \\ \text{literal-1} \end{array} \right\}$ <u>BY</u> identifier-2 [<u>ROUNDED</u>]

    [, identifier-3 [<u>ROUNDED</u>]] . . . [; ON <u>SIZE</u> <u>ERROR</u> imperative-statement]

<u>MULTIPLY</u> $\left\{ \begin{array}{l} \text{identifier-1} \\ \text{literal-1} \end{array} \right\}$ <u>BY</u> $\left\{ \begin{array}{l} \text{identifier-2} \\ \text{literal-2} \end{array} \right\}$ <u>GIVING</u> identifier-3 [<u>ROUNDED</u>]

    [, identifier-4 [<u>ROUNDED</u>]] . . . [; ON <u>SIZE</u> <u>ERROR</u> imperative-statement]

<u>OPEN</u> $\left\{ \begin{array}{l} \underline{INPUT} \text{ file-name-1} \left[\begin{array}{l} \underline{REVERSED} \\ \text{WITH } \underline{NO} \ \underline{REWIND} \end{array} \right] \left[, \text{ file-name-2} \left[\begin{array}{l} \underline{REVERSED} \\ \text{WITH } \underline{NO} \ \underline{REWIND} \end{array} \right] \right] . . . \\ \underline{OUTPUT} \text{ file-name-3 [WITH } \underline{NO} \ \underline{REWIND}] \ [, \text{ file-name-4 [WITH } \underline{NO} \ \underline{REWIND}]] . . . \\ \underline{I\text{-}O} \text{ file-name-5 } [, \text{ file-name-6}] . . . \\ \underline{EXTEND} \text{ file-name-7 } [, \text{ file-name-8}] . . . \end{array} \right\}$ . . .

<u>OPEN</u> $\left\{ \begin{array}{l} \underline{INPUT} \text{ file-name-1 } [, \text{ file-name-2}] . . . \\ \underline{OUTPUT} \text{ file-name-3 [file-name-4]} . . . \\ \underline{IO} \text{ file-name-5 } [, \text{ file-name-6}] . . . \end{array} \right\}$ . . .

<u>PERFORM</u> procedure-name-1 $\left[\left\{ \begin{array}{l} \underline{THROUGH} \\ \underline{THRU} \end{array} \right\} \text{ procedure-name-2} \right]$

<u>PERFORM</u> procedure-name-1 $\left[\left\{ \begin{array}{l} \underline{THROUGH} \\ \underline{THRU} \end{array} \right\} \text{ procedure-name-2} \right] \left\{ \begin{array}{l} \text{identifier-1} \\ \text{integer-1} \end{array} \right\}$ <u>TIMES</u>

<u>PERFORM</u> procedure-name-1 $\left[\left\{ \begin{array}{l} \underline{THROUGH} \\ \underline{THRU} \end{array} \right\} \text{ procedure-name-2} \right]$ <u>UNTIL</u> condition-1

General Format For Verbs

PERFORM procedure-name-1 $\left[\left\{ \begin{array}{l} \underline{\text{THROUGH}} \\ \underline{\text{THRU}} \end{array} \right\} \text{procedure-name-2} \right]$

    <u>VARYING</u> $\left\{ \begin{array}{l} \text{identifier-2} \\ \text{index-name-1} \end{array} \right\}$ <u>FROM</u> $\left\{ \begin{array}{l} \text{identifier-3} \\ \text{index-name-2} \\ \text{literal-1} \end{array} \right\}$

        <u>BY</u> $\left\{ \begin{array}{l} \text{identifier-4} \\ \text{literal-3} \end{array} \right\}$ <u>UNTIL</u> condition-1

    $\left[\underline{\text{AFTER}} \left\{ \begin{array}{l} \text{identifier-5} \\ \text{index-name-3} \end{array} \right\} \underline{\text{FROM}} \left\{ \begin{array}{l} \text{identifier-6} \\ \text{index-name-4} \\ \text{literal-3} \end{array} \right\} \right.$

        <u>BY</u> $\left\{ \begin{array}{l} \text{identifier-7} \\ \text{literal-4} \end{array} \right\}$ <u>UNTIL</u> condition-2

    $\left[\underline{\text{AFTER}} \left\{ \begin{array}{l} \text{identifier-8} \\ \text{index-name-5} \end{array} \right\} \underline{\text{FROM}} \left\{ \begin{array}{l} \text{identifier-9} \\ \text{index-name-6} \\ \text{literal-5} \end{array} \right\} \right.$

        $\left. \left. \underline{\text{BY}} \left\{ \begin{array}{l} \text{identifier-10} \\ \text{literal-6} \end{array} \right\} \underline{\text{UNTIL}} \text{ condition-3} \right] \right]$

<u>READ</u> file-name RECORD [<u>INTO</u> identifier] [; AT <u>END</u> imperative-statement]

<u>READ</u> file-name [<u>NEXT</u>] RECORD [<u>INTO</u> identifier] [; AT <u>END</u> imperative-statement]

<u>READ</u> file-name RECORD [<u>INTO</u> identifier] [; <u>INVALID</u> KEY imperative-statement]

<u>READ</u> file-name RECORD [<u>INTO</u> identifier]

    [; <u>KEY</u> IS data-name]

    [; <u>INVALID</u> KEY imperative-statement]

<u>RECEIVE</u> cd-name $\left\{ \begin{array}{l} \underline{\text{MESSAGE}} \\ \underline{\text{SEGMENT}} \end{array} \right\}$ <u>INTO</u> identifier-1 [; <u>NO DATA</u> imperative-statement]

<u>RELEASE</u> record-name [<u>FROM</u> identifier]

<u>RETURN</u> file-name RECORD [<u>INTO</u> identifier] ; AT <u>END</u> imperative-statement

<u>REWRITE</u> record-name [<u>FROM</u> identifier]

<u>REWRITE</u> record-name [<u>FROM</u> identifier] [; <u>INVALID</u> KEY imperative-statement]

General Format For Verbs

SEARCH identifier-1 $\left[\textbf{VARYING} \left\{ \begin{array}{l} \text{identifier-2} \\ \text{index-name-1} \end{array} \right\} \right]$ [; **AT** **END** imperative-statement-1]

   ; **WHEN** condition-1 $\left\{ \begin{array}{l} \text{imperative-statement-2} \\ \underline{\textbf{NEXT}} \ \ \underline{\textbf{SENTENCE}} \end{array} \right\}$

   $\left[\ ; \ \underline{\textbf{WHEN}} \ \text{condition-2} \left\{ \begin{array}{l} \text{imperative-statement-3} \\ \underline{\textbf{NEXT}} \ \ \underline{\textbf{SENTENCE}} \end{array} \right\} \right]$ ...

<u>SEARCH</u> **ALL** identifier-1   [; **AT** <u>END</u> imperative-statement-1]

   ; <u>**WHEN**</u> $\left\{ \begin{array}{l} \text{data-name-1} \left\{ \begin{array}{l} \text{IS } \underline{\textbf{EQUAL}} \text{ TO} \\ \text{IS } = \end{array} \right\} \left\{ \begin{array}{l} \text{identifier-3} \\ \text{literal-1} \\ \text{arithmetic-expression-1} \end{array} \right\} \\ \text{condition-name-1} \end{array} \right\}$

     $\left[\underline{\textbf{AND}} \left\{ \begin{array}{l} \text{data-name-2} \left\{ \begin{array}{l} \text{IS } \underline{\textbf{EQUAL}} \text{ TO} \\ \text{IS } = \end{array} \right\} \left\{ \begin{array}{l} \text{identifier-4} \\ \text{literal-2} \\ \text{arithmetic-expression-2} \end{array} \right\} \\ \text{condition-name-2} \end{array} \right\} \right]$ ...

   $\left\{ \begin{array}{l} \text{imperative-statement-2} \\ \underline{\textbf{NEXT}} \ \ \underline{\textbf{SENTENCE}} \end{array} \right\}$

<u>SEND</u> cd-name-1 <u>**FROM**</u> identifier-1

<u>SEND</u> cd-name-1 **[** <u>**FROM**</u> identifier-1**]** $\left\{ \begin{array}{l} \textbf{WITH} \text{ identifier-2} \\ \textbf{WITH} \ \underline{\textbf{ESI}} \\ \textbf{WITH} \ \underline{\textbf{EMI}} \\ \textbf{WITH} \ \underline{\textbf{EGI}} \end{array} \right\}$

   $\left[\left\{ \begin{array}{l} \underline{\textbf{BEFORE}} \\ \underline{\textbf{AFTER}} \end{array} \right\} \textbf{ADVANCING} \left\{ \begin{array}{l} \left\{ \begin{array}{l} \text{identifier-3} \\ \text{integer} \end{array} \right\} \left[\begin{array}{l} \textbf{LINE} \\ \textbf{LINES} \end{array} \right] \\ \left\{ \begin{array}{l} \text{mnemonic-name} \\ \underline{\textbf{PAGE}} \end{array} \right\} \end{array} \right\} \right]$

<u>**SET**</u> $\left\{ \begin{array}{l} \text{identifier-1} \ \ [\ , \ \text{identifier-2}] \ \ ... \\ \text{index-name-1} \ [\ , \ \text{index-name-2}] \ ... \end{array} \right\}$ <u>**TO**</u> $\left\{ \begin{array}{l} \text{identifier-3} \\ \text{index-name-3} \\ \text{literal-1} \end{array} \right\}$

<u>**SET**</u> index-name-4 [, index-name-5] ... $\left\{ \begin{array}{l} \underline{\textbf{UP}} \ \underline{\textbf{BY}} \\ \underline{\textbf{DOWN}} \ \textbf{BY} \end{array} \right\} \left\{ \begin{array}{l} \text{identifier-4} \\ \text{literal-2} \end{array} \right\}$

General Format For Verbs

SORT file-name-1 ON $\left\{\begin{array}{l}\text{ASCENDING}\\\text{DESCENDING}\end{array}\right\}$ KEY data-name-1 [, data-name-2] . . .

$\left[\text{ON} \left\{\begin{array}{l}\text{ASCENDING}\\\text{DESCENDING}\end{array}\right\} \text{KEY data-name-3 } [, \text{ data-name-4}] . . .\right] . . .$

$\left\{\begin{array}{l}\underline{\text{INPUT}} \ \underline{\text{PROCEDURE}} \text{ IS section-name-1} \left[\left\{\begin{array}{l}\underline{\text{THROUGH}}\\\underline{\text{THRU}}\end{array}\right\} \text{section-name-2}\right]\\\underline{\text{USING}} \text{ file-name-2 } [, \text{ file-name-3}] . . .\end{array}\right\}$

$\left\{\begin{array}{l}\underline{\text{OUTPUT}} \ \underline{\text{PROCEDURE}} \text{ IS section-name-3} \left[\left\{\begin{array}{l}\underline{\text{THROUGH}}\\\underline{\text{THRU}}\end{array}\right\} \text{section-name-4}\right]\\\underline{\text{GIVING}} \text{ file-name-4}\end{array}\right\}$

START file-name-1 $\left[\underline{\text{KEY}} \left\{\begin{array}{l}\text{IS} \ \underline{\text{EQUAL}} \ \text{TO}\\\text{IS} =\\\text{IS} \ \underline{\text{GREATER}} \ \text{THAN}\\\text{IS} >\\\text{IS} \ \underline{\text{NOT}} \ \underline{\text{LESS}} \ \text{THAN}\\\text{IS} \ \underline{\text{NOT}} <\end{array}\right\} \text{data-name}\right]$

[; __INVALID__ KEY imperative-statement]

__STOP__ $\left\{\begin{array}{l}\underline{\text{RUN}}\\\text{literal}\end{array}\right\}$

__STRING__ $\left\{\begin{array}{l}\text{identifier-1}\\\text{literal-1}\end{array}\right\} \left[\begin{array}{l}, \text{ identifier-2}\\, \text{ literal-2}\end{array}\right] . . . \underline{\text{DELIMITED}} \text{ BY} \left\{\begin{array}{l}\text{identifier-3}\\\text{literal-3}\\\underline{\text{SIZE}}\end{array}\right\}$

$\left[, \left\{\begin{array}{l}\text{identifier-4}\\\text{literal-4}\end{array}\right\} \left[\begin{array}{l}, \text{ identifier-5}\\, \text{ literal-5}\end{array}\right] . . . \underline{\text{DELIMITED}} \text{ BY} \left\{\begin{array}{l}\text{identifier-6}\\\text{literal-6}\\\underline{\text{SIZE}}\end{array}\right\}\right] . . .$

__INTO__ identifier-7 [WITH __POINTER__ identifier-8]

[; ON __OVERFLOW__ imperative-statement]

__SUBTRACT__ $\left\{\begin{array}{l}\text{identifier-1}\\\text{literal-1}\end{array}\right\} \left[\begin{array}{l}, \text{ identifier-2}\\, \text{ literal-2}\end{array}\right] . . . \underline{\text{FROM}} \text{ identifier-m [\underline{ROUNDED}]}$
[, identifier-n [__ROUNDED__]] . . . [; ON __SIZE__ __ERROR__ imperative-statement]

__SUBTRACT__ $\left\{\begin{array}{l}\text{identifier-1}\\\text{literal-1}\end{array}\right\} \left[\begin{array}{l}, \text{ identifier-2}\\, \text{ literal-2}\end{array}\right] . . . \underline{\text{FROM}} \left\{\begin{array}{l}\text{identifier-m}\\\text{literal-m}\end{array}\right\}$

__GIVING__ identifier-n [__ROUNDED__] [, identifier-o [__ROUNDED__]] . . .

[; ON __SIZE__ __ERROR__ imperative-statement]

General Format For Verbs

SUBTRACT $\left\{ \begin{array}{l} \underline{\text{CORRESPONDING}} \\ \underline{\text{CORR}} \end{array} \right\}$ identifier-1 <u>FROM</u> identifier-2 [<u>ROUNDED</u>]

   [; ON <u>SIZE</u> <u>ERROR</u> imperative-statement]

<u>SUPPRESS</u> PRINTING

<u>TERMINATE</u> report-name-1 [, report-name-2] . . .

<u>UNSTRING</u> identifier-1

   $\left[\underline{\text{DELIMITED}} \text{ BY } [\underline{\text{ALL}}] \left\{ \begin{array}{l} \text{identifier-2} \\ \text{literal-1} \end{array} \right\} \left[, \underline{\text{OR}} \ [\underline{\text{ALL}}] \left\{ \begin{array}{l} \text{identifier-3} \\ \text{literal-2} \end{array} \right\} \right] \cdots \right]$

   <u>INTO</u> identifier-4 [, <u>DELIMITER</u> IN identifier-5] [, <u>COUNT</u> IN identifier-6]

     [, identifier-7 [, <u>DELIMITER</u> IN identifier-8] [, <u>COUNT</u> IN identifier-9]] . . .

   [WITH <u>POINTER</u> identifier-10] [<u>TALLYING</u> IN identifier-11]

   [; ON <u>OVERFLOW</u> imperative-statement]

<u>USE</u> <u>AFTER</u> STANDARD $\left\{ \begin{array}{l} \underline{\text{EXCEPTION}} \\ \underline{\text{ERROR}} \end{array} \right\}$ PROCEDURE ON $\left\{ \begin{array}{l} \text{file-name-1 } [, \text{ file-name-2}] \ldots \\ \text{INPUT} \\ \underline{\text{OUTPUT}} \\ \underline{\text{I-O}} \\ \underline{\text{EXTEND}} \end{array} \right\}$.

<u>USE</u> <u>AFTER</u> STANDARD $\left\{ \begin{array}{l} \underline{\text{EXCEPTION}} \\ \underline{\text{ERROR}} \end{array} \right\}$ PROCEDURE ON $\left\{ \begin{array}{l} \text{file-name-1 } [, \text{ file-name-2}] \ldots \\ \text{INPUT} \\ \underline{\text{OUTPUT}} \\ \underline{\text{I-O}} \end{array} \right\}$.

<u>USE</u> <u>BEFORE</u> <u>REPORTING</u> identifier.

<u>USE</u> FOR <u>DEBUGGING</u> ON $\left\{ \begin{array}{l} \text{cd-name-1} \\ [\underline{\text{ALL}} \text{ REFERENCES OF}] \text{ identifier-1} \\ \text{file-name-1} \\ \text{procedure-name-1} \\ \underline{\text{ALL}} \ \underline{\text{PROCEDURES}} \end{array} \right\}$

   $\left[\begin{array}{l} \text{cd-name-2} \\ [\underline{\text{ALL}} \text{ REFERENCES OF}] \text{ identifier-2} \\ \text{file-name-2} \\ \text{procedure-name-2} \\ \underline{\text{ALL}} \ \underline{\text{PROCEDURES}} \end{array} \right]$ . . . .

General Format For Verbs

<u>WRITE</u> record-name [<u>FROM</u> identifier-1]

$$
\left[\begin{array}{l} \underline{\text{BEFORE}} \\ \underline{\text{AFTER}} \end{array} \text{ ADVANCING } \left\{ \begin{array}{l} \left\{ \begin{array}{l} \text{identifier-2} \\ \text{integer} \end{array} \right\} \left[\begin{array}{l} \text{LINE} \\ \text{LINES} \end{array} \right] \\ \left\{ \begin{array}{l} \text{mnemonic-name} \\ \underline{\text{PAGE}} \end{array} \right\} \end{array} \right\} \right]
$$

$$
\left[; \text{ AT } \left\{ \begin{array}{l} \underline{\text{END-OF-PAGE}} \\ \underline{\text{EOP}} \end{array} \right\} \text{ imperative-statement} \right]
$$

<u>WRITE</u> record-name [<u>FROM</u> identifier] [; <u>INVALID</u> KEY imperative-statement]

General Format For Conditions

RELATION CONDITION:

IF $\left\{\begin{array}{l}\text{identifier-1}\\\text{literal-1}\\\text{arithmetic-expression-1}\end{array}\right\}$ $\left\{\begin{array}{l}\text{IS [NOT] }\underline{\text{GREATER}}\text{ THAN}\\\text{IS [NOT] }\underline{\text{LESS}}\text{ THAN}\\\text{IS [NOT] }\underline{\text{EQUAL}}\text{ TO}\\\text{IS [NOT] }>\\\text{IS [NOT] }<\\\text{IS [NOT] }=\end{array}\right\}$ $\left\{\begin{array}{l}\text{identifier-2}\\\text{literal-2}\\\text{arithmetic-expression-2}\end{array}\right\}$

CLASS CONDITION:

IF identifier is [NOT] $\left\{\begin{array}{l}\underline{\text{NUMERIC}}\\\underline{\text{ALPHABETIC}}\end{array}\right\}$

SIGN CONDITION:

IF arithmetic-expression IS [NOT] $\left\{\begin{array}{l}\underline{\text{POSITIVE}}\\\underline{\text{NEGATIVE}}\\\underline{\text{ZERO}}\end{array}\right\}$

CONDITION-NAME CONDITION:

IF condition-name

SWITCH-STATUS CONDITION:

IF condition-name

MESSAGE CONDITION:

IF **MESSAGE** FOR cd-name

COMPOUND CONDITIONS:

IF condition $\left\{\begin{array}{l}\underline{\text{AND}}\\\underline{\text{OR}}\end{array}\right\}$ condition $\left[\left\{\begin{array}{l}\underline{\text{AND}}\\\underline{\text{OR}}\end{array}\right\}\text{ condition}\right]$ ...

NOT CONDITION:

IF **NOT** condition

NOTE: The word "**IF**" is not part of the condition, but is shown in the above formats to improve clarity.

Miscellaneous Formats

QUALIFICATION:

$$\left\{ \begin{array}{l} \text{data-name-1} \\ \text{condition-name} \end{array} \right\} \left[\left\{ \begin{array}{l} \underline{\text{OF}} \\ \underline{\text{IN}} \end{array} \right\} \text{data-name-2} \right] \cdots$$

$$\text{paragraph-name} \left[\left\{ \begin{array}{l} \underline{\text{OF}} \\ \underline{\text{IN}} \end{array} \right\} \text{section-name} \right]$$

$$\text{text-name} \left[\left\{ \begin{array}{l} \underline{\text{OF}} \\ \underline{\text{IN}} \end{array} \right\} \text{library-name} \right]$$

SUBSCRIPTING:

$$\left\{ \begin{array}{l} \text{data-name} \\ \text{condition-name} \end{array} \right\} (\text{subscript} \ [\ , \ \text{subscript}] \ldots)$$

INDEXING:

$$\left\{ \begin{array}{l} \text{data-name} \\ \text{condition-name} \end{array} \right\} (\left\{ \begin{array}{l} \text{index-name} \ [\ (\pm) \ \text{literal-2}] \\ \text{literal-1} \end{array} \right\} \left[, \left\{ \begin{array}{l} \text{index-name} \ [\ (\pm) \ \text{literal-4}] \\ \text{literal-3} \end{array} \right\} \right] \cdots$$

IDENTIFIER: FORMAT 1

$$\text{data-name-1} \left[\left\{ \begin{array}{l} \underline{\text{OF}} \\ \underline{\text{IN}} \end{array} \right\} \text{data-name-2} \right] \cdots \ [\ (\text{subscript-1} \ [\ , \ \text{subscript-2} \ [\ , \ \text{subscript-3}]]) \ ]$$

IDENTIFIER: FORMAT 2

$$\text{data-name-1} \left[\left\{ \begin{array}{l} \underline{\text{OF}} \\ \underline{\text{IN}} \end{array} \right\} \text{data-name-2} \right] \cdots \left[\ (\left\{ \begin{array}{l} \text{index-name} \ [\ (\pm) \ \text{literal-2}] \\ \text{literal-1} \end{array} \right\} \right.$$

$$\left. \left[, \left\{ \begin{array}{l} \text{index-name-2} \ [\ (\pm) \ \text{literal-4}] \\ \text{literal-3} \end{array} \right\} \right] \left[, \left\{ \begin{array}{l} \text{index-name -3} \ [\ (\pm) \ \text{literal-6}] \\ \text{literal-5} \end{array} \right\} \right] \ ] \ ) \right]$$

APPENDIX E
Charts and Tables

1. Successful OPEN Statement

The following chart illustrates what happens when a programmer tries to open a file that may or may not be available to the program. The result depends on whether the file was specified in the **SELECT** clause as an **OPTIONAL** file.

OPEN MODE	FILE IS AVAILABLE	FILE IS UNAVAILABLE
INPUT	Normal open	Open is unsuccessful
INPUT (optional file)	Normal open	Normal open: The first read causes the **AT END** condition
I-O	Normal open	Open is unsuccessful
I-O (optional file)	Normal open	Open causes the file to be created
OUTPUT	Normal open: The file contains no records	Open causes the file to be created
EXTEND	Normal open	Open is unsuccessful
EXTEND (optional file)	Normal open	Open causes the file to be created

2. COBOL 85 Language Subsets

COBOL may not necessarily be COBOL. In other words, CO-
BOL may be many different things. The COBOL language has
been divided into functional modules by the COBOL standardization committees. These modules are:

   Nucleus
   Sequential I-O
   Relative I-O
   Indexed I-O
   Inter Program Communications
   Sort Merge
   Source Text Manipulator
   Report Writer
   Communications
   Debug
   Segmentation

Furthermore, each module may consist of two levels of features
(basic features and advanced features). When a COBOL compiler is released by a vendor, it is described as one of these
subsets:

   Minimum COBOL
   Intermediate COBOL
   High COBOL

In the following chart, four modules (Report Writer, Communications, Debug and Segmentation) need not be included at all
(they are optional); yet a COBOL compiler supplier may still
have a High level compiler.

COBOL SUBSETS	REQUIRED MODULES (required in subsets)							OPTIONAL MODULES (not required in subsets)			
	Nucleus	Sequential I-O	Relative I-O	Indexed I-O	Inter-program communication	Sort-merge	Source text manipulation	Report writer	Communication	Debug	Segmentation
High	2	2	2	2	2	1	2	1	2	2	2
Intermediate	1	1	1	1	1	1	1		1	1	1
Minimum	1	1	Opt	Opt	1	Opt	Opt				

3. COBOL 85 STANDARD-1
ASCII Character Set (American)

b7 b6 b5 →					0 0 0	0 0 1	0 1 0	0 1 1	1 0 0	1 0 1	1 1 0	1 1 1
BITS b4	b3	b2	b1	COLUMN / ROW	0	1	2	3	4	5	6	7
0	0	0	0	0	NUL	DLE	SP	0	●	P	`	p
0	0	0	1	1	SOH	DC1	!	1	A	Q	a	q
0	0	1	0	2	STX	DC2	"	2	B	R	b	r
0	0	1	1	3	ETX	DC3	#	3	C	S	c	s
0	1	0	0	4	EOT	DC4	$	4	D	T	d	t
0	1	0	1	5	ENQ	NAK	%	5	E	U	e	u
0	1	1	0	6	ACK	SYN	&	6	F	V	f	v
0	1	1	1	7	BEL	ETB	'	7	G	W	g	w
1	0	0	0	8	BS	CAN	(	8	H	X	h	x
1	0	0	1	9	HT	EM	)	9	I	Y	i	y
1	0	1	0	10	LF	SUB	*	:	J	Z	j	z
1	0	1	1	11	VT	ESC	+	;	K	[	k	{
1	1	0	0	12	FF	FS	,	<	L	/	l	|
1	1	0	1	13	CR	GS	−	=	M	]	m	}
1	1	1	0	14	SO	RS	.	>	N	^	n	~
1	1	1	1	15	SI	US	/	?	O	__	o	DEL

4. COBOL 85 STANDARD-2 ASCII Character Set (International)

b7 b6 b5					0 0 0	0 0 1	0 1 0	0 1 1	1 0 0	1 0 1	1 1 0	1 1 1
BITS b4	b3	b2	b1	COLUMN / ROW	0	1	2	3	4	5	6	7
0	0	0	0	0	NUL	DLE	SP	0	●	P	`	p
0	0	0	1	1	SOH	DC1	!	1	A	Q	a	q
0	0	1	0	2	STX	DC2	"	2	B	R	b	r
0	0	1	1	3	ETX	DC3	#	3	C	S	c	s
0	1	0	0	4	EOT	DC4	¤	4	D	T	d	t
0	1	0	1	5	ENQ	NAK	%	5	E	U	e	u
0	1	1	0	6	ACK	SYN	&	6	F	V	f	v
0	1	1	1	7	BEL	ETB	'	7	G	W	g	w
1	0	0	0	8	BS	CAN	(	8	H	X	h	x
1	0	0	1	9	HT	EM	)	9	I	Y	i	y
1	0	1	0	10	LF	SUB	*	:	J	Z	j	z
1	0	1	1	11	VT	ESC	+	;	K	[	k	{
1	1	0	0	12	FF	FS	,	<	L	/	l		
1	1	0	1	13	CR	GS	−	=	M	]	m	}
1	1	1	0	14	SO	RS	.	>	N	^	n	~
1	1	1	1	15	SI	US	/	?	O	___	o	DEL

LEGEND for CHARACTER CHARTS

Column/Row	Symbol	Mnemonic and/or Meaning
0/0	NUL	Null
0/1	SOH	Start of Heading
0/2	STX	Start of Text
0/3	ETX	End of Text
0/4	EOT	End of Transmission
0/5	ENQ	Enquiry
0/6	ACK	Acknowledge
0/7	BEL	Bell
0/8	BS	Backspace
0/9	HT	Horizontal Tabulation
0/10	LF	Line Feed
0/11	VT	Vertical Tabulation
0/12	FF	Form Feed
0/13	CR	Carriage Return
0/14	SO	Shift Out
0/15	SI	Shift In
1/0	DLE	Data Link Escape
1/1	DC1	Device Control 1
1/2	DC2	Device Control 2
1/3	DC3	Device Control 3
1/4	DC4	Device Control 4
1/5	NAK	Negative Acknowledge
1/6	SYN	Synchronous Idle
1/7	ETB	End of Transmission Block
1/8	CAN	Cancel
1/9	EM	End of Medium
1/10	SUB	Substitute
1/11	ESC	Escape
1/12	FS	File Separator
1/13	GS	Group Separator
1/14	RS	Record Separator
1/15	US	Unit Separator
2/0	SP	Space (Normally Nonprinting)
2/1	!	Exclamation Point

Column/Row	Symbol	Mnemonic and/or Meaning
2/2	"	Quotation Marks (Diaeresis)
2/3	#	Number Sign
2/4	$ (or ⌼)	Dollar Sign (or open losenge)
2/5	%	Percent Sign
2/6	&	Ampersand
2/7	'	Apostrophe (Closing Single Quotation Mark: Acute Accent)
2/8	(	Opening Parenthesis
2/9	)	Closing Parenthesis
2/10	*	Asterisk
2/11	+	Plus
2/12	,	Comma (Cedilla)
2/13	-	Hyphen (Minus)
2/14	.	Period (Decimal Point)
2/15	/	Slant
3/0 to 3/9	0...9	Digits 0 through 9
3/10	:	Colon
3/11	;	Semicolon
3/12	<	Less Than
3/13	=	Equals
3/14	>	Greater Than
3/15	?	Question Mark
4/0	@	Commercial At
4/1 to 5/10	A...Z	Uppercase Latin Letters A through Z
5/11	[	Opening Bracket
5/12	\	Reverse Slant
5/13	]	Closing Bracket
5/14	^	Circumflex
5/15	__	Underline
6/0	`	Opening Single Quotation Mark (Grave Accent)
6/1 to 7/10	a...z	Lowercase Latin letters a through z
7/11	{	Opening Brace
7/12			Vertical Line
7/13	}	Closing Brace
7/14	~	Tilde
7/15	DEL	Delete

5.   Legal PICTURE Strings

The **PICTURE** procedure chart shows the order of precedure when using characters as symbols in a character-string. An "X" at an intersection indicates that the symbol at the top of the column may precede (but not necessarily immediately), in a given **PICTURE** character-string, the symbol at the left of the row. Arguments appearing in { } indicate that the symbols are mutually exclusive. The currency symbol is indicated by the letters "CS".

SECOND SYMBOL ↓ / FIRST SYMBOL →	B	O	/	,	.	{+ −}	{+ −}	{CR OB}	cs	{Z *}	{Z *}	{+ −}	{+ −}	cs	cs	9	A X	S	V	P	P
NON-FLOATING INSERTION SYMBOLS																					
B	x	x	x	x	x	x			x	x	x	x	x	x	x	x	x		x		x
O	x	x	x	x	x	x			x	x	x	x	x	x	x	x	x		x		x
/	x	x	x	x	x	x			x	x	x	x	x	x	x	x	x		x		x
,	x	x	x	x	x	x			x	x	x	x	x	x	x	x			x		x
.	x	x	x	x		x			x	x		x		x							
{+ −}																					
{+ −}	x	x	x	x	x				x	x	x			x	x	x			x	x	x
{CR OB}	x	x	x	x	x				x	x	x			x	x	x			x	x	x
cs					x																
FLOATING INSERTION SYMBOLS																					
{Z *}	x	x	x	x		x			x	x	x										
{Z *}	x	x	x	x	x	x			x	x	x	x							x		x
{+ −}	x	x	x	x					x			x									
{+ −}	x	x	x	x	x				x			x	x						x		x
cs	x	x	x	x		x								x							
cs	x	x	x	x	x	x								x	x				x		x
OTHER SYMBOLS																					
9	x	x	x	x	x	x			x	x	x		x		x	x	x	x	x		x
A X	x	x	x													x	x				
S																					
V	x	x	x	x		x			x	x	x		x		x	x		x		x	
P	x	x	x	x		x			x	x	x		x		x	x		x		x	
P					x				x									x	x		x

6.   LEGAL MOVEs

Data items in COBOL are categorized according to the following **PICTURE** examples:

```
CATEGORY                    SAMPLE PICTURE

ALPHABETIC                  PICTURE  AAA.
ALPHANUMERIC                PICTURE  XXX.
ALPHANUMERIC-EDITED         PICTURE  XXBXXBXX.
NUMERIC                     PICTURE  999V99.
NUMERIC-EDITED              PICTURE  ZZZ,ZZZ,ZZZ.
```

When **MOVE**ing the contents of data items from one category to another, the following chart indicates the valid and invalid moves.

			CATEGORY OF RECEIVING DATA ITEM		
			Alphabetic	Alphanumeric-Edited Alphanumeric	Numeric integer Numeric noninteger Numeric-Edited
CATEGORY OF SENDING OPERAND		Alphabetic	Valid	Valid	x
		Alphanumeric	Valid	Valid	Valid
		Alphanumeric-Edited	Valid	Valid	x
	NUMERIC	integer	x	Valid	Valid
		noninteger	x	x	Valid
		Numeric-Edited	x	Valid	Valid

7.   Permissible I-O Statements

The following table indicates the various I-O statements that
are permissible for files. The two factors that determine the
permissible statement are File Access mode and the **OPEN**
mode.

			OPEN MODE			
		STATEMENT	INPUT	OUTPUT	I-O	EXTEND
FILE ACCESS MODE	SEQUENTIAL	Read	x		x	
		Write		x		x
		Rewrite			x	
		Start	x		x	
		Delete			x	
	RANDOM	Read	x		x	
		Write		x	x	
		Rewrite			x	
		Start				
		Delete			x	
	DYNAMIC	Read	x		x	
		Write		x	x	
		Rewrite			x	
		Start	x		x	
		Delete			x	

APPENDIX F
COBOL Committees

1. CODASYL 1959

The members of the first CODASYL Executive Committee (July 7, 1959) were:
- Charles Phillips, Chairman
    - The office of the Secretary of Defense
- Joseph F. Cunningham, Vice Chair
    - United States Air Force
- E.J. Albertson
    - U.S. Steel Corporation
- Gregory Dillon
    - DuPont Company
- Mel Grosz
    - Esso Standard Oil Company
- Joseph H. Wegstein
    - National Bureau of Standards
- A. Eugene Smith
    - United States Navy
- Grace M. Hopper, advisor
    - Sperry Rand Company
- Robert W. Bemer, advisor
    - IBM Corporation

Before the end of 1959, a specification for CBL (later COBOL) was developed by the CODASYL Short-Range Committee, whose members were:
- Joseph Wegstein, National Bureau of Standards
- Colonel Alfred Asch, United States Air Force
- William Carter, Honeywell
- Ben F. Cheydleur, RCA
- Mary K. Hawes, Burroughs

- Frances E. Holberton, United States Navy
- Jean E. Sammet, Sylvania
- William Selden, IBM Corporation
- E.F. Somers, Sperry Rand

2.　CODASYL COBOL Committee 1985

The members of the CODASYL COBOL Committee as of September, 1985 are:

Burroughs Corporation
Control Data Corporation
Data General Corporation
Deloitte Haskins and Sells
Digital Equipment Corporation
General Services Administration
Honeywell Information Systems
International Business Machines
Jerome Garfunkel Associates
Micro Focus, Ltd.
National Bureau of Standards
National Computing Centre of England
NCR Corporation
Norfolk Southern
Sperry Corporation
Tandem Computers, Inc.
United States Army
United States Air Force
United States Navy
Wang Laboratories

3.　ANSI COBOL Committee 1985

The organizations represented by members of the American National Standards Institute (ANSI) COBOL technical committee (X3J4) as of June 1985 are:

Burroughs Corporation
Control Data Corporation
Digital Equipment Corporation
DECUS (DEC Users Society)
Hewlett-Packard
Honeywell Information Systems
International Business Machines
ICL
Jerome Garfunkel Associates
Martin Marietta
McDonnell Douglas
Nashoba Systems
National Bureau of Standards
NCR Corporation
Online Systems Support
Perkin-Elmer
Ryan-McFarland
Sperry Corporation
Travelers Insurance Company
United States Army
United States Air Force
Wang Laboratories

4.   ISO COBOL Committee

The countries represented on the international COBOL Committee (ISO TC 97 SC22 WG4) as of February 1986 are:

Austria
Canada
France
Germany
The Netherlands
United Kingdom
United States

APPENDIX G
Glossary

Abbreviated Combined Relation Condition   The combined condition that results from the explicit omission of a common subject or a common subject and common relational operator in a consecutive sequence of relation conditions.

Access Mode   The manner in which records are to be operated upon within a file.

Actual Decimal Point   The physical representation, using the decimal-point characters period (.) or comma (,), of the decimal-point position in a data item.

Alphabet-Name   A user-defined word, in the SPECIAL-NAMES paragraph of the Environment Division, that assigns a name to a specific character set and/or collating sequence.

Alphabetic Character   A character that belongs to the following set of letters: A, B, C, D, E, F, G, H, I, J, K, L, M, N, O, P, Q, R, S, T, U, V, W, X, Y, Z and space. Within the context of contents of data items, the defintion of alphabetic character is extended to include lowercase letters a, b, c, d, e, f, g, h, i, j, k, l, m, n, o, p, q, r, s, t, u, v, w, x, y and z when the computer character set includes such lowercase characters.

Alphanumeric Character   Any character in the computer's character set.

Alternate Record Key   A key, other than the prime record key, whose contents identify a record within an indexed file.

Bit   The smallest unit in a computer's storage structure capable of expressing two distinct alternatives.

Bit Position   The amount of physical storage to store a single bit.

Boolean Character   A unit of information that consists of either of the boolean values zero or one. It may be stored as either a bit or a Standard Data Format character, depending on its usage.

Boolean Data Item   A data item capable of representing some set of boolean values. The particular values that it can represent depend upon the data description clauses used to describe the data item.

Boolean Expression   An identifier referencing a boolean data item; a boolean literal; the figurative constant ZERO (ZEROS, ZEROES) or ALL literal, where literal is a boolean literal; a boolean expression preceded by the unary boolean operator; two boolean expressions separated by one of the binary boolean operators; or a boolean expression enclosed in parentheses.

Boolean Literal   A literal composed of one or more boolean characters delimited on the left by the separator B"and on the right by the quotation mark separator (").

Boolean Operation   The process caused by the evaluation of a boolean expression that results in the establishment of a boolean value.

Boolean Operator   A reserved word used in the construction of a boolean expression to indicate a boolean operation.

Boolean Position   The amount of physical storage required to store a single boolean character. This amount depends on the USAGE specified in the data description entry that defines the data item. If the USAGE is DISPLAY, a boolean position is synonymous with a character position. If the USAGE is BIT, a boolean position is synonymous with a bit position.

Called Program   A program that is the object of a CALL statement combined at object time with the calling program to produce a run unit.

Calling Program   A program that executes a CALL to another program.

Cd-Name   A user-defined word that names an MCS interface area described in a communication description entry within the Communication Section of the Data Division.

Character   The basic indivisible unit of the language.

Character Position   The amount of physical storage required to store a single standard data format character whose usage is

DISPLAY. Further characteristics of the physical storage are defined by the implementor.

Character-String   A sequence of contiguous characters that form a COBOL word, a literal, or a PICTURE character-string.

Class Condition   The proposition, for which a truth value can be determined, that the content of an item is wholly alphabetic or wholly numeric.

Clause   An ordered set of consecutive COBOL character-strings whose purpose is to specify an attribute of an entry.

COBOL Character Set   The complete COBOL character set, exclusive of the contents of nonnumeric literals and comment lines, consists of the characters listed below.

Character	*Meaning*
0, 1, . . . , 9	digit
A, B, . . . , Z	letter
	space
+	plus sign
-	minus sign (hyphen)
*	asterisk
/	slant (solidus)
=	equal sign
$	currency sign (represented as ⊐ in the International Reference Version of International Standard ISO 646-1973)
,	comma (decimal point)
;	semicolon
.	period (decimal point, full stop)
''	quotation mark
(	left parenthesis
)	right parenthesis
>	greater than symbol
<	less than symbol
:	colon

NOTE: In the cases where an implementation does not provide all of the COBOL character set to be graphically
represented, substitute graphics may be specified
by the implementor to replace the characters not
represented. The COBOL character set graphics are
a subset of American National Standard X3.4-1977,
Code for Information Interchange. With the exception of '$', they are also a subset of the graphics
defined for the International Reference Version of
International Standard ISO 646-1973, 7-Bit Coded
Character Set for Information Processing Interchange.

COBOL Word   A character-string of not more than 30 characters that forms a user-defined word, a system-name or a reserved word.

Collating Sequence   The sequence in which the characters
that are acceptable to a computer are ordered for purposes of
sorting, merging, comparing and for processing indexed files
sequentially.

Column   A character position within a print line. The columns
are numbered from 1, by 1, starting at the leftmost character
position of the print line and extending to the rightmost position
of the print line.

Combined Condition   A condition that is the result of con-
necting two or more conditions with the 'AND' and the 'OR'
logical operator.

Comment-Entry   An entry in the Identification Division that
may be any combination of characters from the computer
character set.

Comment Line   A source program line represented by an
asterisk (*) in the indicator area of the line and any characters
from the computer's character set in area A and area B of that
line. The comment line serves only for documentation in a
program. A special form of comment line represented by a slant
(/) in the indicator area of the line and any characters from the

computer's character set in area A and area B of that line causes page ejection prior to printing the comment.

Common Program A program that, despite being directly contained within another program, may be called from any program directly or indirectly contained in that other program.

Communication Description Entry An entry in the Communication Section of the Data Division that is composed of the level indicator CD, followed by a cd-name, and then followed by a set of clauses as required. It describes the interface between the message control system (MCS) and the COBOL program.

Communication Device A mechanism (hardware or hardware/software) capable of sending data to a queue and/or receiving data from a queue. This mechanism may be a computer or a peripheral device. One or more programs containing communication description entries and residing within the same computer define one or more of these mechanisms.

Communication Section The section of the Data Division that describes the interface areas between the message control system (MCS) and the program, composed of one or more communication description areas.

Compile Time The time at which a COBOL source program is translated, by a COBOL compiler, to a COBOL object program.

Compiler Directing Statement A statement, beginning with a compiler directing verb, that causes the compiler to take a specific action during compilation.

Complex Condition A condition in which one or more logical operators act upon one or more conditions. (See Negated Simple Condition, Combined Condition and Negated Combined Condition.)

Computer-Name A system-name that identifies the computer upon which the program is to be compiled or run.

Condition A status of a program at execution time for which a truth value can be determined. Where the term 'condition' (condition-1, condition-2, . . .) appears in these language specifications in or in reference to 'condition' (condition-1, condition-2, . . .) of a general format, it is a conditional expression consisting of either a simple condition optionally parenthesized, or a combined condition consisting of the syntactically correct combination of simple conditions, logical operators and parentheses, for which a truth value can be determined.

Condition-Name   A user-defined word that assigns a name to a subset of values that a conditional variable may assume; or a user-defined word assigned to a status of an implementor-defined switch or device. When 'condition-name' is used in the general formats, it represents a unique data item reference consisting of a syntactically correct combination of a condition-name, together with qualifiers and subscripts, as required for uniqueness of reference.

Condition-Name Condition   The proposition, for which a truth value can be determined, that the value of a conditional variable is a member of the set of values attributed to a condition-name associated with the conditional variable.

Conditional Expression   A simple condition or a complex condition specified in an EVALUATE, IF, PERFORM or SEARCH statement. (See *Simple Condition* and *Complex Condition*.)

Conditional Statement   A statement that specifies that the truth value of a condition is to be determined and that the subsequent action of the object program is dependent on this truth value.

Conditional Variable   A data item one or more values of which has a condition-name assigned to it.

Configuration Section   A section of the Environment Division that describes overall specifications of source and object computers.

Connective   A reserved word that is used to:

   1) associate a data-name, paragraph-name, condition-name or text-name with its qualifier.

2) link two or more operands written in a series.

3) form conditions (logical connectives). (See *Logical Operator*.)

Contiguous Items Items that are described by consecutive entries in the Data Division, and that bear a definite hierarchical relationship to each other.

Control Break A change in the value of a data item that is referenced in the CONTROL clause. More generally, a change in the value of a data item that is used to control the hierarchical structure of a report.

Control Break Level The relative position within a control hierarchy at which the most major control break occurred.

Control Data Item A data item, a change in whose content may produce a control break.

Control Data-Name A data-name that appears in a CONTROL clause and refers to a control data item.

Control Footing A report group that is presented at the end of the control group of which it is a member.

Control Group A set of body groups that is presented for a given value of a control data item or of FINAL. Each control group may begin with a CONTROL HEADING, end with a CONTROL FOOTING and contain DETAIL report groups.

Control Heading A report group that is presented at the beginning of the control group of which it is a member.

Control Hierarchy A designated sequence of report subdivisions defined by the positional order of FINAL and the data-names within a CONTROL clause.

COUNTER A data item used for storing numbers or number representations in a manner that permits these numbers to be increased or decreased by the value of another number, or to be changed or reset to zero or to an arbitrary positive or negative value.

Currency Sign The character '$' of the COBOL character set.

Currency Symbol The character defined by the CURRENCY

SIGN clause in the SPECIAL-NAMES paragraph. If no CUR-
RENCY SIGN clause is present in a COBOL source program,
the currency symbol is identical to the currency sign.

Current Record   In file processing, the record that is available
in the record area associated with a file.

Digit Position   The amount of physical storage required to
store a single digit. This amount may vary depending on the
usage specified in the data description entry that defines the
data item. If the data description entry specifies that usage is
DISPLAY, then a digit position is synonymous with a character
position. Further characteristics of the physical storage are
defined by the implementor.

Division   A collection of zero, one or more sections or paragraphs, called the division body, that are formed and combined in accordance with a specific set of rules. Each division
consists of the division header and the related division body.
There are four divisions in a COBOL program: Identification,
Environment, Data and Procedure

Division Header   A combination of words, followed by a
separator period, that indicates the beginning of a division. The
division headers in a COBOL program are:

> IDENTIFICATION DIVISION.
> ENVIRONMENT DIVISION.
> DATA DIVISION.
> PROCEDURE DIVISION [USING {data-name-1} . . .].

Dynamic Access   An access mode in which specific logical
records can be obtained from or placed into a mass-storage file
in a nonsequential manner and obtained from a file in a sequential manner during the scope of the same OPEN statement.
(See *Random Access* and *Sequential Access*.)

Editing Character   A single character or a fixed two-character
combination belonging to the following set:

Character	Meaning
B	space
0	zero
+	plus
-	minus
CR	credit
DB	debit
Z	zero suppress
*	check protect
$	currency sign
,	comma (decimal point)
.	period (decimal point)
/	slant (solidus)

Elementary Item   A data item that is described as not being further logically subdivided.

End of Procedure Division   The physical position of a COBOL source program after which no further procedures appear.

End Program Header   A combination of words, followed by a separator period, that indicates the end of a COBOL source program. The end program header is:

    END PROGRAM program-name.

Entry   Any descriptive set of consecutive clauses terminated by a separator period and written in the Identification Division, Environment Division or Data Division of a COBOL program.

Environment Clause   A clause that appears as part of an Environment Division entry.

Execution Time   The time at which an object program is executed. The term is synonymous with *object time*.

Explicit Scope Terminator   A reserved word that terminates the scope of a particular Procedure Division statement.

Expression   An arithmetic or conditional expression.

Extend Mode   The state of a file after execution of an OPEN statement, with the EXTEND phrase specified, for that file and before the execution of a CLOSE statement without the REEL or UNIT phrase for that file.

External Data   The data described in a program as external data items and external file connectors.

External Data Item   A data item that is described as part of an external record in one or more programs of a run unit and which itself may be referenced from any program in which it is described.

External Data Record   A logical record that is described in one or more programs of a run unit and whose constituent data items may be referenced from any program in which they are described.

External File Connector   A file connector that is accessible to one or more object programs in the run unit.

External Switch   A hardware or software device, defined and named by the implementor, that is used to indicate that one of two alternate states exists.

Figurative Constant   A compiler-generated value referenced through the use of certain reserved words.

File   A collection of logical records.

File Attribute Conflict Condition   An unsuccessful attempt has been made to execute an input-output operation on a file, and the file attributes, as specified for that file in the program, do not match the fixed attributes for that file.

File Clause   A clause that appears as part of any of the following Data Division entries: file description entry (FD entry) and sort-merge file description entry (SD entry).

File Connector   A storage area that contains information about a file and is used as the linkage between a file-name and a physical file and between a file-name and its associated record area.

File-Control   The name of an Environment Division paragraph in which the data files for a given source program are declared.

File Control Entry   A SELECT clause and all its subordinate clauses that declare the relevant physical attributes of a file.

File Description Entry   An entry in the File Section of the Data

Division that is composed of the level indicator FD, followed by a file-name, and then followed by a set of file clauses as required.

File-Name A user-defined word that names a file connector described in a file description entry or a sort-merge file description entry within the File Section of the Data Division.

File Organization The permanent logical file structure established at the time that a file is created.

File Position Indicator A conceptual entity that contains the value of the current key within the key of reference for an indexed or relative file, or the record number of the current record for a sequential file, or indicates that no next logical record exists, or that the number of significant digits in the relative record number is larger than the size of the relative key data item, or that an optional file is not present, or that the at end condition already exists.

File Section The section of the Data Division that contains file description entries and sort-merge file description entries together with their associated record descriptions.

Fixed File Attributes Information about a file which is established when a file is created and cannot subsequently be changed during the existence of the file. These attributes include the organization of the file (sequential, relative, or indexed), the prime record key, the alternate record keys, the code set, the minimum and maximum record size, the record type (fixed or variable), the collating sequence of the keys for indexed files, the blocking factor, the padding character, and the record delimiter.

Fixed-Length Record A record associated with a file whose file description or sort-merge description entry requires that all records contain the same number of character positions.

Footing Area The position of the page body adjacent to the bottom margin.

Format A specific arrangement of a set of data.

Global Name A name that is declared in only one program but which may be referenced from that program and from any program contained within that program. Condition-names, data-names, file-names, record-names, report-names and some special registers may be global names.

Group Item   A data item that is composed of subordinate data items.

High Order End   The leftmost character of a string of characters.

I-O-CONTROL   The name of an Environment Division paragraph in which object program requirements for sharing of same areas by several data files and multiple file storage on a single input-output device are specified.

I-O-CONTROL Entry   An entry in the I-O-CONTROL paragraph of the Environment Division that contains clauses that provide information required for the transmission and handling of data on named files during the execution of a program.

I-O Mode   The state of a file after execution of an OPEN statement, with the I-O phrase specified, for that file and before the execution of a CLOSE statement without the REEL or UNIT phrase for that file.

I-O Status   A conceptual entity that contains the two-character value indicating the resulting status of an input-output operation. This value is made available to the program through the use of the FILE STATUS clause in the file description entry or file control entry for the file.

Identifier   A syntactically correct combination of a data-name, with its qualifiers, subscripts and reference modifiers, as required for uniqueness of reference, that names a data item. The rules for 'identifier' associated with the general formats may, however, specifically prohibit qualification, subscripting or reference modification.

Imperative Statement   A statement that either begins with an imperative verb and specifies an unconditional action to be taken or is a conditional statement that is delimited by its explicit scope terminator (delimited scope statement). An imperative statement may consist of a sequence of imperative statements.

Implementor-Name   A system-name that refers to a particular feature available on that implementor's computing system.

Implicit Scope Terminator   A separator period that terminates the scope of any preceding unterminated statement, or a phrase of a statement that by its occurrence indicates the end of the scope of any statement contained within the preceding phrase.

Index   A computer storage area or register, the contents of which represent the identification of a particular element in a table.

Index Data Item   A data item in which the values associated with an index-name can be stored in a form specified by the implementor.

Index-Name   A user-defined word that names an index associated with a specific table.

Indexed File   A file with indexed organization.

Indexed Organization   The permanent logical file structure in which each record is identified by the value of one or more keys within that record.

Initial Program   A program whose program state is initialized, whenever the program is called, to the same state as when that program was first called in the run unit. During this initialization process, all local data items in the program whose description includes a VALUE clause are initialized to that defined value; but any item whose description does not include a VALUE clause is initialized to an undefined value.

Input File   A file that is opened in the input mode.

Input Mode   The state of a file after execution of an OPEN statement, with the INPUT phrase specified, for that file and before the execution of a CLOSE statement without the REEL or UNIT phrase for that file.

Input-Output File   A file that is opened in the I-O mode.

Input-Output Section   The section of the Environment Division that names the files and the external media required by an object program and provides information required for transmission and handling of data during execution of the object program.

Input Procedure   A set of statements, to which control is given during the execution of a SORT statement, for the purpose of controlling the release of specified records to be sorted.

Integer   A fixed-point numeric literal or a numeric data item that does not include any digit position to the right of the assumed decimal point. Where the term 'integer' appears in general formats, integer must not be a numeric data item, and must not be signed, nor zero unless explicitly allowed by the rules of that format.

Internal Data   The data described in a program excluding all external data items and external file connectors. Items described in the Linkage Section of a program are treated as internal data.

Internal Data Item   A data item that is described in one program in a run unit. An internal data item may have a global name.

Internal File Connector   A file connector that is accessible to only one object program in the run unit.

Intra-Record Data Structure   The entire collection of groups and elementary data items from a logical record that is defined by a contiguous subset of the data description entries that describe the record. These data description entries include all entries whose level-number is greater than the level-number of the first data description entry describing the intra-record data structure.

Invalid Key Condition   A condition, at object time, caused when a specific value of the key associated with an indexed or relative file is determined to be invalid.

Key   A data item that identifies the location of a record, or a set of data items which serve to identify the ordering of data.

Key of Reference   The key, either prime or alternate, currently being used to access records within an indexed file.

Key Word   A reserved word whose presence is required when the format in which the word appears is used in a source program.

Level Indicator   Two alphabetic characters that identify a specific type of file or a position in a hierarchy. The level indicators in the Data Division are: CD, FD, RD and SD.

Level-Number   A user-defined word, expressed as a one or two digit number, that indicates the hierarchical position of a data item or the special properties of data description entry. Level-numbers in the range 1 through 49 indicate the position of a data item in the hierarchical structure of a logical record. Level-numbers in the range 1 through 9 may be written either as a single digit or as a zero followed by a significant digit. Level-numbers 66, 77 and 88 identify special properties of a data description entry.

Library-Name   A user-defined word that names a COBOL library that is to be used by the compiler for a given source program compilation.

Library Text   A sequence of text words, comment lines, or the separator space, or the pseudo-text delimiters in a COBOL library.

LINAGE-COUNTER   A special register whose value points to the current position within the page body.

Line   A division of a page representing one row of horizontal character positions. Each character position of a report line is aligned vertically beneath the corresponding character position of the report line above it. Report lines are numbered from 1, by 1, starting at the top of the page. The term is synonymous with *report line*.

Line Number   An integer that denotes the vertical position of a report line on a page.

Linkage Section   The section in the Data Division of the called program that describes data items available from the calling program. These data items may be referred to by both the calling and the called program.

Literal   A character-string whose value is implied by the ordered set of characters comprising the string.

Logical Operator   One of the reserved words AND, OR or

NOT. In the formation of a condition, either AND or OR, or both, can be used as logical connectives. NOT can be used for logical negation.

Logical Page   A conceptual entity consisting of the top margin, the page body and the bottom margin.

Logical Record   The most inclusive data item. The level-number for a record is 01. A record may be either an elementary item or a group item. The term is synonymous with *record*.

Low Order End   The rightmost character of a string of characters.

Mass Storage   A storage medium in which data may be organized and maintained in both a sequential and nonsequential manner.

Mass Storage Control System (MSCS)   An input-output control system that directs, or controls, the processing of mass-storage files.

Mass Storage File   A collection of records that is assigned to a mass-storage medium.

MCS   Message control system; a communication control system that supports the processing of messages.

Merge File   A collection of records to be merged by a MERGE statement. The merge file is created and can be used only by the merge function.

Message   Data associated with an end of message indicator or an end of group indicator. (See *Message Indicators*.)

Message Control System (MCS)   A communication control system that supports the processing of messages.

Message Count   The count of the number of complete messages that exist in the designated queue of messages.

Message Indicators   EGI (end of group indicator), EMI (end of message indicator) and ESI (end of segment indicator) are conceptual indications that serve to notify the message control system that a specific condition exists (end of group, end of message, end of segment). Within the hierarchy of EGI, EMI and ESI, an EGI is conceptually equivalent to an ESI, EMI and

EGI. An EMI is conceptually equivalent to an ESI and EMI. Thus, a segment may be terminated by an ESI, EMI or EGI. A message may be terminated by an EMI or EGI.

Message Segment　Data that forms a logical subdivision of a message, normally associated with an end of segment indicator. (See *Message Indicators*.)

Mnemonic-Name　A user-defined word that is associated in the Environment Division with a specific implementor-name.

MSCS　Mass storage control system; an input-output control system that directs, or controls, the processing of mass storage files.

Native Character Set　The implementor-defined character set associated with the computer specified in the OBJECT-COMPUTER paragraph.

Native Collating Sequence　The implementor-defined collating sequence associated with the computer specified in the OBJECT-COMPUTER paragraph.

Negated Combined Condition　The 'NOT' logical operator immediately followed by a parenthesized combined condition.

Negated Simple Condition　The 'NOT' logical operator immediately followed by a simple condition.

Next Executable Sentence　The next sentence to which control will be transferred after execution of the current statement is complete.

Next Executable Statement　The next statement to which control will be transferred after execution of the current statement is complete.

Next Record　The record that logically follows the current record of a file.

Noncontiguous Items　Elementary data items, in the Working-Storage and Linkage Sections, that bear no hierarchic relationship to other data items.

Nonnumeric Item　A data item whose description permits its content to be composed of any combination of characters taken from the computer's character set. Certain categories of nonnumeric items may be formed from more restricted character sets.

Nonnumeric Literal   A literal bounded by quotation marks. The string of characters may include any character in the computer's character set.

Numeric Character   A character that belongs to the following set of digits: 0, 1, 2, 3, 4, 5, 6, 7, 8, 9.

Numeric Item   A data item whose description restricts its content to a value represented by characters chosen from the digits '0' through '9'; if signed, the item may also contain a '+', '-', or other representation of an operational sign.

Numeric Literal   A literal composed of one or more numeric characters that may contain either a decimal point, or an algebraic sign, or both. The decimal point must not be the rightmost character. The algebraic sign, if present, must be the leftmost character.

OBJECT-COMPUTER   The name of an Environment Division paragraph in which the computer environment, within which the object program is executed, is described.

Object Computer Entry   An entry in the OBJECT-COMPUTER paragraph of the Environment Divison that contains clauses that describe the computer environment in which the object program is to be executed.

Object of Entry   A set of operands and reserved words, within a Data Divison entry of a COBOL program, that immediately follows the subject of the entry.

Object Program   A set or group of executable machine language instructions and other material designed to interact with data to provide problem solutions. In this context, an object program is generally the machine language result of the operation of a COBOL compiler on a source program. Where there is no danger of ambiguity, the word 'program' alone may be used in place of the phrase *object program*.

Object Time   The time at which an object program is executed. The term is synonymous with *execution time*.

Obsolete Language Element   A COBOL language element in this revision of American National Standard COBOL that is currently planned for deletion in a subsequent revision of American National Standard COBOL.

Open Mode   The state of a file after execution of an OPEN statement for that file and before the execution of a CLOSE statement without the REEL or UNIT phrase for that file. The particular open mode is specified in the OPEN statement as either INPUT, OUTPUT, I-O or EXTEND.

Operand   Whereas the general definition of operand is 'that component that is operated upon', for the purposes of this document, any lowercase word (or words) that appears in a statement or entry format may be considered to be an operand and, as such, is an implied reference to the data indicated by the operand.

Operational Sign   An algebraic sign, associated with a numeric data item or a numeric literal, to indicate whether its value is positive or negative.

Optional File   An input file which is declared as being not necessarily present each time the object program is executed. The object program causes an interrogation for the presence or absence of the file.

Optional Word   A reserved word that is included in a specific format only to improve the readability of the language and whose presence is optional to the user when the format in which the word appears is used in a source program.

Output File   A file that is opened in either the output mode or extend mode.

Output Mode   The state of a file after execution of an OPEN statement, with the OUTPUT or EXTEND phrase specified, for that file and before the execution of a CLOSE statement without the REEL or UNIT phrase for that file.

Output Procedure   A set of statements to which control is given during execution of a SORT statement after the sort function is completed, or during execution of a MERGE statement after the merge function has selected the next record in merged order.

Padding Character   An alphanumeric character used to fill the unused character positions in a physical record.

Page   A vertical division of a report representing a physical separation of report data, the separation being based on internal reporting requirements and/or external characteristics of the reporting medium.

Page Body   That part of the logical page in which lines can be written and/or space.

Page Footing   A report group that is presented at the end of a report page as determined by the report writer control system.

Page Heading   A report group that is presented at the beginning of a report page as determined by the report writer control system.

Paragraph   In the Procedure Division, a paragraph-name followed by a separator period and by zero, one or more sentences. In the Identification and Environment Divisions, a paragraph header followed by zero, one or more entries.

Paragraph Header   A reserved word, followed by the separator period, that indicates the beginning of a paragraph in the Identification and Environment Divisions. The permissible paragraph headers in the Identification Division are:

    PROGRAM-ID.
    AUTHOR.
    INSTALLATION.
    DATE-WRITTEN.
    DATE-COMPILED.
    SECURITY.

The permissible paragraph headers in the Environment Division are:

    SOURCE-COMPUTER.
    OBJECT-COMPUTER.
    SPECIAL-NAMES.

FILE-CONTROL.
I-O-CONTROL.

Paragraph-Name   A user-defined word that identifies and begins a paragraph in the Procedure Division.

Phrase   A phrase is an ordered set of one or more consecutive COBOL character-strings that form a portion of a COBOL procedural statement or of a COBOL clause.

Physical Page   A device-dependent concept defined by the implementor.

Physical Record   The term is synonymous with *block*.

Prime Record Key   A key whose contents uniquely identify a record within an indexed file.

Printable Group   A report group that contains at least one print line.

Printable Item   A data item, the extent and contents of which are specified by an elementary report entry. This elementary report entry contains a COLUMN NUMBER clause, a PICTURE clause and a SOURCE, SUM or VALUE clause.

Procedure   A paragraph or group of logically successive paragraphs, or a section or group of logically successive sections, within the Procedure Division.

Procedure-Name   A user-defined word used to name a paragraph or section in the Procedure Division. It consists of a paragraph-name (which may be qualified), or a section-name.

Program-Name   In the Identification Division and the end program header, a user-defined word that identifies a COBOL source program.

Program Name Entry   An entry in the PROGRAM-ID paragraph of the Identification Division that contains clauses that specify the program-name and assign selected program attributes to the program.

Pseudo-Text   A sequence of text words, comment lines, or the separator space in a source program of COBOL library bounded by, but not including, pseudo-text delimiters.

Pseudo-Text Delimiter　 Two contiguous equal sign (=) characters used to delimit pseudo-text.

Punctuation Character　 A character that belongs to the following set:

Character	Meaning
,	comma
;	semicolon
:	colon
.	period (full stop)
"	quotation mark
(	left parenthesis
)	right parenthesis
	space
=	equal sign

Qualified Data-Name　 An identifier that is composed of a data-name followed by one or more sets of either of the connectives OF and IN followed by a data-name qualifier.

Qualifier　 (1) A data-name or a name associated with a level indicator that is used in a reference either together with another data-name that is the name of an item that is subordinate to the qualifier or together with a condition-name.

(2) A section-name used in a reference together with a paragraph-name specified in that section.

(3) A library-name used in a reference together with a text-name associated with that library.

Queue　 A logical collection of messages awaiting transmission or processing.

Queue Name　 A symbolic name that indicates to the message control system the logical path by which a message or a portion of a completed message may be accessible in a queue.

Random Access　 An access mode in which the program-specified value of a key data item identifies the logical record that is obtained from, deleted from or placed into a relative or indexed file.

Record The most inclusive data item. The level-number for a record is 01. A record may be either an elementary item or a group item. The term is synonymous with *logical record*.

Record Area A storage area allocated for the purpose of processing the record described in a record description entry in the File Section of the Data Division. In the File Section, the current number of character positions in the record area is determined by the explicit or implicit RECORD clause.

Record Description The total set of data description entries associated with a particular record. The term is synonymous with *record description entry*.

Record Description Entry The total set of data description entries associated with a particular record. The term is synonymous with *record description*.

Record Key A key whose contents identify a record within an indexed file. Within an indexed file, a record key is either the prime record key or an alternate record key.

Record-Name A user-defined word that names a record described in a record description entry in the Data Division of a COBOL program.

Record Number The ordinal number of a record in the file whose organization is sequential.

Reel A discrete portion of a storage medium, the dimensions of which are determined by each implementor, that contains part of a file, all of a file or any number of files. The term is synonymous with *unit* and *volume*.

Reference Format A format that provides a standard method for describing COBOL source programs.

Reference Modifier The leftmost-character-position and length used to establish and reference a data item.

Relation The term is synonymous with *relational operator*.

Relation Character A character that belongs to the following set:

(See table on page 302)

Character	Meaning
>	greater than
<	less than
=	equal to

Relation Condition   The proposition, for which a truth value can be determined, that the value of an arithmetic expression or data item has a specific relationship to the value of another arithmetic expression or data item. (See *relational operator*.)

Relational Operator   A reserved word, a relation character, a group of consecutive reserved words or a group of consecutive reserved words and relation characters used in the construction of a relation condition. The permissible operators and their meanings are:

Relational Operator	Meaning
IS [NOT] GREATER THAN IS [NOT] >	Greater than (or not greater than)
IS [NOT] LESS THAN IS [NOT] <	Less than (or not less than)
IS [NOT] EQUAL TO IS [NOT] =	Equal to (or not equal to)
IS GREATER THAN OR EQUAL TO IS >=	Greater than or equal to
IS LESS THAN OR EQUAL TO IS <=	Less than or equal to

Relative File   A file with relative organization.

Relative Key   A key whose contents identify a logical record in a relative file.

Relative Organization   The permanent logical file structure in which each record is uniquely identified by an integer value greater than zero, which specifies the record's logical ordinal position in the file.

Relative Record Number   The ordinal number of a record in a file whose organization is relative. This number is treated as a numeric literal which is an integer.

Report Clause   A clause, in the Report Section of the Data Division, that appears in a report description entry or a report group description entry.

Report Description Entry   An entry in the Report Section of the Data Division that is composed of the level indicator RD, followed by the report-name, followed by a set of report clauses as required.

Report File   An output file whose file description entry contains a REPORT clause. The contents of a report file consist of records that are written under control of the report writer control system.

Report Footing   A report group that is presented only at the end of a report.

Report Group   In the Report Section of the Data Division, an 01 level-number entry and its subordinate entries.

Report Group Description Entry   An entry in the Report Section of the Data Division that is composed of the level-number 01, an optional data-name, a TYPE clause and an optional set of report clauses.

Report Heading   a report group that is presented only at the beginning of a report.

Report Line   A division of a page representing one row of horizontal character positions. Each character position of a report line is aligned vertically beneath the corresponding character position of the report line above it. Report lines are numbered from 1, by 1, starting at the top of the page.

Report-Name   A user-defined word that names a report described in a report description entry within the Report Section of the Data Division.

Report Section   The section of the Data Division that contains one or more report description entries and their associated report group description entries.

Report Writer Control System (RWCS)   An object time control system, provided by the implementor, that accomplishes the construction of reports.

Report Writer Logical Record   A record that consists of the report writer print line and associated control information necessary for its selection and vertical positioning.

Reserved Word   A COBOL word specified in the list of words that may be used in a COBOL source program, but that must not appear in the programs as user-defined words or system-names.

Resource   A facility or service, controlled by the operating system, that can be used by an executing program.

Resultant Identifier   A user-defined data item that is to contain the result of an arithmetic operation.

Run Unit   One or more object programs that interact with one another and function, at object time, as an entity to provide problem solutions.

RWCS   Report Writer Control System; an object time control system, provided by the implementor, that accomplishes the construction of reports.

Section   A set of zero, one or more paragraphs or entries, called a section body, the first of which is preceded by a section header. Each section consists of the section header and the related section body.

Section Header   A combination of words followed by a separator period that indicates the beginning of a section in the Environment, Data and Procedure Division. In the Environment and Data Divisions, a section header is composed of reserved words followed by a separator period. The permissible section headers in the Environment Division are:

    CONFIGURATION SECTION.
    INPUT-OUTPUT SECTION.

The permissible section headers in the Data Division are:

    FILE SECTION.
    WORKING-STORAGE SECTION.
    LINKAGE SECTION.
    COMMUNICATION SECTION.
    REPORT SECTION.

In the Procedure Division, a section header is composed of a section-name, followed by the reserved word SECTION, followed by a segment-number (optional), followed by a separator period.

Section-Name   A user-defined word that names a section in the Procedure Division.

Segment-Number   A user-defined word that classifies sections in the Procedure Division for purposes of segmentation. Segment-numbers may contain only the characters '0', '1', . . . , '9'. A segment-number may be expressed either as a one or two digit number.

Sentence   A sequence of one or more statements, the last of which is terminated by a separator period.

Separately Compiled Program   A program that, together with its contained programs, is compiled separately from all other programs.

Separator   A character or two contiguous characters used to delimit character-strings.

Sequential Access   An access mode in which logical records are obtained from or placed into a file in a consecutive predecessor-to-successor logical record sequence determined by the order of records in the file.

Sequential File   A file with sequential organization.

Sequential Organization   The permanent logical file structure in which a record is identified by a predecessor-successor relationship established when the record is placed into the file.

Sign Condition   The proposition, for which a truth value can be determined, that the algebraic value of a data item or an arithmetic expression is either less than, greater than or equal to zero.

Simple Condition   Any single condition chosen from the set:
    relation condition
    class condition
    condition-name condition
    switch-status condition
    sign condition
    (simple-condition)

Sort File   A collection of records to be sorted by a SORT statement. The sort file is created and can be used by the sort function only.

Sort-Merge File Description Entry   An entry in the File Section of the Data Division that is composed of the level indicator SD, followed by a file-name and then followed by a set of file clauses as required.

Source   The symbolic identification of the originator of a transmission to a queue.

SOURCE-COMPUTER   The name of an Environment Division paragraph in which the computer environment, within which the source program is compiled, is described.

Source Computer Entry   An entry in the SOURCE-COMPUTER paragraph of the Environment Division that contains clauses that describe the computer environment in which the source program is to be compiled.

Source Item   An identifier designated by a SOURCE clause that provides the value of a printable item.

Source Program   Although it is recognized that a source program may be represented by other forms and symbols, in this book it always refers to a syntactically correct set of COBOL statements. A COBOL source program commences with the Identification Division; a COPY statement; or a REPLACE statement. A COBOL source program terminates with the END PROGRAM header, if specified, or by the end of the Procedure Division.

Special Character   A character that belongs to the following set:

Character	Meaning
+	plus sign
-	minus sign
*	asterisk
/	slant (solidus)
=	equal sign
$	currency sign

,	comma (decimal point)
;	semicolon
.	period (decimal point, full stop)
"	quotation mark
(	left parenthesis
)	right parenthesis
>	greater than symbol
<	less than symbol
:	colon

Special Character Word   A reserved word that is an arithmetic operator or a relation character.

SPECIAL-NAMES   The name of an Environment Division paragraph in which implementor-names are related to user-specified mnemonic-names.

Special Names Entry   An entry in the SPECIAL-NAMES paragraph of the Environment Division that contains clauses that provide means for specifying the currency sign, choosing the decimal point, specifying symbolic characters and relating implementor-names to user-specified mnemonic-names and for relating alphabet-names to character sets or collating sequences.

Special Registers   Certain compiler generated storage areas whose primary use is to store information produced in conjunction with the use of specific COBOL features.

Standard Data Format   The concept used in describing data in a COBOL Data Division under which the characteristics or properties of the data are expressed in a form oriented to the appearance of the data on a printed page of infinite length and breadth, rather than a form oriented to the manner in which the data is stored internally in the computer or on a particular external medium.

Statement   A syntactically valid combination of words and symbols, beginning with a verb, written in a COBOL source program.

Sub-Queue   A logical hierarchical division of a queue.

Subject of Entry   An operand or reserved word that appears immediately following the level indicator or the level-number in a Data Division entry.

Subprogram   A program which is the object of a CALL statement combined at object time with the calling program to produce a run unit. The term is synonymous with *called program*.

Subscript   An occurrence number represented by either an integer, a data-name optionally followed by an integer with the operator + or - or an index-name optionally followed by an integer with the operator + or -, which identifies a particular element in a table.

Subscripted Data-Name   An identifier that is composed of a data-name followed by one or more subscripts enclosed in parentheses.

Sum Counter   A signed numeric data item established by a SUM clause in the Report Section of the Data Division. The sum counter is used by the Report Writer Control System to contain the result of designated summing operations that take place during production of a report.

Switch-Status Condition   The proposition, for which a truth value can be determined, that an implementor-defined switch, capable of being set to an 'on' or 'off' status, has been set to a specific status.

Symbolic-Character   A user-defined word that specifies a user-defined figurative constant.

System-Name   A COBOL word used to communicate with the operating environment.

Table   A set of logically consecutive items of data that are defined in the Data Division of a COBOL program by means of the OCCURS clause.

Table Element   A data item that belongs to the set of repeated items comprising a table.

Terminal   The originator of a transmission to a queue, or the receiver of a transmission from a queue.

Text-Name   A user-defined word that identifies library text.

Text Word   A character or a sequence of contiguous characters between margin A and margin R in a COBOL library, source program or in pseudo-text that is:

1) a separator, except for: space; a pseudo-text delimiter; and the opening and closing delimiters for nonnumeric literals. The right parenthesis and left parenthesis characters, regardless of context within the library, source program or pseudo-text, are always considered text words.

2) a literal including, in the case of nonnumeric literals, the opening quotation mark and the closing quotation mark that bound the literal.

3) any other sequence of contiguous COBOL characters except comment lines and the word 'COPY', bounded by separators, that is neither a separator nor a literal.

Top Margin   An empty area that precedes the page body.

Transitional Element   A COBOL language element in this revision of American National Standard COBOL that is currently planned for deletion in a subsequent revision of American National Standard COBOL.

Truth Value   The representation of the result of the evaluation of a condition in terms of one of two values: true, false.

Unary Operator   A plus (+) or a minus (-) sign, that precedes a variable or a left parenthesis in an arithmetic expression and has the effect of multiplying the expression by +1 or -1, respectively.

Unit   A discrete portion of a storage medium, the dimensions of which are determined by each implementor, that contains part of a file, all of a file or any number of files. The term is synonymous with *reel* and *volume*.

Unsucessful Execution   The attempted execution of a statement that does not result in the execution of all the operations specified by that statement. The unsuccessful execution of a statement does not affect any data referenced by that statement, but may affect status indicators.

User-Defined Word   A COBOL word that must be supplied by the user to satisfy the format of a clause or statement.

Variable   A data item whose value may be changed by execution of the object program. A variable used in an arithmetic-expression must be a numeric elementary item.

Variable-Length Record   A record associated with a file whose file description or sort-merge description entry permits records to contain a varying number of character positions.

Variable-Occurrence Data Item   A table element that is repeated a variable number of times. Such an item must contain an OCCURS DEPENDING ON clause in its data description entry, or be subordinate to such an item.

Verb   A word that expresses an action to be taken by a COBOL compiler or object program.

Volume   A discrete portion of a storage medium, the dimensions of which are determined by each implementor, that contains part of a file, all of a file or any number of files. The term is synonymous with *reel* and *unit*.

Word   A character-string of not more than 30 characters which forms a user-defined word, a system-name or a reserved word.

Working-Storage Section   The section of the Data Division that describes working storage data items and constants, composed either of noncontiguous items or working storage records or of both.

77-Level-Description-Entry   A data description entry that describes a noncontiguous data item with the level-number 77.

VI

COBOL 85

Index

"All my dreams are in COBOL."